DEVELOPMENT CENTRE STUDIES

MINING AND METALLURGY INVESTMENT IN THE THIRD WORLD:

THE END OF LARGE PROJECTS?

BY

OLIVIER BOMSEL

WITH

ISABEL MARQUÈS, DJIBRIL NDIAYE, PAULO DE SA

DEVELOPMENT CENTRE
OF THE ORGANISATION FOR ECONOMIC CO-OPERATION AND DEVELOPMENT

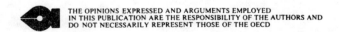

This study was carried out in conjunction with the Development Centre's research project on Foreign Direct Investment and Industrialisation in Developing Countries, as part of the theme on Financing of Development, under the direction of Charles Oman.

Also available

Development Centre Studies

THE WORLD ECONOMY IN THE 20TH CENTURY by Angus Maddison (1989)
(41 89 05 1) ISBN 92-64-13274-0, 146 pp.   £17.00   US$30.00   FF140   DM58

NEW FORMS OF INVESTMENT IN DEVELOPING COUNTRY INDUSTRIES:
Mining, Petrochemicals, Automobiles, Textiles, Food by Charles Oman
(1989)
(41 89 02 1) ISBN 92-64-13188-4, 276 pp.   £28.00   US$48.50   FF230   DM95

FINANCIAL POLICIES AND DEVELOPMENT by Jacques J. Polak (1989)
(41 89 01 1) ISBN 92-64-13187-6, 234 pp.   £17.00   US$29.50   FF140   DM58

RECYCLING JAPAN'S SURPLUSES FOR DEVELOPING COUNTRIES by
T. Ozawa (1989)
(41 88 05 1) ISBN 92-64-13177-9, 114 pp.   £11.00   US$19.00   FF90   DM37

Development Centre Seminars

ONE WORLD OR SEVERAL? edited by Louis Emmerij (1989)
(41 89 04 1) ISBN 92-64-13249-X, 320 pp.   £19.50   US$34.00   FF160   DM66

Forthcoming

Development Centre Studies

BUILDING INDUSTRIAL COMPETITIVENESS: New Technologies and
Capabilities in Developing Countries by Sanjaya Lall

TABLE OF CONTENTS

Chapter I

TRANSFORMATION OF THE GROWTH MODE OF THE MINING AND METALS INDUSTRIES: THE END OF THE BIG PROJECTS

Chapter II

CARAJAS

Chapter III

LES GUELBS

Chapter IV

PT INCO

Chapter V

CERRO MATOSO

Chapter VI

SELEBI-PHIKWE

Chapter VII

BOUGAINVILLE COPPER LTD

Chapter VIII

OK TEDI

Chapter IX

ALBRAS/ALUNORTE

Chapter X

VALESUL

ACKNOWLEDGEMENTS

The Development Centre is grateful to Olivier Bomsel and his team at the Centre for Natural Resource Economics (CERNA) of the Mining School of Paris for their initiative and generosity in undertaking this study. The Centre is also indebted to Mrs. Christiane Lapier, of the CERNA, for her tireless efforts to process the manuscript for publication.

The authors wish to extend a special note of gratitude to Charles Oman, head of the Development Centre's research programmes on new forms of investment and on foreign investment and industrialisation in developing countries. His guidance, questions and criticism were particularly stimulating, and induced us not only to carry out this study but to rethink our own analytical categories. We also thank Marion Radetski, Martin Brown and an anonymous reviewer for helpful comments on an earlier draft.

This study has benefited from ten years of research on the evolution of the mining and metallurgical industries at CERNA. The study owes much to Pierre-Noel Giraud, Director of CERNA, who has continuously provided valuable advice and encouragement.

PREFACE

Multinational mining companies have often been seen as exploiting developing countries' mineral resources for the benefit of industrialised countries. One reason for this perception is the traditional concentration of world demand for raw materials in the industrialised countries, which has also made the North dependent on mineral resources from the South. The other reason is the desire of developing country governments to retain from foreign operators a growing proportion of income to be derived from their mineral resources.

Regardless of the degree of truth to this perception in the past, it has become increasingly evident since the early 1980s that the degree of control exercised by OECD-based multinational mining and metals companies over many of the extractive and processing activities they once dominated in developing countries, has declined significantly. Closely related to this decline have been the sharp increase in the role of international debt capital and the transformation of corporate investment strategies. The forms of competition in the industry have also been modified, as have the dynamics of interaction between the companies and other key actors in the sector, notably developing country government and state enterprises, multinational banks and lending organisations, national and regional development banks, and aid organisations.

The original inspiration for this study came from results of the Centre's research on new forms of investment (cf. Charles Oman, *New Forms of Investment in Developing Country Industries: Mining, Petrochemicals, Automobiles, Textiles, Food*, 1989). In the course of preparing an analysis of the new forms of investment in the mining industry for that project, Olivier Bomsel and his team at the prestigious Mining School of Paris came to realise the importance of this approach for understanding the profound transformation of the global mining industry that is now underway.

The present study provides a detailed behind-the-scenes look at the objectives and behaviour of the often numerous participants in developing-country mining investments -- local and foreign mining companies, governments, suppliers of technology and equipment, purchasers or marketers of output and a myriad of suppliers of financial capital -- as well as their complex interaction and evolution. It does this for nine recent minerals projects in Africa, Asia and Latin America which account for over $9 billion in investment and are among the largest investment projects ever undertaken in developing countries. In doing so it provides fascinating insights into the global transformation of the industry, into the role of foreign direct investment in the mining sector in developing countries, and into their implications for public policy as well as private investment in the years ahead.

Louis Emmerij
President
OECD Development Centre
January 1990

10

INTRODUCTION

FROM THE NEW FORMS OF INVESTMENT TO THE LOGIC OF INVESTMENT

Between the end of the Second World War and the end of the 1970s, the mining and metallurgical companies achieved their expansion through "traditional" investment, largely self-financed[1], aimed at allowing them to develop new operations, alone and for their own account, anywhere in the world, as and when new deposits were discovered. The need for mastery of the techniques of geological prospecting, mine operation, and the processing and marketing of ores and metals, together with the capital-intensive nature of the industry, were at that time dissuasive barriers to entry.

Thus, at the end of the 1960s, when companies were seen to work together and associate with governments, agree to sell their technologies and marketing services, manage mines of which they were not the exclusive owner, seek the involvement of consumers in their operations, and rely on the banking system to finance an increasing share of their investments, certain economists quite rightly saw in these phenomena the emergence of "new forms of investment" (NFI). These NFI attracted attention because they were a sign of a change in North-South relations on the issue of international investment. Stressing the increased role of Third World states in the control of investments on their territory, Charles Oman has defined new forms of investment in the broad sense as the set of methods by which a foreign company has been able to undertake, and even in certain cases to stimulate the creation of production capacity in a host country without having to rely on equity ownership to assert partial or total control over the investment project[2]. In the mining industry, NFI became substantially dominant during the 1970s[3].

At the end of 1985, the Development Centre of the OECD, which was beginning a study of the significance of new forms of investment in the general evolution of North-South relations and the industrial development of Third World countries, asked us to interpret the emergence of NFI in the mining industry. It just so happened that at that time the mining industry was entering the fifth year of the biggest crisis in its history, which lasted until the middle of 1987, when the prices of ores and metals very suddenly shot up again. The majority of the projects under way -- and indeed the firms involved in them -- were experiencing serious financial difficulties which sometimes even led to the abandonment of operations that were

11

scarcely completed. But for very few exceptions[4], none of them were able to repay their debts according to the schedule originally planned. In short, the majority of mining and metallurgical projects appeared to be failures. Because of this, the problem of the forms of investment initially seemed to us of minor importance compared with that of the economic rationality of the projects and the causes of their difficulties. In a sense, we then thought that NFI in the mining sector corresponded to a calling into question of the 1960s and 1970s, a period in which new actors emerged. In fact, they were concerned, over and above the interplay between actors, with the very logic of investment and the behaviour of investors, major questions for the 1980s and 1990s.

We took a sample of mining and metallurgical projects and analysed in detail the logic of the actors involved. We worked on the hypothesis that if their projects were conceived, developed and sometimes continued despite the initial lack of success, the actors running them could not have been simply irresponsible or unlucky. They must at least have had strong, conherent motives with a particular economic rationale. Our aim was thus to understand the economic, financial and political logics which, at the time the relevant project studies were being carried out, led to the decision to go ahead and determined the choice of the form of investment.

This procedure enabled us to better identify what we call the *growth logic* of the mining and metallurgical firms, i.e. the dynamic through which the firms conceived their growth on their markets. A firm's growth is not in fact a continuous and homogeneous phenomenon, but proceeds by fits and starts. These movements correspond to decisions and choices that engage the firm's development in a direction defined by a product or by the regional location of an operation, as a function of the general context -- the world market and prices -- and the relative power of the firm over this context. Getting involved in a project is a choice that engages the firm and its relationship with the context. Each project is an illustration of the way in which firms, and indeed the other actors involved, make these choices.

The thesis that this book demonstrates through analysing the selected projects is that the growth mode of mining and metallurgical firms -- defined in terms of the relative position of the firm on the market -- has changed. This is how we explain the discrepancy between the logic of the conception of the majority of these projects and the conditions of their implementation. In this approach, the NFI are analysed as one factor in the mining and metallurgical industry crisis of the 1980s that cannot be dissociated from the overall dynamic of the firms involved: they are indicative of the way in which different economic logics were able to converge so that increasingly technologically and financially risky operations were undertaken, thus accentuating the market imbalances. They translate the ways in which the different actors perceived and shared the risks. This is how an analysis of forms of investment led to a more global study of the rationale of the actors through a systematic examination of a number of significant big projects implemented in the Third World in recent years.

METHODOLOGY: ANALYSIS OF THE PROJECTS AND OF THE RATIONALE OF THE ACTORS

We selected seven of the biggest ore mining operations developed in the Third World since the beginning of the 1970s (cf. Table 1). Apart from the Cuajone copper mine in Peru, the Boké and Kindia bauxite mines in Guinea, the exploitation of tin and bauxite deposits in Brazil and the development of deposits oriented towards domestic demand in India and China, there were no other (non-energy) mining projects on a comparable scale during this period[5]. This sample may thus be considered fully representative of the export-oriented mining operations implemented during this period.

TRENDS IN MINING INVESTMENT IN THE WESTERN WORLD
(Thousand million 1980 dollars)

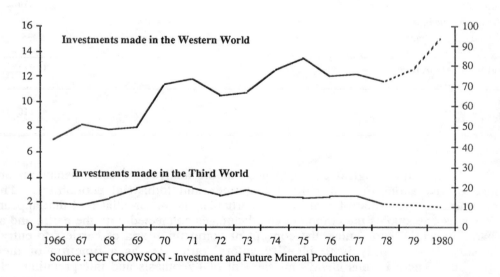

Source : PCF CROWSON - Investment and Future Mineral Production.

In addition to these mining projects we have taken two aluminium smelter projects which have in common with the mining operations the fact that since electrolytic smelting is extremely energy-intensive, many such smelters were built in the late 1970s with the aim of exploiting, generally for export, the natural resource constituted by energy potential.

13

Table 1: Summary of the projects studied

Project	Country	Industrial partners	Product	Investment million US$ (1980)
Carajás	Brazil	CVRD	Iron ore	3 053
Guelbs	Mauritania	Snim	Iron ore concentrates	303
PT Inco	Indonesia	Inco	Nickel matte	809
Cerro-Matoso	Colombia	Billiton, Hanna Mining	Ferro nickel	539
Selebi-Phikwe	Botswana	Amax-AAC	Copper-nickel matte	568
Bougainville	Papua-New Guinea	CRA	Copper concentrates and gold	1 029
Ok Tedi	Papua-New Guinea	BHP-Amoco-MG	Copper concentrates and gold	1 078
Subtotal mining projects				7 379
Albrás/Alunorte	Brazil	CVRD	Aluminium	297
Valesul	Brazil	CVRD	Aluminium	1 435
Subtotal aluminium				1 732
Grand total				9 110

The methodological concepts used in the analysis of actor behaviour are those of the economics of natural resources and industrial economics. The principle concept is that of rent, and in particular the differential rent that appears as soon as one studies the comparative advantages connected with the earth, and as regards industrial economics, the concept of competition and of barriers to entry[6]. The aim of our study is to identify actors' rationales as a function of their behaviour. There is thus always an element of hypothesis and interpretation[7]. In the case we are concerned with, the existence of economic rents is considered an intrinsic feature of the dynamics of extractive industries. The basic hypothesis is that differential and absolute rents, because they are a major factor in regulating competition in the sector, constitute an important factor explaining the behaviour of actors, which varies according to its own logic, determined by their history, their environment, and the way in which they perceive it.

Each of the mining or metallurgical projects studied has a chapter of its own (Chapters 2 to 10), presenting the technical and economic features of the project and the history of its implementation, including in particular the evolution of its legal and financial structure[8]. The slowness of the evaluation and maturation processes in all the projects should be stressed. In most cases, the period elapsing between the discovery of the deposit or the realisation that investment would be justified and the initiation of construction work was far longer than the construction phase proper. What is more, there were major technical design changes during the implementation of many projects, bringing about changes in the legal and financial conditions initially decided[9].

Analysing these processes makes it possible to understand how actors' economic approaches have evolved over the last twenty years. The task usually involves a degree of interpretation, the references for which are not limited solely to the implementation conditions of the project itself, but include external economic factors such as the global strategy of the industrial operators concerned and of their competitors, the economic dynamic of the host country and the international market situation. In this respect, Chapters 2 to 10 of this book are more than descriptive monographs of the conditions under which the different operations were implemented and of the associated forms of inventment. Each constitutes in itself a research study based on a broad knowledge of the problems and issues of the world mining and metallurgical sector and contributes, through its own findings, to the overall view. We have grouped these chapters by type of product so that the reader can keep in mind the specific features of each of the metal markets concerned. The first two are iron ore projects (Chapters 2 and 3), the next three nickel (Chapters 4 to 6), the next two copper (Chapters 7 and 8) and the last two aluminium (Chapters 9 and 10).

It is this overall picture that we intend to trace in the first chapter, which is both a synthesis of the findings and a guide to the reading of the individual case studies. In order to evaluate the role played by NFI in the evolution of the sector and the way in which they are likely to contribute to its future development, it was necessary to understand the historical and economic logic in which these NFI appeared in the mining and metallurgical sector. This is what we have tried to do in establishing as broad a picture as possible of what we have called the transformation of the mode of growth of the mining industry. This description provides a global interpretation of the evolution of the industry in which the behaviours of the actors involved in the projects are cited as reference points, but which also includes evaluations concerning the general context of the industry derived from other sources.

SUMMARY OF FINDINGS

As regards the actors engaged in the economic development of the Third World, the findings of this study, apart from the interpretation of the growth dynamic of the mining and metallurgical industries proposed, may be summarised as follows:

i) Exporting raw materials, and thus exploiting a natural comparative advantage, no longer guarantees a net transfer of resources from the outside world to the host country. The destabilisation of raw materials markets has made the financial benefits to be expected from the exploitation of natural resources very uncertain. Natural resources can no longer be regarded as buried treasure.

ii) The intervention of development banks and co-operation organisations promoting investment in the Third World through projects oriented towards international markets, so as to promote the transfer of resources to these countries, has resulted in the funding of financially vulnerable operations. Stabilization of the results of these operations depends on a financial structure able to withstand wide variations in cash flow.

iii) Operations which have encountered technical, commercial or financial difficulties have generally resulted in adjustment measures which have furthered the industrial experience of the host countries. In every case, the rehabilitation of an operation in difficulty poses a problem of industrial and financial strategy. If the mineral deposits have a comparative advantage, the initial difficulties of the projects, where they are due to technical inexperience, the financial structure or bad timing, may be compensated for in the longer term by efforts made by national actors to make the operation profitable.

iv) National actors are all the more able to adjust their industrial tool to the cyclical variations of the markets where the latter do not occupy a central place in the economy of the country. The "mining countries", heavily dependent on their minerals exports, are the ones which encounter the greatest difficulty in adjusting their mining enterprises.

v) The economics of a mining and metallurgical project are difficult to reconcile with the risks associated with the increased instability of raw materials markets. In future, only close links between the producers and consumers of raw materials will make it possible to limit the commercial risk of operations far upstream in the production chain. The NFI, while they contributed to the destabilization of markets through lowering the barriers to entry, have nevertheless made it possible to establish new vertical links in the industrial chain.

NOTES AND REFERENCES

1. See MANSEAU (1979) and RADETZKI (1980).

2. Among these methods, Charles OMAN *et al.* (1989) mentions in particular joint-ventures in which the foreign participation does not exceed 50 per cent, licensing agreements, management contracts, marketing franchises, turnkey and product-in-hand projects, production-sharing and international subcontracting.

3. A statistical survey by Charles OMAN (*ibid.*) of all the mining and metals projects studied or developed since the beginning of the 1970s, based on data gathered from the specialist press (*Engineering and Mining Journal*), shows that two-thirds of the major base metals projects (iron, copper, aluminium) correspond to NFI.

4. Notably gold mines in the industrialised countries.

5. These seven mining projects implemented between 1970 and 1984 represent a cumulative investment of $US(1980) 7.4 billion. The only global estimations of cumulative investment available for the mining sector world-wide are those by CROWSON (1982), who estimates the sums invested in the Third World between 1970 and 1980 at about $US(1980) 2 billion a year. This figure includes investments concerned with uranium -- very substantial after 1973 -- and also takes into account expenditure on the maintenance and extension of existing capacities, which was high due to the very capital-intensive nature of the industry. On this basis, it can thus reasonably be considered that our sample is significant in terms of capital invested.

6. By differential rents, we mean the differences in the productivity of the factors of production capital and labour caused by qualitative variations in deposits, or in other words the differences in production prices (total production cost plus "average" profit) between different operations producing for the same market. The basic reference is the classical theory of rent (in particular RICARDO'S theory of differential rent) and its recent development in France (CHEVALIER 1973, ANGELIER 1976, BENZONI 1982). By absolute rent we mean the excess profits realized by the industry as a whole, including marginal producers, imputable to the capacity of a group of actors to control supply. As regards absolute rents, many references are taken from industrial economics, in particular with regard to the notion of industry, of competition (PORTER 1980) and barriers to entry (BAIN 1956). The latter identifies four major factors making it possible to keep competition at bay: cost advantages (connected with technology or

nature), product differentiation, economies of scale and high capital intensity.

7. This exercise is very close to what PORTER (1980) calls "analysis of competition", except that we apply it not only to firms, but to all the actors engaged in an industrial operation, and in a retrospective fashion. According to PORTER, "The aim of strategic analysis is to study the nature and degree of success of the strategic changes which, in all probability, each competitor could make, the probable reactions of each competitor to the possible strategic moves of the other firms, and their reaction in response to all the evolutions of the sector and to all the broader changes that could occur in the environment" (Chapter 3, page 52). See also the methodological work on the analysis of competition in the mining and metallurgical industries in the thesis by Paulo de SA (1988).

8. In this approach we make frequent reference to the analyses by MIKESELL (1982).

9. It should be added that we have deliberately chosen not to examine mining projects that were abandoned in the course of realisation, like Tenké Fungurumé in Zaïre, stopped in 1978, Cerro Colorado in Panama, 1983, or Exmibal in Guatemala, written off shortly after construction was completed in 1983.

Chapter I

TRANSFORMATION OF THE GROWTH MODE OF THE MINING AND METALS INDUSTRIES: THE END OF THE BIG PROJECTS

OLIGOPOLY AS THE GROWTH MODE OF THE MINING AND METALS INDUSTRIES

The big projects that we shall study in this book were symptoms of major changes taking place in the mining and metals industries. These changes affected not only the investment choices and the financial equilibrium of the companies concerned, but also the structure of their activities, the organisation of their markets and their relations with their customers. With the introduction of the concept of "growth mode" we shall attempt to describe the overall dynamic in which these changes took place and the role played by new forms of investment. But before discussing what changed, it is worthwhile recalling what the growth mode of the mining and metals industries had been since the end of the Second World War and how foreign direct investment was adapted to it.

Until the end of the 1960s, the strong growth of the mining and metals industries was based on the three following factors:

-- *The fairly uninterrupted growth in demand for ores and metals* at an exponential rate, based essentially on the industrial dynamic of Fordist growth[1], the development of heavy industries and the production of capital goods. The industrialised countries consumed over 90 per cent of the non-ferrous metals and 80 per cent of the steel. Demand was fairly inelastic to short-term prices[2] and its relatively steady growth, despite cyclical fluctuations, meant that producers could anticipate it. The producers were in fact supported in this by the consuming industries, who saw their needs increasing and were prepared to pay a price for their raw materials that enabled their suppliers to extend production capacities. Since it is a highly capital-intensive industry, the customers considered it reasonable to allow the ore and metal producers a sufficient margin to enable them to finance new investment.

-- *The discovery of new deposits, richer or more accessible than those already being exploited,* thanks in particular to the development and internationalisation of mining exploration, which enabled new investments to be made on cost criteria, independently of short-term demand trends, and even going against the cycle. The search for lower cost deposits implied a globalisation of the activities of mining companies, which had in fact started to look outside their own countries as early as the second half of the nineteenth century[3]. Until the end of the 1950s, mining companies who discovered rich deposits in any country at all were in a position to appropriate for themselves the greater part of the resulting differential rents, which they could then use to finance their expansion.

-- The ability of certain big operators to control prices through taking advantage of their dominant position on the ores and metals markets assured the existence of absolute rents. These producers were able to ride out the inevitable cyclical fluctuations in demand by reducing their sales in periods of recession and anticipating the upturn by makingcounter-cyclical investments. The industry was thus in a situation of permanent structural overcapacity, but with absolute rents that were more than enough to finance the resulting additional costs. The oligopolistic control of markets was possible only because there was a consensus among all the producers (generally few in number on any given market) to maintain ther respective market shares more or less fixed, generally by means of a compartmentalisation of regional markets[4]. There was generally no explicit and concerted regulation, but rather a balance of power between a leader and a number of followers, all of whom derived advantage in accepting the status quo[5]. Commercial rivalries appeared only on the new markets resulting from the increase in global demand. The regular growth of demand made it possible on the whole to reduce the effect of the contradictions resulting from the diversity of investment strategies and to moderate the effects of competition.

Oligopoly was thus not simply a "market structure" defined by the static conditions of concentration of supply. In fact, the maintenance of a concentrated supply in the face of a strongly growing demand implied investment strategies on the part of the actors aimed at maintaining a dissuasive structural overcapacity[6] in addition to short-term price regulation. What is more, the financial and technical barriers specific to this industry, maintained by the system of price adjustment, facilitated the access of already-established producers to differential rents. *Oligopoly defined de facto an industrial growth mode* in which the limitation of competition, i.e. the controlled anticipation of the structure of supply on the world scale, determined the production and development strategies of the mining and metallurgical companies:

i) The growth of world demand was the necessary condition;

ii) The regulation of markets by controlling world supply was the sufficient condition;

iii) The creation and reinvestment of rents was the financial logic.

Direct investment that guaranteed exclusive control of supply and maintenance of the barriers to entry was without doubt the form of investment best suited to this growth mode. There was a consensus[7] among all the actors (producers and consumers of mineral raw materials) to leave to the upstream industry leaders the task of ensuring the balanced growth of production. They did it through controlling prices, allowing all producers the margins necessary to finance their increases in capacity. The existence of a consensus brought about a convergence of the economic logics of all the actors, in particular on the supply side, to the extent that it is possible to speak, over and above the specific logic of each enterprise, of the *mining and metals industry* as a coherent whole, taken in a homogenous historic dynamic.

THE EMERGENCE OF NEW ACTORS: THE SECTOR BECOMES "GEOPOLITICAL"

The geopolitical transformations of the 1960s, marking the end of the colonial era, were to radically change the growth mode of the mining industry. The leaders gradually lost their exclusive power to control world supply. The difficulties encountered by firms operating in the Third World caused them to look for outside financing and made consumer countries fear that the mining sector would no longer be able to ensure its growth. It is significant that the economic problems of the sector then appeared, at least in France at the beginning of the 1980s, as being more a matter of geopolitics than of economics or industrial strategy[8].

State intervention

Globalisation was a characteristic feature of mining industry growth. The search for differential rents, and also the need to develop new deposits to preserve their market shares, led mining companies to invest outside the consumer countries. Mining projects, conceived as real adventures, were thus able to be set up in the midst of civilisations far removed from our western societies, not only in the geographical sense, but also in the ethnological and economic sense. The development of mining in Africa, and more recently in Papua-New Guinea, are significant examples here.

Until the end of the 1960s, there were still certain regions of the world where the companies were able to look on mining investments as local operations, isolated from any socio-economic, historical or political context, as witnessed in particular by the enclave development of most mining sites. In the course of time however, and with the emergence of the less developed countries as autonomous economic and political entities, the mining companies who had hitherto been "transnational" (i.e. extending across nations), had to integrate themselves with the regions in which they were operating to such an extent that they became "multinationals", i.e. fitting into the specific historical processes of the host countries. This process, which might be called the "multinationalisation of the mining companies" corresponded to an irreversible engagement of these companies in the economic and political history of the host countries, or what might even be termed a *de facto* "nationalisation" of them (though without there necessarily being appropriation of capital by the state). The increasing appropriation of mining rents by the host countries, generally by means of taxation, was just one of the symptoms of this process which was in fact extremely complex. In most cases, it proceeded slowly enough for the companies to be able to recover the capital already invested, but it did give rise to doubts about the profitability of new investment[9].

By and large, the mining sector has always been attractive for developing countries with a restricted domestic market. The possibility of producing for a foreign demand thought to be growing, and of benefitting from export earnings and budget revenue capable of financing transfers to the rest of the national economy has often been considered by host countries as offering a cheap way out of domestic economic difficulties. Thus in the case of Third World mining and metallurgical industries, a distinction should be made between those countries with a large domestic market (India, Brazil, China, etc.) in which the mining industry produces to a large extent for national requirements, and the "mining countries"[10] in which the mining industry is the main industrial activity and produces essentially for export. In countries of the first category, the mining and metals industries developed and will continue to develop in connection with the needs of the domestic market. It is within this economic logic that the Brazilian Valesul project in particular, the subject of Chapter 10, was conceived. In countries of the second category, the export mining industry has been developed for two main reasons:

-- First, because there was a rapidly growing need on the international market for mineral raw materials, thought to ensure guaranteed outlets for underground resources;

-- Second, because certain countries enjoyed natural advantages that could give rise to differential rents.

From the formal standpoint, mining rents represent an income over and above the "normal" remuneration of the factors of production and thus constitute a form of financial transfer from the consumer to the producer. In many cases over a period of several decades, they brought forms of financial support from the rest of the world to the economies of the countries exporting mineral raw materials. Thus during the 1970s, companies like Codelco in Chile and Gécamines in Zaïre were at the origin of regular transfers of several hundred million dollars a year to those countries. More often than not, however, these transfers from abroad, far from going to finance the development of industrial or agricultural activities, were used instead to subsidise sectors in crisis, compensating the effects of their weakness through imports and internal transfers of incomes (development of administrative jobs, subsidies for basic products, etc.). This type of economic dynamic, common to the majority of countries having enjoyed rents -- ever since the Spain of the Conquistadores -- has been the subject of many economic analyses, especially since the first oil crisis revealed the very substantial rents of the oil-exporting countries. We shall limit ourselves here, in a secondary analysis, to characterising the "mining countries" as countries having known a rentier economic dynamic based on the rents of an export-oriented mining sector[11].

In most mining countries, it can be seen that there was a coincidence between the political choice of the state, often in association with foreign operators, to set up an exporting sector capable of generating rents, and a latent crisis in the traditional productive sectors oriented towards the domestic market (agriculture, consumer goods production). These economic policy choices always resulted in a compartmentalisation of the economies of mining countries into two completely dissociated sectors: the mining sector, generating budget revenue and foreign currency, making it possible in particular to finance imports, and the rest of the economy, based on a fragile productive apparatus, largely supported by an extended redistribution system[12]. What is more, this was a cumulative process, in which the amount of transfers to be reinjected into the economy to compensate the structural imbalances never stopped growing. In the late 1970s, foreign debts rapidly came to reinforce the transfers coming from the mining sector. In the space of a few years, the mining countries became some of the most indebted countries in the world, in terms of the debt as a proportion of GDP[13]. In certain mining countries, the disappearance of rents has brought a very real risk of the collapse of the redistribution system and the associated state structure. The development of new sources of mining income has been a means of deferring the breakdown in these countries. In several of them (Peru, Mauritania, Tunisia, etc.) it can be seen that substantial investments have been made less on the criteria of long-term profitability, than following a logic of increasing or maintaining the turnover of a mining sector threatened by marginalization. The development of the Guelbs mining project (Chapter 3) in Mauritania followed this logic, with strong support from the development banks.

The 1960s saw an acceleration in the process of integrating the transnational mining companies into the economic dynamic of the host countries. *The most important consequence was to be the emergence of states as new actors in the sector.* The fact is that in order to negotiate their share of the rents and control the activities of the foreign firms, states began to actively intervene in the sector through establishing stricter mining regulations and even by assuming, with or without a financial contribution, part of the equity of the operations. Within a few years, in all the mining countries, there were to be significant changes in the conditions under which foreign companies were received and could operate. This is seen notably in the process of renegotiation of the Bougainville agreement (Chapter 7) and the establishment of that for Ok Tedi[14] (Chapter 8) in Papua-New Guinea. The Bougainville operation, coinciding with the decolonisation of Papua-New Guinea was implented on the initiative of the mine operator (CRA, an Australian subsidiary of RTZ) with symbolic participation by the local administration. Ok Tedi, for which planning began only three years after the Bougainville decision, encountered much stronger pressure from the host government, which did not even hesitate to lead the process of choosing an operator.

Among the forms of state intervention in projects, it has been possible to identify:

-- Majority involvement of a state company in the capital of the operation: this is the case in particular of Carajas in Brazil (Chapter 2), a strategic project for the economic integration of Amazonia and for the development of the state company CVRD. The Brazilian government imposed the majority capital participation of CVRD on US Steel, the finder of the deposit. As a result, US Steel withdrew and CVRD found itself alone. In view of the political and economic importance of the project, the Brazilian government took the responsibility of giving the national enterprise exclusive control of the operation. From this standpoint, the Guelbs project in Mauritania is very similar.

-- Minority participation by the state or a public enterprise in the capital of a joint-venture intended to make it possible to control operations from the inside and to derive the best advantage from the technical experience. This type of intervention in new projects initially scared off foreign investors, as was the case with Hanna Mining in Cerro Matoso (Chapter 5), Kennecott in Ok Tedi and Reynolds in Valesul, who at that time thought they would lose control over the implementation of the project. Later on however, the foreign operators realized the advantage they could derive from this intervention through sharing the industrial and financial risks of the operation with the state. With the advent of the crisis in the 1980s, which will be discussed below, the majority of the states involved as minority shareholders in mining projects had difficulties with their partners over the rescheduling of the debts of these projects and the revision of their taxation or contractual agreements (Guinea, Papua-New Guinea, Colombia, Botswana, Albras and Alunorte in Brazil [Chapter 9][15]).

-- Refusal to play a direct part in the mining investment, which enabled host states to establish themselves as observers capable of taking their share of any rents without having to commit any capital. This was the stance generally adopted by South Africa and Australia, big promotors of mining projects, or among the examples we have analysed, Indonesia in the PT Inco project (Chapter 4). In this particular case, the state, even though it had negotiated the possiblity of becoming a shareholder in the case of success, was able to remain aloof from the financial difficulties encountered by Inco. In this type of situation, the state has generally been able to play on the different aspects of its sovereignty to appropriate the rents, using not only taxation, but also charges for public services (electricity, transport, infrastructures, etc.), or foreign exchange legislation, all without its own financial liability being engaged in the project.

Whatever the mode of their intervention, the host states thus appeared during the 1960s and 1970s as the actors best able *in the long term* to appropriate for themselves the lion's share of the rents of mining operations and to change the course of their realization. They thus modified the financial logic of transnational investment through limiting the profits that could be expected by companies investing their own funds, so that foreign operators had to face higher industrial and financial risks[16].

Intervention by the banks

The mining operations gradually came to seek greater leverage for the remuneration of their equity capital, and increasingly resorted to bank financing, all the more so because during the 1960s and 1970s real interest rates were low or even negative. What is more, using the banks made the companies appear less isolated in their negotiations with states, as the power and cohesion of the international financial community could be used as a guarantee of the stability of the agreements concluded[17]. The banks that inaugurated the technique of "project financing" rapidly became significant actors in the mining sector. They made it possible to set up projects with a far greater share of borrowed funds than in the past[18]. In the majority of the projects examined in this book, equity capital does not exceed 30 per cent of the investment.

Although it is difficult to measure, it would appear that the appearance of large quantities of petrodollars to be recycled after the first oil crisis stimulated the interest of the commercial banks in big, capital-intensive projects. Furthermore, the revival of exports from the industrialised countries after the first oil shock, together with the development of supply policies by these states, favoured the creation of export credits associated with the sale of capital goods produced in the industrialised countries. We shall return to this point in detail.

This growing involvement of the banks in the sector during the 1970s at first led to a dilution of the industrial risks of projects, and this influenced investors' decisions. The latter could in fact embark on operations in which, because they initially committed less own capital, they could support higher risk, all the more so because "project financing" generally meant off balance sheet indebtedness for the mining companies. The operators embarked on the Selebi-Phikwe (Chapter 6) and PT Inco (Chapter 4) projects with their own equity share making up less than 5 per cent of the effective total investment.

The development banks, and in particular the World Bank, played an important role in setting up the outside financing for many projects. Their intervention made it possible to delay the conflicts between states and operators by differentiating between the financing allocated to production units and that allocated to infrastructures, so that the responsibilities of the different actors could be kept separate. In the case of Selebi-Phikwe, the free share of the Botswana State could be limited to 15 per cent of the joint-venture capital and compensated for by the creation of infrastructures financed by the World Bank. What is more, this made it possible to stabilize the agreements between the actors involved in projects thanks to obtaining state guarantees on the loans. The intervention of the development banks was based in the first place on the realisation that it was necessary to stabilize the new relations between states and operators through promoting the financing of projects to meet the long-term growth of demand. From this standpoint the development banks saw their role as continuing the regulation of markets[19], which had always existed up to then, through stabilizing investment flows. In addition, it was based on the idea that the Third World countries needed capital and the mining industry could constitute a pole of accumulation capable of both enabling the loans to be repaid and, in the longer term, of providing the exporting countries with foreign exchange resources[20]. From this standpoint, the geopolitical aspects of projects sometimes took precedence over economic rationality. In the extreme case of the Guelbs project in Mauritania, the intervention of the development funds was a regional geopolitical act: in the economic situation obtaining between the two oil crises and with the war in western Sahara, the country deliberately stirred up competition between the OPEC Development Fund and the Western development banks (World Bank, European Investment Bank, Caisse Centrale de Coopération Economique, bilateral and multilateral development funds).

Resorting to bank financing was seen until the end of the 1970s as a way of limiting the risk of mining operations. It is in fact striking to realise that it was not until the end of the 1970s, at a time when the banks were becoming more circumspect in the financing of projects, that observers began to express concern about the destabilizing effects of their interventions[21]. The rise in interest rates as from 1980 and the amplification of monetary fluctuations affecting the repayment of debts suddenly aggravated the financial risks associated with outside financing, on top of which came the industrial and commercial risks which had hitherto been underestimated.

Summarising, during the 1960s and 1970s, the banks made it possible for new projects to go on being implemented after the earlier logic of the mining companies self-financing their growth had been seriously compromised by the intervention of host countries.

At the same time, the consumers, i.e. the metal processing industries in the industrialised countries and also metallurgical companies that were not integrated upstream, realized with concern that the mining companies were no longer willing to develop the sector alone, and decided to become more active themselves. During the 1970s, "supply policies" were developed in all the ore and metal importing countries, aimed at promoting the development of new capacities through the granting of financing associated with the conclusion of long-term purchase contracts.

In fact, after the first oil crisis, the consumer industries in the industrialised countries became concerned about their dependence on the producers of raw materials. Without seriously fearing cartellisation, consumers were worried that control of the supply of ores and metals might permanently escape from their traditional suppliers. Furthermore, the modification of vertical integration patterns in the industry, due in particular to the increasing intervention of host countries in the furthest upstream stages of the production chain, raised new supply problems for the consumer firms, even though overall final demand was generally satisfied. Thus for example, the development of the copper industry in Japan created a new demand for copper concentrates for export at the very moment when many of the producers of the South were integrating downstream. Certain European metallurgical companies -- Metallgesellschaft (MG) and Union Minière, for example -- were also encountering serious supply difficulties. At the same time, the oil price rise caused the shutdown of the Japanese aluminium smelters supplied by oil-fired power stations, so that the structure of the flows of raw materials imported by this country was greatly changed. Between 1979 and 1982, Japan became the world's biggest aluminium importer and adjusted its supply strategy accordingly. To deal with these difficulties, the governments of the industrialised countries supported their companies' supply strategies, in particular by means of syndicating their interests and granting low-interest credits through their financial institutions. These credits, even though they were financing high-risk operations, could nevertheless be advantageous for the consuming countries if they had the effect of reducing the upward trend of imported raw materials prices.

The intervention of Japanese or German consumers often took the form of complex consortiums bringing together a large number of enterprises, generally srongly unified about national commercial strategies. These consortiums were always in a position of strength in the implementation of projects thanks to the synergies of their groupings. In exchange for product purchase guarantees and tied financing, they were able to sell equipment and services on advantageous terms. Examples are the sale of European firms' consultancy services and equipment to the Guelbs project in Mauritania or the resale by the Japanese consortium engaged in the Albras project in Brazil of the aluminium smelting technology developed by Péchiney during the 1950s.

However, the involvement of consumers was always aimed at ensuring a reliable and suitable supply, while limiting the risks of upstream integration, the best situation being that of a big customer of an operation, without being directly involved in either its capital or its funding. The different forms of intervention may be ranked in order of decreasing risk:

-- Provision of equity capital and bank financing in exchange for part of the production (the case of the Japanese consortium in Albras and Alunorte and of the German KE consortium -- where we find MG -- in the first phase of Ok Tedi;

-- Capital investment in association with other actors in exchange for exclusive refining rights (the case of Amax in Selebi-Phikwe and the Japanese refiners in PT Inco);

-- Provision of financing in exchange for exclusive marketing rights giving control over the product (characteristic of MG's strategy in Selebi-Phikwe and Ok Tedi);

-- Provision of financing and guarantees to take the product (the case of European and Japanese steelmakers in Carajas and the Japanese smelters in Bougainville);

-- Provision of financing by the bilateral and multilateral development banks (World Bank, European Investment Bank, Caisse Centrale de Coopération Economique) of the consumer countries, without any guarantees to take the product on the part of the consuming industries (case of the Guelbs project in Mauritania).

Whatever the mode of intervention, the essential point is that the consumers contributed to the promotion of projects much more than in the past. It is thus clear that the earlier form of consensus aimed at entrusting responsibility for ensuring the growth of supply to the mining companies alone, even though the raw materials prices might be a little higher, was no longer acceptable.

Consequences: lowering of barriers to entry and disorganisation of supply

The appearance of states, banks and consumers in the mining sector meant that the industry lost its independence, notably financial, with respect to the development of its mode of growth. Recourse to bank financing enabled new actors (private mining and metallurgical firms operating outside the traditional markets, Third World state enterprises, often encouraged by the consumers) to overcome the barrier of the high capital intensity of the industry[22].

The technological barriers were also lowered when certain operators, pushed into it by consumers[23], agreed to supply their technology to new entrants. Once the operators realized that the barriers to entry to the industry would no longer be able to resist the pressure of the new actors, some of them did not hesitate to take part in the movement and turn their new competitors into customers. They thus tended to limit their equity participation in projects or (as in the of Hanna Mining in Cerro Matoso and Reynolds in Valesul) associate it with the sale of different kinds of services or know-how: consultancy, technology, management, marketing, financing, etc. In most cases however, where they were heavily committed in the capital of the operations, the mining companies derived only marginal profits from the sale of services in comparison with the overall risk involved in the investment.

The multiplication of the actors involved in projects gave rise to new forms of investment[24]. *During the 1960s and 1970s, the NFI contributed to the lowering of barriers to entry to the mining and metals industry*, barriers that were connected with the growth dynamic and the market regulation specific to what we have called the oligopolistic growth mode. This change in itself would not have been enough to put an end to this mode of growth, for as we have stressed, the concentration of supply was not in itself an indispensable precondition for the functioning of the oligopoly. On the other hand, as we shall see below, the lowering of the barriers undermined the authority of the leaders and weakened the consensus among suppliers regarding the ways in which regulation should be exercised.

Once it was possible to get round the financial and technical barriers by resorting to banks and the purchase of services, there was nothing to stop new actors from trying to profit from any rents and establishing themselves in their turn on the oligopoly markets. Thus, wishing to diversify on the nickel market and taking advantage of the lowering of the barriers to entry, Amax got involved in the confused Selebi-Phikwe project in association with the government of Botswana, Anglo-American and the European consumers. In Cerro Matoso, Billiton, associated with the Colombian government, tried to take advantage of the same opportunity. With the second oil crisis, the Brazilian public operator CVRD tried, in association with the Japanese aluminium companies, to move into the world aluminium market in a big way with the Albras/Alunorte project.

These candidates for entry to the new markets found powerful allies in the oil operators[25] seeking to reinvest in the mining sector the considerable cash flows generated by the two oil crises. The interventions by Shell and its subsidiaries in Cerro Matoso and Valesul, and those by BHP and Amoco in Ok Tedi were partly due to this logic. These enterprises with abundant funds were looking for major investments to strengthen their positions in the mining sector.

Thanks to the NFI, certain marginal producers were able to develop extended capacity with the support of external actors: SNIM, a "small" iron ore producer just managing to take national control of its operations after the departure of the expatriate management due to the Polisario war, was able to embark on the big Guelbs project thanks to the support of the consumers and the development banks.

In addition, the big "new"[26] Third World monoproducers, producing for export and enjoying high differential rents in their working mines and with

29

abundant low-cost reserves, were trying to reinforce their position, thinking that they in their turn could become the leaders of an oligopoly. To a large extent, the development by CVRD of the Carajas iron ore mine in Brazil, which benefitted from the support of the consumers and the development banks, fitted into this pattern. State enterprises on other markets, e.g. phosphate and phosphoric acid in the case of l'Office Chérifien des Phosphates (OCP) in Morocco and copper for Codelco and Enami in Chile, had similar strategies.

The traditional leaders reacted in very different ways to these changes. In fact, while some of them (like Reynolds in Valesul) agreed to sell their technology[27] and prepared to give up their dominant positions on the primary metals markets (aluminium and zinc in particular), others tried to react by increasing their installed capacity at all costs. This was notably the case of Amax in North America on the molybdenum market and, in our sample, of the PT Inco nickel mining and concentrating complex in Indonesia. Initially conceived as a project oriented to the Japanese market, PT Inco was first developed as an NFI with the participation of Japanese consumers and the financing of American and Japanese public bodies. As from 1974, the oil price rise considerably changed the technical and economic parameters of the project, which was very energy-intensive. The Japanese consumers refused to follow Inco in a very expensive extension of the project, the only way to achieve economies of scale. Inco then went into this adventure alone, thinking that through maintaining its market share it would be able to control price levels, so that the project would still be profitable, whatever the cost. As we shall see, this industrial logic, typical of the oligopolistic mode of growth, turned out to be catastrophic when Inco lost control of the market.

Generally speaking, the appearance of new actors and new forms of investment confused producers' strategies[28] on the oligopolistic markets and upset the earlier forms of consensus on the mode of growth. The leaders were contested and some of them reacted in conservative fashion, usually ineffectively. The consumers broke the earlier consensus by favouring the appearance of new entrants. The resulting disorganisation of supply, or rather its reorganisation through the intervention of states, banks and consumers, caused the producers to lose a degree of freedom as regards adjusting the rate of output of their operations[29]. Through becoming dependent on increasingly numerous and heterogenous actors, supply lost some of its flexibility and its controllability during this period. The virtuous dynamic which previously existed between the installation of excess capacity and the short-term supply-side adjustment of the market under the control of the industry leaders, had come to an end.

THE SLOWDOWN IN GROWTH OF CONSUMPTION AND THE END OF METAL MARKET REGULATION

In parallel with the disorganisation of supply, the 1970s saw a very marked deceleration of the rate of growth of demand both in the industrialised countries and in the Third World. This break in the trend[30], clearly illustrated in Figure 5, was the result not only of reduced overall economic growth in the industrialised countries, but also to a change in structure of these economies (more services, less material objects) and above all a reduction in the *intensity of use* of ores and metals (economies, substitution) in the industrial production of the countries with a high standard of living. In this situation, the effects of recycling metals, favoured by the increased stocks of scrap, took on considerable proportions.

The slowdown corresponded much more to a structural saturation of requirements than to a temporary reduction of consumption. It reflected a basic change in the *mode of metal consumption,* i.e. in the design of manufacturing processes and the choice of industrial inputs. In other words, the consumers of materials acquired considerable freedom of choice during the 1970s in what they could use as inputs. This was due on the one hand to the rise of materials industries outside the traditional metallurgical sector (plastics, composites) and on the other to the development of new supply strategies resulting from the desire of manufacturers to adapt the materials used as closely as possible to the evolution of their products.

What is more, consumers in the industrialised countries ceased to fear a long-term breakdown in their supplies of metals. Refined metals and even semi-finished products became commodities, i.e. standard products for which only cost criteria count. The relations of the processing industries with their suppliers of commodities became purely commercial and were influenced by short-term considerations. The strategic reasons which had made consumers willing to pay a high price for raw materials to finance the expansion of upstream capacities disappeared once the growth of the volume of demand slowed down. The earlier consensus was broken: consumers were no longer willing to finance the oligopolistic regulation of markets.

It can be seen in retrospect that despite the slower growth of demand in the second half of the 1970s and despite the change in patterns of consumption, the level of investment in the mining sector continued to grow in constant money terms during this period[31]. Thus, for example, according to Radetzki and Van Duyne (1984)[32], in 1974, the capacity expansion planned for the next five years in the copper industry corresponded to an anticipated growth rate of 6 per cent per annum, whereas the real rate was 1.6 per cent. Similarly, it is estimated that the total capacity of planned aluminium smelter projects after the second oil crisis amounted to 40 per cent of worldwide installed capacity, while the average annual growth rate of world demand had dropped from 9.2 per cent in the period 1950-73 to 1.7 per cent in the period 1974-85.

It is likely that in this situation the industry, in its old structure, would have underestimated the slowdown of demand and would have overinvested against the cycle as was its habit. However, as we have seen, the appearance of new actors and the disorganisation of supply had brought new motivations for greater investment quite independent of, not to say in spite of, the basic change in requirements. This very high level of investment, which was not compensated by the shutdown of the oldest capacities, led to the appearance of considerable overcapacities in the early 1980s[33].

From a static standpoint, this situation was nothing new in itself, since as we have seen, the industry was traditionally in a state of permanent structural overcapactity. But there were two factors that indicated something had changed:

-- The sheer volume of excess capacity: almost twice the effective consumption in the nickel industry in 1982;

-- The duration of the phase difference with respect to the revival of demand, which was constantly expected but never came.

The "necessary condition" of demand catch-up ceased to be fulfilled. Before long, the short-term financial constraints weighing on operators, whether they were heavily-indebted private companies or public enterprises in the exporting countries of the Third World caught up in the crises of their national economies, led the most vulnerable to start price wars, in which they were followed by the stronger companies[34]. In 1982, the prices of most ores and metals fell to their lowest level since 1945. In the case of nickel and aluminium, introduced on the commodity markets at the beginning of the crisis in the late 1970s, the collapse of prices led to the reference to producer prices being abandoned.

In particular, those mining and metallurgical projects that were in the start-up phase in the early 1980s whatever their comparative advantages, experienced financial difficulties. Certain companies decided purely and simply to close down production units that had scarcely been completed. Apart from Bougainville, which started up in 1972, all the projects studied in this book had to be financially restructured. The contradictions between the different actors involved in individual projects became sharper. The new forms of investment which had made it possible in the design phase to share the risks between all the actors led to conflicts once these risks materialised. The first difficulties appeared between shareholders and bankers when the rise in interest rates combined with the fall in prices compromised the debt-servicing of several projects (PT Inco, Selebi-Phikwe, Cerro Matoso). In all cases the companies had to put up equity capital. In that of PT Inco the parent company was obliged to consolidate the project debt in its balance sheet. But the need for equity capital further aggravated the tensions between shareholders, with some companies deciding on strategic withdrawal (Amax in Selebi-Phikwe), while others, trapped in the operations, were trying not to have to suffer all the consequences of the situation on their own. Technical difficulties gave rise to disputes over the sharing of responsibility (Selebi-Phikwe, Ok Tedi). The host states, whatever their degree of financial involvement, tried to prevent the disengagement of the foreign operators. Even though, as we shall see, other factors contributed to the overall rigidity of supply during this phase of overcapacity[35], it is clear that the difficulties encountered in each of the projects studied prevented them from reacting in a flexible way to the slowing of demand.

The fact is that far from reflecting a temporary imbalance between supply and demand, this collapse in prices had revealed the serious disorganisation of all the markets. The traditional regulation practices had lasted a long time, but the disorganisation of supply now meant that it was no longer sufficient for a dominant supplier to temporarily reduce his sales on a market to see prices suddenly move up. On the contrary, the majority of producers who tried to apply this type of measure in order to preserve the old system ended up by losing some of their outlets to the benefit of their more aggressive competitors. In the space of a few years, the producers became fiercely competitive. The commercial rivalries which had previously been concentrated mainly on the marginal increase in demand, suddenly shifted to market shares already attributed. The aggressive inroads of certain producers wishing to extend their markets broke down the earlier regional compartmentalisation. This generalised disorder was amplified by the increased and unforeseeable intervention of Eastern bloc countries on Western markets (USSR for nickel, China for tungsten and tin). The traders who had been the catalysts for these phenomena were then themselves competed against by the producers.

The disorganisation of the markets first of all meant the end of the absolute rents received by all producers in a given branch (aluminium, nickel, molybdenum, tin, etc.). But more than this, the undifferentiated nature of the products made competition between the producers of what were now commodities especially fierce, all the more so because the barriers to market exit were high. On certain markets this competition held prices for a considerable time (notably in 1982 and 1986) below the costs of the most advantaged producers, so that differential rents disappeared for a while. When the markets emerged from oligopolistic control differential rents no longer sufficed to ensure firms' margins.

CRISIS IN THE OLIGOPOLISTIC MODE OF GROWTH

The raw materials crisis thus temporarily shattered the financial logic of the growth mode of the industry. But can it be concluded from this that the oligopolistic strategies in the mining and metallurgical sector are now a thing of the past? Or can it be thought on the other hand that the restructuring brought about by price wars on the markets will reduce overcapacity and enable new giants to re-establish regulation? We do not think so, because as we are going to show, it is not only the financial logic but also the industry mode of growth itself that was condemned by the crisis. In fact, the three basic conditions have ceased to be fulfilled:

1. Demand is now growing only slowly and has become unpredictable: in the industrialised countries the basic trend is that the overall mass of objects produced by industry is increasing very little, or even diminishing. *Most markets for material objects have become replacement markets.* Even when a new market appears for a metal, this market remains very competitive and is saturated within a few years. Zinc, which penetrated the motor vehicle industry very strongly as from 1984 to protect bodywork steels against corrosion, now covers on average about 40 per cent of these steels, which seems close to the maximum. So in five years this new segment has already become a replacement market.

Consumption is growing faster in the Third World. According to Phillip Crowson[36], between 1977 and 1987 the developing countries' share of metal consumption increased from 10 to 18 per cent for aluminium and copper, and from 16 to 24 per cent for zinc. In the newly industrialized countries (NICs), the average consumption of metal has increased at an average rate of 6-7 per cent per annum during the 1980s. Five countries -- India, Taiwan, Brazil, Mexico and South Korea -- account for almost half the consumption of the developing countries. But it would appear that the industrial dynamic that is readjusting the pattern of consumption towards the developing countries is also bringing the development of national mining and metallurgical industries[37] in the new consumer countries. As the adjustment of national production to consumption sometimes results in massive imports and sometimes in unexpected exports (Valesul), this is a further factor adding to the destabilisation of international markets. Not only is the trend of consumption in the Third World difficult to forecast, but its impact on markets is even more so.

The earlier representations of global long-term demand for metals and for fertilizers (exponential growth) have become obsolete[38], and what is more, the traditional correlations between economic growth and mineral raw materials consumption which used to form the basis for demand analysis no longer exist. In the industrialised countries, in fact, strong growth stimulated by the service sector no longer brings about *a priori* an increase in the consumption of mineral raw materials, while a temporary and localized increase in the activity of a branch of industry[39] in a given country may have the effect of sharply but precariously increasing the demand for a product in one region of the world, bringing about a market disequilibrium without anybody being able to say whether it will be durable or not. The cyclical fluctuations in demand which used to be smoothed out in the longer term by the exponential growth are now of considerable importance.

It has become impossible to forecast medium and long-term global demand for ores and metals.

2. Without regulation, differential rents may be reduced or even disappear.

Competition between raw materials producers has caused spectacular restructuring, bringing about in particular a narrowing of the cost scale and a relative reduction in differential rents. The fact is that the impossibility of differentiating products has turned the mining and metallurgy industry, formerly highly protected, into one of the most competitive activities that can be, because competition can be exercised only through costs. This competition has been made worse by monetary instability in the industrialized countries, sometimes favouring the European or Japanese producers (as was the case between 1982 and 1985 when the dollar was very strong relative to the Japanese and European currencies), sometimes the North American ones (as has been the case since 1985), inciting in turn the group of producers disadvantaged by the monetary situation to look more actively for productivity gains. The price pressure exerted between 1982 and 1987 favoured the optimisation of factor allocation and of mine operating techniques, in some cases bringing unit costs down by as much as 40 per cent in real terms[40].

In addition, in the mineral raw materials exporting countries whose economic dynamic was based essentially on the creation of mining rents and their redistribution in the domestic economy, those we have called the mining countries, the reduction of these rents caused structural imbalances which resulted in particular in currency devaluations. These monetary phenomena also contributed to the overall movement towards reduced costs. Zambia, which everyone considered at the beginning of the 1980s to be a very high cost copper producer, has shown in recent years that it could continue to produce despite depressed prices, thanks to develuations of the Kwacha. In the Zambian economy, as in the majority of countries in which mining exports weigh heavily in the balance of trade, there is a strong correlation between the value of the local currency and that of the ores and metals exported[41]. This analysis shows that in the absence of market regulation the structure of differential rents has undergone great changes, the general trend being the reduction of the cost scale in the industry. *In the time of the oligopolies, the absolute rents preserved the differential rents.* It is very possible that the 1987 price rise will bring about another rise in the costs of the industry[42]. But on the one hand it is not certain that this upward readjustment will once again increase differential rents, or in other words that costs will increase more rapidly in marginal operations, and on the other, it appears today that costs and prices are closely linked[43], so that what appears to be a comparative advantage in a period of high prices may be significantly diminished when price pressure concentrates the competition on costs.

3. Without the prospect of demand growth, the industry is ceasiing to invest.

As a result of the crisis, excess capacities have to a large extent been eliminated on most markets (with the notable exception of the iron ore market). The upturn in metals consumption registered in the second half of 1987 caught all producers by surprise. The prices of aluminium and copper doubled, while the price of nickel increased five-fold (see Figures 1-4). These phenomena are in themselves nothing new, and such price movements had escaped the regulatory capacity of the producers more than once in the past[44].

What is new this time is that while in the past (nickel in 1969, aluminium in 1973, molybdenum in 1976) these movements were systematically accompanied by big waves of investment, spearheaded by the leaders, anxious not to be overtaken by the growth of the market and to keep out potential new entrants, no sign of this has been seen since 1987. Everyone has been waiting for demand to fall again, and in the meantime has patched up his financial wounds and constituted reserves ready to face new price battles[45]. A summary stocktaking of investments made in the eighteen months following the 1987 turnaround shows that the expenditure of the enterprises having survived the best has been much more concerned with taking over competitors than with starting to build new operations[46]. The mining and metallurgical companies no longer seem to believe in growth on their traditional markets. However, without strong growth of the industry, regulation of supply, at least in its earlier form, is not possible. And vice-versa.

The crisis of the 1980s was perceived by the operators as the end of the oligopolistic regulation of markets. In the absence of regulation, it appeared that prices could lastingly remain at very low levels, thus compromising the profitability of any new investment. Being a very capital-intensive industry, with margins limited by the tax systems of host countries, producing a mining or metallurgical commodity, i.e. a standard product enjoying no qualitative advantage, for an unpredictable international demand, has become a high-risk activity. Those companies that had relied on their natural advantages[47] to increase their production and eliminate their competitors encountered such resistance that they were obliged to abandon this strategy. Furthermore, attempts at regulation aimed at restoring profits through limiting competition, because of a lack of clear possibilities for growth on the markets, failed. This was notably the case of the European zinc producers' attempt to group together, announced in 1987, the weak point in which was to try to reduce production capacities in Europe without at the same time defining the growth strategies of the companies involved. The same problem also appeared in the reduction of excess steelmaking capacity in the EEC.

In other words, it is the whole of what we have called the growth mode of the industry, i.e. *the dynamics of investment by enterprises and of market regulation, taken as being indissociable,* which came into crisis. The new forms of investment, and this is an important finding of our research, contributed to the appearance of this crisis because, through the introduction of new actors, they made possible a dissociation between the dynamic of oligopolistic investment and regulation by mining and metallurgical enterprises. *The NFI facilitated the entry to the industry of actors foreign to the former regulating practices.*

THE SEARCH FOR OTHER MODES OF GROWTH

The questions raised by the crisis thus concern at one and the same time both the regulation of raw materials markets and the future of the mining and metallurgical industry.

The regulation of commodity markets

Once they had escaped from the control of producers, adjustments of supply and demand were made with much greater price variations than in the past. As from the beginning of the 1980s, the majority of metals transactions -- formerly based on "producer prices" -- have been indexed on the commodity exchanges, while the financial instruments markets have developed remarkably. Metals have thus become financial products subject to the investment and arbitrage logic of the operators on this kind of market. Judging by the vigorous growth of the activity of commodity exchanges, the financial mass invested around metals trading has greatly increased. As a result, the anticipations provoked by only small variations in the fundamentals[48] of the metals markets have caused very spectacular price jumps (see Figures 1-4). Furthermore, with the reduction of stocks at each stage in the processing chain together with the new rigidities in supply of which we have spoken, the equilibrium of the fundamentals has become more sensitive. This structural instability and the price movements it provokes are upsetting to consumers and encourage substitions leading to an irreversable decline in metals demand for certain applications.

The creation of new forms of regulation is an open question. A return to the former system of supply-side regulation seems not to be desired, because everybody fears the effects of overcapacity if the consensus between suppliers and buyers is not re-established. Why in fact should the producers, whether private or public operators, reinvest their profit margins in installing excess capacity likely to cause a fall in prices?

New directions for the growth of enterprises

During the 1980s, commodity producers in the industrialised countries have been actively trying to diversify their products and their activities, abandoning the uni-directional growth associated with the regulation of commodity markets. This uni-directional growth was in fact what gave its meaning to the concept of *the industry*[49]. The mining and metallurgical industry was a set of enterprises developing on markets on which they assumed the management of the equilibrium. These enterprises now have to find new directions for growth, which is likely to make the growth dynamic of each one of them more individual.

Already during the 1970s, certain big mining and metallurgical companies, unable to reinvest their profits in their traditional markets, had tried to diversify into other markets. This was notably the case of Amax, molybdenum market leader in the 1960s, who successfully diversified into coal, copper, nickel and aluminium. But this diversification was into other commodity markets, which Amax thus helped to destabilize. What is new in the present situation is that there are no longer any mineral commodity markets offering a growth potential capapable of offering an alternative to the saturated traditional markets of the big groups. To return to the example of Amax, this company has had to abandon its activities in copper and nickel, and can no longer hope today to grow through expanding its production of aluminium or coal. Furthermore, having lost its dominant position on the molybdenum market, the company has to act as a marginal producer, forced to greatly reduce its production when demand falls in order to avoid the price collapse which would hurt Amax much more than its competitors[50]. Thus, while making every effort to remain competitive in their basic activities, the mining and metallurgical companies now have to find growth processes that enable them to get out of commodity markets.

This transformation can be achieved in the context of large-scale financial restructuring, either through the mining and metallurgical company being absorbed by an outside industrial group whose logic will become dominant (the case of Boliden's takeover by Trelleborg in Sweden in 1987), or through the company liquidating its mining assets and redeploying into other sectors (the case of the diversification of the French Imetal group since 1986).

A slower and more complicated method is the process of industrial diversification of commodity producers trying to develop new products for new clients on the basis of the company's existing know-how. However, the growth mode being, as we have said, "the growth logic of the industry examined in its relationship with markets", innovating in the mode of growth means for the company a change in its relationship with the market. But as we have seen, this relationship with the market, i.e. the perception of demand and the method of dealing with competition, was specific to oligopolistic growth. Demand was perceived as a global figure forming the horizon for the strategic vision. The leaders on the major markets (Inco for nickel and Alcoa for aluminium) carried out research to develop demand, not with the aim of finding new sources of value-added in new products, but with the aim of increasing overall demand for the metal for the industry in general and themselves in particular, so as to be able to continue in the long term to grow while keeping the competition within certain limits. Now, in order to conceive new products, the mining and metallurgical companies have to replace the concept of demand by that of "client" which is based on the existence, over and above the simple deal, of new relationships with the downstream operators and the orientation of production to their needs. The sellers of semi-finished metal products now spend more time with their clients than in their own companies and research is carried out jointly by materials producers and users, materials suppliers take part in the marketing of the finished product, etc. The aim of these processes is to manage to add to the commodity a service or additional treatment that differentiates it and in turn promotes specialisation into new activities.

The diversification of commodity producers is starting to bring new modes of growth. In these processes, the question of the relationship with the market, i.e. with other producers and with clients, or if one prefers, dealing with the competition, has given rise to the concept of *know-how*. Each company having its own industrial experience, it is from the accumulated experience of its own individual history that the fields of specialisation are induced or its competitiveness can be guaranteed. "Know-how" now identifies the accumulated knowledge of the firm and embodies the results of its economic history[51]. The use of this concept in the concrete analysis of the diversification processes of commodity producers[52] reveals a differentiation of the firms operating on a given market that calls into question the earlier concept of "the industry". We increasingly find groups of enterprises that used to be mining and metallurgical companies, but have nothing else in common. In the industrialised countries, there is now little in common between Phelps Dodge and Metallgesellschaft, Noranda and Boliden, Péchiney and Alcan. In the Third World countries, the monoproducers of commodities for export still remain fairly similar. It is likely that they will have to differentiate themselves more in the future, for example through diversifying on their domestic markets. The host states, if they cease to promote mining exports, might try to reorient them in this direction. With diversification, other new forms of investment are appearing, connected with the evolution in client-supplier relations upstream and downstream of the metallurgical firms (partnership), growth through the takeover of customers or competitors, and financing through the market.

This trend is drastically changing the transnational nature of the former relationship with demand, because downstream linkage implies not only geographical proximity, but also technical and economic proximity to customers and final consumers. The producers who have gone furthest along this road have generally begun by finding potential downstream industrial partners in their home country or region. The exporting producers of the Third World, hitherto favoured essentially by natural advantages, are likely to be at a disadvantage in their search for forms of diversification on distant markets. This is why, in our opinion, the big Third World mining companies, accustomed to producing for export regardless of the trends in their own national economies, could very well, in the next few years, find themselves forced to find ways of extending their activities, preferably oriented towards the development of domestic production and markets.

This has already begun in the Third World countries with buoyant domestic markets. But, as can be seen through the example of the Valesul aluminium project in Brazil, orientation towards the domestic market does not in itself suffice to protect an enterprise from commercial risks. In fact, the refusal of the Brazilian processors to participate in the project meant that the company got into commercial difficulties when the domestic market turned down. In this precise case, it was the state that indirectly took responsibility for the corresponding risk. It appears that in future new links need to be forged with Brazilian consumer enterprises in order to better guarantee market outlets for the national producer. The establishment of these links will be a contradictory process because it changes earlier commercial practices. It is clear that in this field there is room for new forms of investment actually within a developing country[53].

On the other hand, there is in our opinion, little future for the big Third World export-oriented projects. Managing internationally competitive operations in rentier coutries has become more difficult. What is more, the effects on precariously balanced markets of the coming on stream of big operations have become something to be feared. Big exporters (Zambia and Chile for copper)[54] can even be seen seeking shares in processing units in the consumer countries.

In conclusion, it may be noted that the new forms of investment, of which we have said that they contributed to the crisis of the earlier mode of growth, have also participated in the establishment of a new mode of growth through limiting the involvement of mining and metallurgical companies in the production of commodities, going into assocation with consumer clients and introducing innovative forms of financing. By and large, it can be seen that if the commodity markets have become uncontrollable, it is necessary to strengthen direct links between producers and consumers, or even between suppliers and customers. Commodity production having become structurally more risky, the consumer industries are going to have to take more responsibility for ensuring the security of outlets for these operations. *The NFI, which favoured the decoupling of oligopolistic growth and the regulation of commodity markets, are now permitting the establishment of international vertical links in industrial production chains, thus marginalising recourse to the markets.* Through this, they are participating in the evolution of the world economy towards greater integration.

NOTES AND REFERENCES

1. Concept developed by AGLIETTA (1976).

2. At least so it was thought, because prices were then relatively stable. Cf. NAPPI (1985).

3. This does not mean that prospecting for rich and distant deposits was the only way to get in at the low end of the supply curve of the industry. The Americans became the leading copper producers at the end of the nineteenth century thanks to the invention of large-scale exploitation techniques that enabled them to exploit the low-grade porphyritic deposits that had hitherto been uneconomic. However, given constant exploitation technology, the search for new, low-cost deposits was at the origin of the development of the mining industry far from the consumption centres.

4. Thus, for example, although there was never a formal oligopoly on the world copper market, the exclusive commercial rights of American companies on the United States domestic market made it possible to establish a producer price on this market. Cf. NAPPI (1985).

5. On this subject, see the studies on the technical and economic characteristics of the mining industry, notably in BOSSON and VARON (1977), Chapter 1, and GIRAUD (1983).

6. On this observation see the analysis of P. de SA (1988) on supply side regulation mechanisms on mineral raw materials markets, in "Structural Changes and Price Formation in the Minerals and Metals Industries".

7. The notion of consensus, traditional in oligopoly theories (in particular CAVES and PORTER, 1978) to designate the implicit agreement between producers, should also be extended to producer-consumer relations. The relationship between producer and consumer in which the price established reflected the long-term cost of production rather than the short-term equilibrium of the market was certainly a form of consensus.

8. Cf. GIRAUD (1983).

9. In certain cases (e.g. ZCCM in Zambia), it can be seen that the increasing state share of the capital of the company during the 1970s was matched by a policy of strategic retreat on the part of foreign operators when the disappearance of mining rents in the more or less distant future (due to the exhaustion of reserves) appeared inevitable. In other situations, (e.g. that of the nationalisation of the copper industry in Chile in 1971), nationalisation coincided with the refusal of the foreign operator to continue investments on which rents were to be taxed, while the state at the same time expressed

its intention to seek rents for itself. In fact, in the 1955 "Nuevo Trato" binding the Chilean state and the big United States copper companies (Kennecott, Anaconda), the government agreed to reduce taxation as an incentive to encourage the foreign companies to invest in capacity expansion. With the state taking an increasing share of company income, this agreement was repudiated during the 1960s. To increase copper production, the state had no other choice but to nationalise the entire sector in 1971. See BOMSEL (1986).

10. The principal mining countries may be defined *a priori* as those countries whose ore and metal exports make up over 40 per cent of total exports. The countries embraced by this definition, used in particular in a study by NANKANI (1979), are: Chile, Peru, Bolivia, Morocco, Mauritania, Guinea, Liberia, Niger, Togo, Zaïre, Zambia, Zimbabwe, Botswana, Jamaica, Guyana and Papua-New Guinea. These mining countries may be described as countries where the economic dynamic depends on rents generated by a mining sector producing for export.

11. The study of rent-based economic dynamics has given rise to an abundant literature, notably concerned with the case of the oil-exporting countries. See in particular CORDON and NEARY (1982) and NEARY and VAN WIBERGEN (1986). The theses put forward in this chapter concerning the creation and circulation of mining rents in the exporting countries of the Third World are developed in BOMSEL (1986).

12. This compartmentalisation which was at the origin of rent-based economic dynamics has not always been able to survive. In many mining countries (Bolivia, Peru, Zambia, Liberia, Mauritania, etc.) the dynamics of income redistribution affects the mining sector itself, breaking down the partition between the production sector and the distribution sector and hastening the marginalisation of the exporting sector.

13. The increasing indebtedness of the mining countries was accelerated by the second oil crisis, which brought about a net reduction in their "rent balance". The rents paid through oil imports were subtracted from those received through mining product exports. In 1982, the outstanding foreign debt for all mining countries was over 30 per cent of GNP, and was over 60 per cent for seven of the countries cited in note 10 above (BOMSEL 1986).

14. Most of the companies involved in these projects (RTZ, Asarco Phelps Dodge, Billiton, BHP, Amoco, etc.) invested in order to take advantage of differential rents. In fact, it would appear that only RTZ in its Bougainville investment, which benefitted from particularly favourable economic circumstances, was able, during a short period (four years) and thanks to skilled management, to appropriate a significant share of the mining rents. It should be noted that this was possible only because the company was able to repatriate these rents before getting too involved in the internal contradictions of Papua-New Guinea development.

15. In this last case, it was not strictly speaking a minority share because CVRD formally holds 51 per cent of the capital. It should be noted however that CVRD relied very much on the financing capacity of its Japanese partners whose power of decision over the realisation of the project was considerable.

16. The companies were well aware of what was happening however, as is shown by the fact that despite the ouvertures made to foreign operators since the beginnings of the 1980s by Chilean President Pinochet, the big United States, European and Australian mining companies have been suspicious of what the macroeconomic constraints weighing on the Chilean government may have on taxation in the longer term. Although the mineral reserves offered to foreign operators appeared likely to generate substantial differential rents, these operators turned out to be more than hesitant about investing. The recent decisions to invest in Chilean projects (Escondida, El Indio), the only new Third World export projects of the late 1980s, where taken on the one hand through fear of a shortage of copper concentrates for non-integrated metallurgists and on the other because it seemed to consumers that despite its precarious socio-political situation, Chile was no doubt the least unstable of the copper exporting countries.

17. On this subject, see MANSEAU (1979) and GIRAUD (1983), Chapter 5.

18. There was in fact a shift, according to RADETZKI (1980) from outside financing of no more than 10 to 20 per cent of the total before the 1960s, to levels of over 60 and even quite often as much as 70 or 80 per cent.

19. The World Bank services responsible for monitoring the mineral raw materials markets in fact produced the most exaggeratedly "optimistic" medium-term demand forecasts in the 1970s, not so much in our opinion because of scientific blindness as because of the conviction that it was the duty of the Bank to promote the development of capacity in this sector. (Cf. studies published by the market forecasting service of the World Bank in the late 1970s).

20. This argument regarding support for Third World raw materials exporting countries is one of the central theses in the work by BOSSON and VARON (1977).

21. All the authors we have cited (MANSEAU, RADETZKI, GIRAUD) in fact mention the role of the banks as a safety barrier for the risk run by the firms. They are then judged much more as inhibitors of the realisation of new projects than as incitors of investment.

22. This movement was considerably amplified at the beginning of the 1980s when the oil companies, wishing to reinvest the financial surpluses resulting from the second oil crisis, moved in to buy mining assets on a massive scale. Cf. de SA (1986).

23. In certain cases, this movement was initiated by consumers hoping to favour the development of supply. The Japanese, reselling technology bought elsewhere (flash smelting of copper, aluminium smelting) were particularly active in this field.

24. See the analyses by OMAN (1989) and those by LEBEN, more centred on the legal mechanisms through which NFI appeared.

25. On this subject see de SA *et al.* (1986).

26. Enterprises taken over by the State in the 1960s and 1970s.

27. This was also the case with Alcoa and Péchiney in aluminium, Outokumpu in copper, Vieille-Montaigne in zinc, etc.

28. It confused the issue to such an extent that all the producers tried to offest the fragility of their position by diluting the risks. This risk dilution often led to poor evaluation of the difficulty of implementing projects, leading to serious technical problems (Selebi-Phikwe, PT Inco, Ok Tedi, etc.). The failure of these projects after a few years of operation, or even before production had been built up to full capacity, brought the reality of the financial risk to the surface again and forced the actors with a share of the capital to face up to the obligations that they too had largely underestimated.

29. The constraints connected with bank debts or with state control constituted obstacles to reducing the production rate of the new units. In fact, on the one hand the external financing of the projects incited the companies to produce more to cover the debt servicing of the project, and on the other, the host countries put pressure on to maintain the level of production (the case of the Indonesian government in PT Inco and of Papua-New Guinea in Ok Tedi). In certain cases, the companies preferred to shut down the operation completely rather than to run at a reduced rate (the case of Inco in Guatemala).

30. This break in the trend was noticed only at the beginning of the 1980s. It was subsequently studied extensively by the mineral economists. See in particular GIRAUD *et al.* (1985), TILTON (1986) and ROBERTS (1988).

31. A calculation based on an average mine life of 20 years, a construction time of 6 years and a capital intensity in the industry of 3 (ratio of the initial investment to annual turnover) shows that a reduction in the rate of growth of demand from 5 to 2 per cent would have required the annual volume of investment to be divided by 2. It is possible to object to the bases of this calculation, admittedly very crude, but the fact remains that the high capital intensity of the mining industry leads to a high investment "accelerator" (or "decelerator") coefficient. See BOMSEL, GIRAUD, de SA (1985).

32. RADETZKI and VAN DUYNE (1984) examine the specific difficulties of adjusting a highly capital-intensive industry to a sharp reduction in the growth of demand. Without going into great detail, they interpret the delay observed in the adjustment of investment in the copper industry to the inertial effect of capital intensity on the one hand and divergencies in the rationale of the supply-side actors involved on the other hand.

33. See BOMSEL, GIRAUD, de SA (1985).

34. On the nickel market it was Amax, a highly-indebted marginal producer, who triggered the price war in 1982. On the copper market, the price war

was due to the Chileans' desire to oust the United States producers at a time when the Zambians, even less favourably placed on the cost scale, could scarcely close down an industry whose exports accounted for 98 per cent of the country's foreign exchange earnings.

35. HUMPHREYS (1988) shows that capacity utilisation rates of copper, lead, and zinc mines and of aluminium smelters on the whole varied little between the two periods 1975-81 and 1982-86.

36. CROWSON (1989).

37. This is the case of China, India and Brazil. In this last country, the state has also recently limited foreign participation in the mining sector to 25 per cent. (*Le Monde*, 4th May 1988).

38. The freedom of choice of materials that consumers now have suggests that demand has ceased to be a purely structural phenomenon which can be assigned for example to GDP per head in such and such a country. It is now also dependent on rapidly evolving processes connected with the dynamism and adjustment capability of the industrial chains in which competition between materials is becoming more common. In countries with a comparable standard of living, aluminium has penetrated drink packaging much further in the United States than in Europe, where glassmakers, steelmakers and above all drink producers (brewers, winemakers, etc.) have created different consumption habits. In each country, the constitution and maintenance of market shares in competing materials has depended and will go on depending on the dynamism of national suppliers.

39. Thus, for example, the revival of the building and public works industry in Japan in the second half of 1987 created a sudden shortage on the non-ferrous metals markets. This phenomenon, which had not been foreseen, was not perceived as the sign of a stable revival of metals consumption in the OECD countries however.

40. See de SA (1987).

41. It should be noted however that in Zambia the short-term maintenance of mining sector competitiveness through devaluation of the currency at the same time aggravated the domestic economic situation and led to deterioration in the productive apparatus of the copper industry, unable to import the equipment necessary for the proper maintainance of the plant and machinery.

42. This point is practically established in HUMPHREYS (1988).

43. See in particular CROWSON (1984).

44. HUMPHREYS (1988) also stresses that the fact that no one perceived or forecast the turnaround in prices is worrying for the evolution of minerals economics, whose ambition for the last 20 years has been to model raw materials market equilibria.

45. The price upturn even brought a return of conflicts over the sharing of economic rents which was thought to be a thing of the past. Thus, in the Dominican Republic, following a five-fold increase in the nickel price in the first quarter of 1988, the state tried to impose a royalty of 25 per cent on Falconbridge's nickel exports. The company, whose operations in this country, begun at the end of the 1970s, had never covered costs, was forced to suspend its exports to negotiate a more favourable sharing of rents with the state, arguing in particular that a fall in the price of the product was imminent. This example shows how the companies have lost their ability to appropriate the rents for themselves, especially where the appearance of these rents has ceased to depend on them.

46. Certain projects were relaunched, but often as an extension of existing capacities, and these movements have been insignificant in comparison with the sums involved in takeovers. The best example no doubt is the comparison between the Neves Corvo mining project in Portugal, decided by RTZ in 1985 for £ 500 million -- one of the rare projects developed during the 1980s -- and the takeover of BP Minerals in 1988, again by RTZ, for $4.5 billion. In the annual survey of the *Engineering and Mining Journal* for 1989, the number of mining and metallurgical projects has fallen from 480 in 1988 to 430, with the corresponding cumulative investment down 13 per cent.

47. This was above all the case with certain state enterprises in the Third World for which the maximisation of rents (or export earnings) was to be the prime objective, margins not being limited by having to share the rents with a foreign actor. Thus for example, the relative failure of Codelco's aggressive attempt to expand on the copper market (with certain American competitors it was trying to oust recording profits in 1986 despite the lower prices) called the company's strategy into question. The United States copper industry, whose production capacity has admittedly been reduced, nevertheless emerged from the crisis with a more competitive production tool.

48. I.e. the supply/demand equilibrium for physical metal.

49. See OMAN (1989), Chapters 3 and 5.

50. This is explained by the fact that Amax's new competitors on the market obtain molybdenum as a byproduct of copper, hence at virtually zero cost.

51. DETRIE and RAMANANTSOA (1983) define know-how as "all the knowledge that it is necessary to possess, absolutely, to be competitive in a given activity".

52. This research is currently under way at the CERNA under the title: *Diversification latérale des producteurs de commodités*, 1989.

53. China is already participating in a joint-venture with CRA in Australia for the development of a captive iron ore mine.

54. This strategy is even more marked on the part of Australian producers -- Australia being considered an industrialised country, even though highly specialised in natural resources and hence a rentier -- who export to Europe and South East Asia.

Figure 1

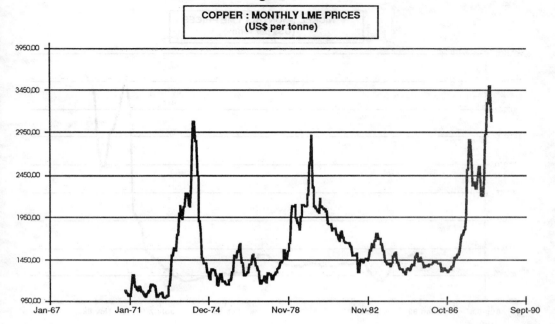

COPPER : MONTHLY LME PRICES
(US$ per tonne)

Figure 2

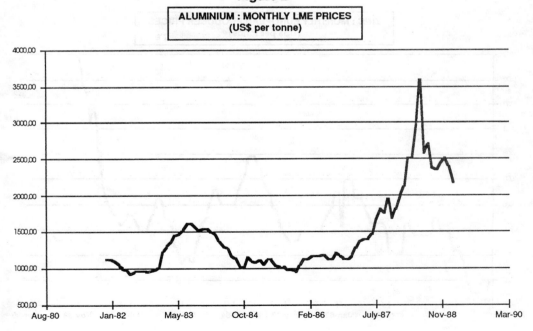

ALUMINIUM : MONTHLY LME PRICES
(US$ per tonne)

Figure 3

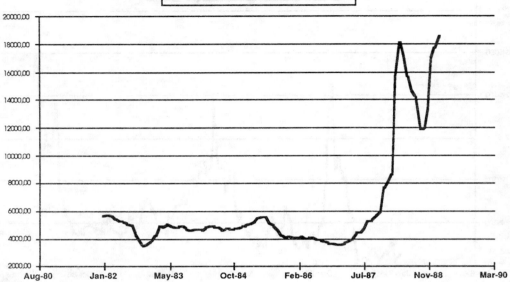

NICKEL : MONTHLY LME PRICES
(US$ per tonne)

Figure 4

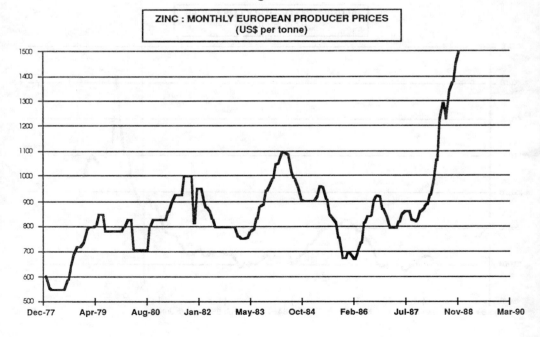

ZINC : MONTHLY EUROPEAN PRODUCER PRICES
(US$ per tonne)

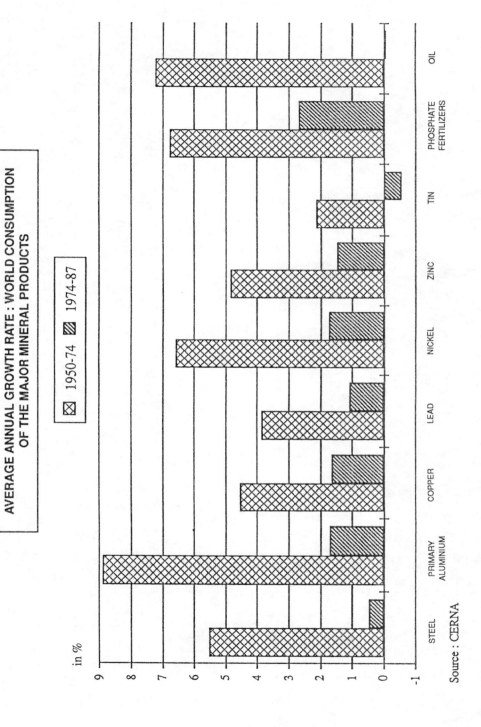

Figure 5

AVERAGE ANNUAL GROWTH RATE : WORLD CONSUMPTION
OF THE MAJOR MINERAL PRODUCTS

1950-74   1974-87

Source : CERNA

51

Chapter II

CARAJAS*

INTRODUCTION

With an investment of almost $4 billion in the early 1980s and the construction of a railway 900 kilometres long through Amazonia, Carajas is the biggest ore mine project since the opening up of the African Copperbelt at the end of the 19th century. The proven reserves of the deposit amount to almost 20 years of world iron ore consumption at the present rate. The realisation of this project, drastically changing the structure of the world iron ore market, brought in, alongside the Brazilian public operator CVRD (Companhia Vale Rio Doce), supported by its government, the world's biggest iron ore importers (in particular European and Japanese), concerned about the equilibrium of the market. This chapter illustrates how the strategies of CVRD, the world's biggest iron ore producer, the Brazilian state, and the world's biggest iron ore importers fitted together in this operation.

HISTORY OF THE PROJECT

The Carajas iron ore deposit was discovered in 1967 by US Steel geologists prospecting for manganese deposits capable of taking over from the company's reserves mined in the south of the country since 1910. News of the size and quality of US Steel's discovery spread rapidly in Brazilian government circles, arousing the interest in particular of CVRD, Brazil's biggest iron ore producer, anxious to increase its influence on the world iron ore market.

---

* Chapter prepared by Isabel Marquès.

Because of the scale of the project, the Brazilian government suspended the granting of licences from 1967 to 1969 in order to impose the entry of CVRD as majority shareholder. US Steel, not particularly interested in exploiting the deposit as its real aim was to find manganese, nevertheless agreed to participate in the evaluation work. It was to this end that in 1970 CVRD and US Steel created a subsidiary, AMZA (Amazonie Mineraçao SA), CVRD holding 51 per cent and US Steel 49 per cent.

Differences soon appeared between the two partners over the size of the project: US Steel wanted a medium-sized operation with the output being transported by river, while CVRD wanted a very large operation with a railway and a large capacity port to enable it to export the ore to distant countries, notably Japan[1].

The potential of the Carajas project was way beyond US Steel's needs and marketing ambitions, this company being mainly interested in the supply of feedstocks for its steelworks in the United States. Furthermore, the stagnation of iron ore prices since 1973, connected with the steel crisis, did not argue in favour of a large-scale operation . In view of the investment costs envisaged by CVRD for a production of 35 million tonnes ayear (see Inset), US Steel[2] withdrew, selling its share in AMZA to CVRD in 1977 for $50 million, so that CVRD became sole shareholder in the project.

CVRD is a public enterprise[3], the biggest exporter of iron ore to Europe. Its industrial experience in mining, treating, transporting and marketing iron ore put it in a strong position for commercial and financial negotiations.

In order to obtain long-term sales contracts (up to the year 2000) -- a guarantee demanded by the lenders -- CVRD embarked on commercial negotiations with the biggest buyers of iron ore as from 1979. The resulting contracts, negotiated before 1981, covered a volume of 24.65 million tonnes a year, or about 70 per cent of Carajas' total production capacity. Of this volume, 9.3 million tonnes a year represented substitution for tonnage at that time coming from the mines in the south of the country (see Table 2.1).

Table 2.1.: Sales contracts for Carajás iron ore
(Million tonnes)

Importer (Country)	1985	1986	1987	1988/89	Substitution for southern system	Net additional exports
Italsider (Italy)	2.50	2.50	2.50	2.50	1.20	1.30
Salzgitter (Germany)	0.50	0.50	0.50	0.50	0.30	0.20
Thyssen (Germany)	2.40	2.40	2.40	2.40	0.90	1.50
Mannesmann (Germany)	0.80	0.80	0.80	0.80	0.30	0.50
Krupp (Germany)	1.00	1.00	1.00	1.00	0.50	0.50
Klockner (Germany)	0.50	0.50	0.50	0.50	0.50	
Korf (Germany)	0.50	0.50	0.50	0.50		0.50
Dillinger (Germany)	0.25	0.25	0.25	0.25		0.25
Usinor (France)	1.70	1.70	1.70	1.70	0.80	0.90
Solmer (France)	1.40	0.60	1.00	1.50	0.30	1.20
Arbed (Bel/Lux/Germany)		1.00	1.00	2.00		2.00
Japanese Steel Mills (Japan)	7.00	8.50	10.00	10.00	4.50	5.50
Pohang (Korea)	1.00	1.00	1.00	1.00		1.00
Total	**19.55**	**21.25**	**23.15**	**24.65**	**9.30**	**15.35**

Source : CVRD

These contracts made an impression on institutional lenders, sensitive to the strategic interests of the iron ore buyers and the need to ensure the long-term competitiveness of supplies for the western steel industry.

The constitution of the financing package for the Carajas project bears witness to CVRD's skill in being able to obtain very substantial outside financing in a somewhat unfavourable economic context (Brazil being highly indebted and the iron ore market depressed). The World Bank, applied to in 1981, gave a favourable opinion in May 1982. Negotitations were completed in August 1982 with the approval of the financing plan. Tables 2.2, 2.3 and 2.4 show the overall Carajas financing package and the details of the Brazilian contribution.

Table 2.2. : Carajás financial resources and expenditure – 1982 plan
(Million dollars)

Resources	
Equity capital	1 820.4
Brazilian financing	1 218.6
Tied credits	130.7
IBRD & US financing	331.5
Japanese financing	495.4
European financing	530.0
Provisions[4]	400.0
Total resources[5]	
Hypothesis I)	4 526.6
Hypothesis II)	4 926.6
Expenditure	
Physical investment	3 504.4
Working capital	212.9
Interim interest	559.6
Provisions	
Hypothesis I)	249.7
Hypothesis II)	649.7
Total expenditure	
Hypothesis I)	4 526.6
Hypothesis II)	4 926.6

Source : CVRD

Table 2.2 shows that:

1. Sixty-seven 67 per cent of the funding was from local sources, 40 per cent being CVRD's equity capital. The proportion of foreign financing was thus limited to 33 per cent. The overall debt/equity ratio was 60:40.

2. CVRD arranged the financing package in such a way that the funds raised more than covered the physical investment, the payment of interim interest, pre-operational expenditure and working capital, thus constituting a contingency reserve of about 5 per cent of the total. This provided a security to cover the completion guarantee that the

company had to provide. What is more, an additional $400 million of foreign loans were raised as a financial provision.

3. Commercial bank loans usually being more expensive, their share was limited to 37 per cent of the foreign credits or 20 per cent of the total, excluding financing negotiated by way of provision.

Table 2.3. : Breakdown of the foreign loans for Carajás

	Million $	Per cent
- Non-tied credits		
IBRD	304.5	6.7
Morgan Guarantee Corp[6]	27.0	0.6
- Japan (long-term contracts : 10 million t/yr)		
Eximbank of Japan	50.0	1.1
Import loan (Japanese commercial banks)	250.0	5.6
Bank syndicate	150.0	3.3
Loan stock issue in Japan	45.4	1.0
- Europe (long-term contracts : 14 million t/yr)		
ECSC	400.0	8.8
KFW	130.0	2.9
- Credits tied to the import of equipment		
European banks	36.7	0.8
Eximbank of Japan	36.0	0.8
US Eximbank	58.0	1.3
Sub-total	**1 487.6**	**32.9**

Source: CVRD

Table 2.4. Breakdown of Brazilian financing in 1982

- Equity capital

	Million dollars	Per cent
Self-financing	1 438.2	31.8
State reinvestment of dividends	257.2	5.7
Convertible loan stock	125.0	2.7
Total equity capital	**1 820.4**	**40.2**

- Local loans

BNDES	697.0	15.4
FINAME	321.4	7.1
Bank of Amazonia	75.2	1.7
Convertible loan stock	125.0	2.7
Total local loans	**1 218.6**	**26.9**
Total loans (Tables 2.3 and 2.4)	**2 706.2**	**59.8**

Source : CVRD

The large-scale granting of soft loans by the financial institutions of the major iron ore importing countries and the limiting of credits tied to the import of equipment to 9 per cent of the international funding is an indication of the European and Japanese steelmakers' interest in the realisation of this project.

This financing package enabled the risks to be shared among many financial institutions. In addition, the funds raised were sufficient not only to finance the construction costs of the project (up to 1988), but also to be able to cope with any delay or cash flow problem. This consitituted an additional guarantee for the lenders. Furthermore, during the construction phase, CVRD had a safety margin limiting the amount of equity capital to be contributed in the case of unforeseen problems. In addition:

-- The World Bank requested and obtained absolute priority for loan repayments;

-- The Brazilian government gave a complementary formal guarantee covering 70 per cent of the foreign loans;

-- The overall foreign exchange risk was reduced by the diversity of currencies in which loans were subscribed. The project was protected from the effects of overvaluation of the dollar[7];

-- CVRD gave its guarantee for the additional financial needs caused by delays in construction or underestimation of investment requirements (completion guarantee).

DIFFICULTIES ENCOUNTERED

An operation of this size requires a considerable co-ordination effort, special relationships between the different actors, and above all, government-to-government discussions concerning the involvement of the multilateral financing bodies. The main difficulties encountered are enumerated below.

Difficulties in setting up the financing package

a) In order to obtain the intervention of the *World Bank*, CVRD had to prove that Carajas was vital to its long-term growth and the maintenance of its position on the international iron ore market, basing its arguments in particular on the importance of this export sector to Brazil's balance of trade.

Certain countries, worried about the consequences that the realisation of Carajas would have on the development of smaller projects, notably in Africa, exerted pressure to prevent EEC involvement. What is more, the legislature of the State of Minnesota, acting in the name of the United States iron ore producers who saw Carajas as a threat to their industry, put pressure on the World Bank.

b) It was the setting up of the *Japanese loans* that gave rise to the most protracted and difficult negotiations. CVRD received the direct support of the Brazilian government.

The proposal by the Export-Import Bank of Japan that its loans to CVRD should transit via the Japanese steelmakers was strongly opposed by the latter. Lengthy negotiations between all the institutions concerned (governments, banks, steel firms and traders) were required before agreement could be reached on the details of the Japanese participation. As a result:

i) The Export-Import Bank of Japan granted a loan directly to Carajas, an exceptional event as up to then its credit lines had been exclusively reserved for the energy sector. This loan was guaranteed by the Brazilian government;

ii) The "import loan" was more difficult to negotiate because the traditional form of this loan did not suit the steel firms[8] and raised problems of a legal and contractual nature for CVRD.

In order to get round these difficulties, with the steelmakers refusing individually to lend to CVRD and the latter being unable to accept certain of the clients' contract clauses, the following arrangement, backed by the Brazilian government, was set up:

a) The Japanese steelmakers set up a specific firm, Nippon Carajas Iron Ore Company, to receive the credits from the Export-Import Bank of Japan (70 per cent) and the private banks (30 per cent) and transmit them to CVRD through the import loan;

b) A "payment account"[9] was created to service the debt, the contractual arrangements here being acceptable to CVRD;

c) The following credit operations were mounted in Europe:

i) The *Kreditanstalt für Wiederaufbau* (KFW) in Germany decided in 1982 to limit its financial support for Carajas to 80 per cent of the sum initially fixed during the preliminary discussions. This forced CVRD to seek the aid of other regional banks to make up the difference;

ii) The *European Coal and Steel Community* (ECSC), one of the functions of which is to ensure ore supplies for the European steel industry, and which could allocate credits to enterprises engaged in development projects, hesitated before taking a decision. After protracted discussions that began in 1978 on the socio-economic and political implications of the project for Europe, the Council of Ministers of the Europe of Ten approved the granting of a credit in 1982. The contract consisted of a main contract (Loan Agreement Facility) and a number of specific subsidiary contracts (Individual Loan Agreements) for each loan operation. The EEC insisted on a guarantee by the Brazilian state in addition to the bank guarantees brought by the stand-by credits consituted for each operation. This request met with some token resistance from the Brazilian government.

A difficult domestic and international environment

The establishment of the financing package took place in a difficult international climate characterised by the deterioration of Brazil's financial relations with its lenders and the reduction of capital flows into the country (both for direct investment and, above all, for the financing of national investment projects). The payments crisis that Brazil got into as from 1981, with its corollory of recourse to the IMF, brought new financial constraints, both domestic and with regard to access to the international capital market.

The Brazilian economic crisis and the measures recommended by the IMF had their effect on the development of Carajas. In fact, the restrictive monetary policy resulted in tight government control of the investments of public enterprises in Brazil. As a result, CVRD's relations with the public financial institutions which were to provide the greater part of the local currency credits became more strained. What is more, Brazil's restricted access to international financial markets caused the drawdown on foreign credits in 1983 and 1984 to be lower than initially envisaged.

On top of all this, CVRD's cash flow was reduced because of the fall in iron ore prices. Lastly, although in 1982 the disbursement of international loans had been higher than envisaged in the financing plan, in 1983 CVRD had to finance the construction of the project -- at a reduced rate -- with the international contribution of the World Bank only and local financing at a much lower level than that initially planned.

Effects on the construction phase

All these difficulties caused changes in the investment programme and the financing package:

1. The physical investment cost was brought down from $3 504 million to $3 104 million through reducing the cost of the infrastructures and mining equipment;

2. The ratio of local currency to foreign currency expenditure, initially estimated at 70:30, was increased to 80:20. Two factors led to this change:

    -- The devaluation of the cruzeiro by about 17 per cent in real terms with respect to the dollar in 1973, which meant a reduction in local costs converted into dollars;

    -- Very fierce competition between Brazilian capital goods manufacturers who, because of the recession, had to lower their prices to be able to sell.

3. The total financing requirement was reduced from $4 520 million to $3 600 million. This reduction was achieved partly through savings in the physical investment and partly through the rescheduling of the construction period interest payments to a period 5 to 10 years after the commencement of operations;

61

4. The financing package was adjusted, with CVRD announcing its intention not to draw on the foreign credit of $200 million or the $400 million provision;

5. CVRD's equity capital contribution was reduced with respect to the initial estimates. In this new financing package -- local and foreign credits of $1 160 million and $1 387 million respectively -- CVRD's own contribution was reduced to $1 120 million, or a saving to CVRD of 38 per cent with respect to the initial estimates and a readjustment of the debt/equity ratio ratio to 70:30. This additional safety margin came on top of the other provisions mentioned above.

This further increase in the provisions put CVRD and the lenders in a comfortable position. The technical and financial risks of the project before production reached full capacity, planned for 1988, were thus able to be adequately covered.

The operational phase

The success of the operational phase, during which the project has to rely solely on its own cash flow to service the debt and provide a return on the investment, depends very much on the iron ore price level and the firm's commercial strategy.

It would appear at present, assuming that the mine produces at full capacity and with price levels on the order of those obtaining since the beginning of the decade, the cash flow would suffice to service the debt, but would give only a very low return on equity capital.

The building of the railway (46 per cent of the physical investment) was and still remains the main reason for the low profitability of the Carajas project, making it unattractive to the private sector. It was thus precisely here that the influence of the state was exercised, all the more so because the Brazilian government wanted to make the railway a major axis for the economic colonisation of the Amazon region. The enormous investment necessary for its construction and the risks this entailed led the government to devise a scheme for sharing the risks between CVRD and the Brazilian public financing institutions in order to limit the financial consequences if the project should have failed.

The poor return on the project was the target for criticism of the opponents of Carajas, particularly those in North America. They pointed to it as a project typical of public enterprises in the Third World, stressing the fact that it could be implemented only with the aid of a government more concerned with increasing its foreign currency earnings than satisfying the profitability criteria for market economy investment. However, while it is true that the decision to develop Carajas was greatly influenced by the policy of the Brazilian government (in particular with respect to foreign exchange earnings and regional development), we still think that the commercial logic resulting from CVRD's own strategy remains the main reason for this choice.

CONCLUSION: STRATEGIES OF THE ACTORS

One may wonder why a project disadvantaged by its technical and economic parameters (scale of operations, cost, profitability) and by many external economic factors (Brazil's financial difficulties, saturation of the iron ore market, crisis in the consuming industries) was nevertheless supported by so many actors whose interests were *a priori* so diverse. The different logics behind the intervention of the principal actors involved are analysed below.

The European and Japanese steelmakers

The European and Japanese steelmakers were the essential actors in the realization of Carajas. The fact is that since the beginning of the 1970s, most of the steel experts had been predicting a certain tightness on the iron ore markets as from about 1985, which would be likely to cause a lasting increase in ore prices. At the end of the 1970s, the steelmakers' main concern was to be able to have adequate sources of supply if, as was still hoped, steel demand in the industrialised countries should pick up again. However, the concentration of the steel industry that had been achieved since the end of the 1960s had put ore buyers in a strong position if they were not integrated upstream and were free to make their ore suppliers compete with one another. The non-integrated steelmakers in Europe and Japan were thus trying to promote the development of new capacity in the late 1970s, but without having to actually integrate upstream[10]. Their poor financial results in fact provided excellent reasons to justify their refusal to heavily invest equity capital in mining operations. The governments of ore consuming countries therefore stepped in to finance the implementation of the project through public credits. This situation was the occasion for the development of new forms of investment, in that the consumers, while not providing capital, were active in arranging the financing package for the project. In particular, they did not hesitate to commit themselves to long-term purchasing contracts in order to help the operator to obtain loans.

Lastly, it should be noted that for the non-integrated steelmakers the realisation of Carajas made it possible to remove the danger of future difficulties on the market through supporting just one project. What is more, the sheer size of Carajas could but work in the direction of lower prices in the longer term.

It was nevertheless thanks to the intervention of the World Bank that it was possible to mount the financing package. The World Bank's participation in an operation of this scale made it possible to overcome the reticence of the commercial banks, reluctant to get any further involved with the highly indebted Latin American countries. This intervention led to criticism from operators, notably in North America, who pointed out that it was not justifiable for the World Bank to favour a CVRD strategy whose effect for the firm's competitors could but be a fall in ore prices.

The fact is that since the end of the 1960s, the World Bank's policy with respect to the mining industry in the Third World has been to aid the financing of the development or maintenance of capacity producing for export. In order to obtain World Bank support therefore, CVRD demonstrated, as shown in Table 2.5, that the reserves of its biggest mines in the south of Brazil were likely to be exhausted before the end of the century, thus compromising the company's iron ore export capability beyond that date unless it developed other deposits. Carajas being the most favourable operation from CVRD's standpoint, it was only right that the company should exploit this deposit.

CVRD

The decision to build Carajas corresponded to CVRD's desire to remain a dominant iron ore producer in the longer term despite the impending exhaustion of its mining reserves in the Minas Gerais and to take advantage of the opportunity to increase its production capacity and its volume of sales on the international market. For CVRD, there were thus two determining factors associated with the development of Carajas:

-- Increasing the flexibility of its operations and remaining active on the domestic market;

-- Reinforcing its commercial position on the international market.

a) Flexibility of operations and CVRD's position on the domestic market

At the beginning of the 1980s, CVRD wanted to be able to take advantage of the strong growth of iron ore demand forecast for both the Brazilian domestic market and the international market, but the foreseeable exhaustion in the medium term of Caue and Conceicao-Dois Corregos, its two biggest mines in the southern system, would have prevented CVRD from satisfying this anticipated future demand. The Carajas project thus gave CVRD the possibility of maintaining flexibility of operation:

Table 2.5. : CVRD, Forecast iron ore supply and demand 1984-88
(Million tonnes)

	1984	1985	1986	1987	1988	Foreseeable (1) present rate of production	exhaustion at (2) planned rate of production
I - Demand							
Domestic market	25.4	28.7	30.0	30.0	30.0		
Exports							
Southern mines[11]	53.0	44.0	44.0	44.0	44.0		
Carajás	--	10.3	12.0	13.9	15.4		
Total demand	**78.4**	**83.0**	**86.0**	**87.9**	**89.4**		
II - Production							
Caué	30	30	26	26	20	1994	2000
Conceição / Dois Córregos	20	20	20	15	15	1999	2014
Timbopeba	2.5	7.5	7.5	7.5	7.5		
Capanema	6.5	8.5	10.5	10.5	10.5		
Carajás	--	5	15	25	35		
Other mines	5	5	3.9	3.9	3.9	Piçarrao : 1985 (1.1 Mt/yr)	
Total production	**64.0**	**76.0**	**82.9**	**87.9**	**91.9**		
III - Balance[12]	14.4	7.0	3.1	--	2.5		

Source : CERNA

-- Carajas would make it possible, as from 1988, to export 9.5 million tonnes a year, taking over from the southern system and allowing a reduced rate of exploitation of Caue and Conceicao-Dois Corregos;

-- If necessary, CVRD could operate Carajas at full capacity, even without new contracts, by switching all the sales contracts of the southern system to Carajas and using the southern mines as buffer capacity in the case of an upturn in world demand. If this should happen, Carajas would provide the bulk of the export ore, while the southern system would mainly cover domestic demand[13].

b) CVRD's strategy on the world iron ore market

Since the beginning of the 1970s, it has been the price resulting from the annual negotiations with German steelmakers that has been the reference price for the marketing of ore exported to Europe. With Carajas, CVRD wanted to retain its role as leader on the international iron ore market.

Through increasing its production capacity, CVRD believed it would be possible to precipitate the marginalisation of certain producers and even cause certain competing mines, notably in Latin America, to close down, and at the same time to prevent the development of new projects, in particular in West Africa. However, this agressive strategy came into action at a time when the world iron ore market was depressed, which thus caused internal competition between CVRD's two production systems. The project came on stream at a time when steelmakers were putting pressure on volumes and prices, and the commercial synergies that CVRD had hoped to be able to take advantage of turned against it.

In the longer term, it is likely that an upturn in demand will enable the company, which will long remain the dominant producer on the market, to gradually stabilize its production system. The consumers, who wanted to maintain the abundance of supply, are now trying to maintain its diversity in order to moderate the effects of this situation. Thanks to the new forms of investment, CVRD has been able to provide itself with a very substantial production capacity which would have been difficult for the company to finance through traditional forms of investment, despite its considerable resources.

Table 2.6. : Iron ore exports as a percentage of Brazil's total exports (1974-1983)

Year	74	75	76	77	78	79	80	81	82	83
Percentage	7.2	10.5	9.9	7.5	8.4	8.4	7.7	7.5	9.5	7.0

Source : UNCTAD

Table 2.7. : World Bank credits (disbursed) granted to Brazil (1983-85) (Million dollars)

Year	1983	1984	1985 (E)
Total	1200	1300	1500
Carajás	111	66	81

Source : World Bank ; E : CERNA estimate

Inset 1: Technical and economic description

The Carajas iron ore deposit is located in Amazonia, in the north of Brazil, about 550 kilometres from Belem. The reserves are estimated at 18 billion tonnes of iron ore, low in phosphor and with an average Fe content of 66 per cent, sufficient to guarantee about 250 years of exploitation at a production rate of 35 million tonnes a year. The mining complex consists of an open-cast mine and crushing, grinding and separating plant with an annual capacity of 35 million tonnes of sinter feed and calibrated ore. The very friable ore favours the production of fine products. Production work-up began in February 1985 and nominal capacity was expected to be reached in 1988.

The Carajas project included the construction of an 890 kilometre railway and the port of Ponta de Madeira in the State of Maranhao, designed to take ships of up to 280 000 dwt.

The operator and sole shareholder is the Brazilian public enterprise CVRD (Companhia Vale Rio Doce). The financing requirements of the project, defined in agreement with the World Bank in August 1982, amounted to $4.5 billion. The capital costs amounted to $3.5 billion, broken down as follows:

	Million dollars	Percentage
Mining	622.8	17.8
Railway	1702.0	48.6
Harbour	230.7	6.6
Towns	178.9	5.1
Management	435.0	12.4
Indian programme	13.6	0.4
Financial provisions	321.4	9.1
TOTAL	3504.4	100.0

Source : CVRD

The operating costs at full capacity were estimated[14] in 1981 at $5.64 a tonne. The total production costs, taking into account financial charges and general expenses, were estimated at that time at about $29.5 a tonne.

The forecasts of demand and price trends[15] made in 1982 gave an internal rate of return for the project in the order of 10.6 per cent for a production of 35 million tonnes a year, which could be increased to 12.9 per cent if the project were to be expanded to 50 million tonnes a year, a possibility that was envisaged at the time. This rate of return was considered satisfactory for a new project requiring very heavy fixed capital investment. However, the feasibility study had shown that the rate of return was very sensitive to ore prices and to any delays in the implementation of the project.

NOTES AND REFERENCES

1. For reasons of economies of scale, the choice of the transport infrastructure to a large extent determines the scale of the mining operation.

2. The first explicit disagreements arose in 1975, following US Steel's refusal to increase the capital of AMZA.

3. The Brazilian Treasury held 64.3 per cent of the company's capital in 1981. As from 1982, CVRD issued $181 million of loan stock convertible into ordinary shares to help finance Carajas. In 1984, the state's direct holding was reduced to 53 per cent, the rest of the 75 per cent of the ordinary shares required to control the board of directors being held mainly by a few public financial institutions and private investors.

4. These $400 million were available to CVRD in case of need. They thus increased its margin of cover until completion of the project in 1988. This foreign currency provision was financed half by the European Coal and Steel Community (ECSC) and half by the commercial banks in cofinancing with the World Bank.

5. Hypothesis I: without the provision of $400 million. Hypothesis II: with this provision.

6. Entirely disbursed in 1981.

7. It was not protected against a rise in the yen, however, which disadvantaged the project during the start up phase.

8. In fact the steelmakers could either invest directly in the project, or lend, in both cases by means of financing through the special lines of credit of the Eximbank or the private banks. As the steelmakers did not want to invest directly, it was the loan option that was studied. However, being a loan, the guarantee had to cover the share of the future income from the project to be retained by the lender-buyer when he paid for the imported products, which could have the effect of biasing the marketing negotiations for the sale of the product.

9. Nevertheless, this payment account, very similar to a trust account, caused new difficulties in the negotiations with the other lenders, who considered it to be an additional guarantee given to the creditor which should be extended to all the other contracting parties. Similarly, the guarantee given by the Brazilian state for this import loan created a contractual distinction vis-à-vis the earlier financial engagements which could expose CVRD to a situation of default in the case of non-respect of its obligations under these last contracts. CVRD therefore had to stress the large proportion of public

loans in this import loan and persuade other private banks to modify certain contractual formulations in order to avoid this risk.

10. The Japanese steelmakers who had never been integrated upstream were the first to promote this type of strategy. As from the 1960s they systematically took minority shareholdings in iron ore mines in Australia and Brazil. This participation was not so much aimed at achieving integration as to gain access to inside information to enable them to better conduct price negotiations.

11. Exports only: the domestic consumption of ores appears in the accounts under "domestic market".

12. CVRD bought 3.5 million tonnes a year from smaller producers; in 1984 it was mainly for building up stocks.

13. It was expected that between 1984 and 1994 the net foreign currency gain to Brazil would be at least five times the total sum invested in dollars. What is more, 75 per cent of the income from the project would constitute payments to the national economy.

14. Estimate made on the basis of the cost structure of CVRD operations in the Minas Gerais, in the south of the country.

15. The estimates of future demand (1986-1990) for iron ore were made on the basis of two hypotheses for the growth of steel production: *(i)* one of 2.7 per cent a year, which would mean a supply shortfall of 30 million tonnes in 1986 rising to 82.6 million tonnes in 1990; *(ii)* the other of 1.8 per cent, meaning a surplus of 7 million tonnes in 1986 but a shortfall of 17 million tonnes in 1988, the year in which the installed capacity was to come into full production. Other sources, such as Amax, forecast additional ore requirements of about 12 million tonnes a year by 1985.

As regards prices, the feasibility study considered that between 1983 and 1985 prices would not increase in real terms (taking account of the real increase of 5 per cent in 1982), but after 1985, and because of the upturn in the market, prices would increase between 1986 and 1990 at a real rate of 1.5 per cent a year.

Chapter III

LES GUELBS*

INTRODUCTION

The Guelbs complex extracts iron ore in the Mauritanian Sahara. The project, decided on at the end of the 1970s, was conceived as an investment to extend the capacity of a state enterprise in a mining country, i.e. a country whose exports of mineral raw materials have structured the dynamic of the domestic economy since the 1960s. Unlike the Carajas project (cf. Chapter 2), also an extension project for a state enterprise, the Guelbs project -- for which the amount invested was on the same order of magnitude as Mauritania's gross national product -- is an operation of considerable size, not so much in absolute terms, but with respect to the scale of the operator, SNIM (Société Nationale Industrielle et Minière) and the economy of the country. The issues raised by this investment, encouraged by SNIM's traditional customers and financed by the development banks, concern:

-- The industrial logic of an investment decided on the basis of geopolitical considerations;

-- The running of a project involving many subcontractors by an inexperienced public operator;

-- The sharing of technical and financial responsibilities in an operation largely financed through loans.

---

* Chapter prepared with the aid of Paulo de Sa.

Discovered by French geologists in 1935, the Kédia deposits were not developed until towards the end of the 1950s. The realisation of this operation coincided with Mauritania's independence. The iron ore mine, built right in the Sahara, required the construction of a 600 kilometre railway through the desert and represented an investment of almost $200 million at the beginning of the 1960s. The existence of other iron ore deposits near Kédia (the Guelbs) argued in favour of the project. The World Bank, approached in 1957, granted $66 million towards financing the project in 1960. The operating company was called Miferma and its capital was held as follows:

Shareholder	Holding (per cent)
BRGM[1]	24
IMETAL	11
Usinor	15
British Steel	20
Finsider	15
German steelmakers	5
Sundry	5
Mauritanian state	5

The Kédia mine started up in 1963 with an output of 1.3 million tonnes of high grade hematite (65 per cent iron). Production gradually rose to a maximum of 12 million tonnes in 1973, the output being sold through long-term purchasing contracts concluded with the shareholders.

The desire to continue operations beyond the 1990s, when the Kédia deposits were expected to be exhausted, led to surveys being carried out on other deposits, including the Guelbs, in 1967. The ores here were *very different*, magnetites with a 40 per cent iron content, requiring enrichment and thus necessarily involving higher operating costs. However, geological tests were carried out and a pilot plant was set up at Zouérate.

In 1972, the Mauritanian government set up the SNIM (Société Nationale Industrielle et Minière) whose function was to manage all the economic activities of the Mauritanian public sector (i.e. an explosives plant; a steelworks with an electric furnace, using imported scrap exclusively; a gypsum quarry; oil product refining and distribution).

In 1974, the government decided to nationalise Miferma, paying generous compensation of $90 million to the shareholders (after 10 years of operation the Kédia project was virtually amortized). The mining activity at Kédia was taken over by Cominor, 100 per cent controlled by SNIM. There were few changes on the operational side and production remained the responsibility of expatriate staff. There was no serious interruption of ore sales.

In 1975, the Akjoujt copper mine, opened in 1971 and already with heavy losses, was nationalised in its turn. It was closed down in 1978.

With the support of Socomine -- a French project study company made up of former Miferma staff -- SNIM continued to study the possibility of exploiting the Guelbs magnetite deposits, and more specifically those of Guelb El Rhein and Guelb Oum Arwagen, considered the most favourable. The market conditions of the time made it better to look for large deposits of low-grade ore rather than small deposits of rich ore.

The pilot plant came on stream in 1974 and the results of the tests served as the basis for a feasibility study presented in 1976 to obtain financing for the project, notably from the World Bank.

During the course of 1977, the war in the western Sahara brought repeated attacks on the Zouérate mining area and the railway, seriously interfering with production and causing the departure of many expatriates. It was in this troubled context that the *real* nationalisation of SNIM took place, i.e. Mauritanian nationals taking responsibility for production. Despite the difficulties associated with taking over the control of operations at Kédia -- this was the first time Mauritanians had assumed such economic responsibility -- the new SNIM management was in favour of launching the Guelbs project.

The studies for the project were entrusted to the French firms Socomine and Sofresid. The feasibility studies were based on projected prices (an increase of 5 per cent a year as from 1979) that soon turned out to be very over-optimistic. The planned output was to be almost 14 million tonnes a year over the period 1985-95, but this target was abandoned in 1980.

Negotiations with financial backers for the Guelb El Rhein project were completed in 1978-79, the total cost of the project being estimated at $501 million. The decision to go ahead with the project was very clearly based on geopolitical considerations[2]. In order to finance it, Mauritania managed to stir up competition between Arab oil exporters keen to establish a bridgehead in Sub-saharan Africa and western backers (World Bank, European Investment Bank, Caisse Centrale de Coopération Economique) anxious not to loose their influence in this part of the world.

The backers' agreement was conditional upon the restructuring of SNIM: disengagement from various loss-making activities[3] other than iron ore mining (Cominor accounted for 90 per cent of SNIM's earnings and represented 95 per cent of its assets) and conversion into a semi-public company by opening up the capital structure to Arab money from various sources. The financing package for the operation was planned so that foreign contributions covered virtually all of the foreign exchange requirements of the project. This foreign financing took the form either of shareholdings -- totalling $120 million -- or bank loans granted to SNIM or the Mauritanian state. The overall financing of the project was broken down as follows[4]:

Equity capital	$162.7 million
Loans	$338 million
Debt/equity ratio	32:68

SNIM's capital, totalling 9 billion ouguiyas[5] (UM) was held as follows:

Shareholder	Percentage holding
Islamic Republic of Mauritania	70.89
Kuwait Foreign Trading Contracting and Investment Co.	9.64
Arab Mining Company	7.61
Irak Fund for External Development	6.17
Bureau de Recherches et de Participations Minières (Morocco)	3.09
Islamic Development Bank	2.41
Private Mauritanian investors	0.19

The development banks granted 61 per cent of the credits, Arab funds 38 per cent (Saudi Arabia 19 per cent, Kuwait 13 per cent, Abu Dhabi 6 per cent) and OPEC funds 1 per cent.

Unlike the financing of a traditional project where the loans are guaranteed by the future cash flow of the operation, usually with a completion guarantee given by the operator, the financing of the Guelbs project was based on a system where the guarantees were on the product of sale or even on the ore itself. In this particular case the bankers had an additional right of inspection of the progress of operations, continuously monitoring the management of production and marketing and the cash flow situation of the enterprise.

In fact, SNIM, the Mauritanian Central Bank and the lenders agreed on the opening of a bank account in Paris into which all receipts were to be paid, SNIM being obliged to specify this condition in all its sales contracts. SNIM therefore did not have the possibility of selling its products under barter agreements.

Table 3.1. : Breakdown of financing

	Million dollars	Percentage of total
1-Loans granted to the Mauritanian government and retroceded to SNIM :		
-Special OPEC fund	5	1
-Saudi fund	65	19
-African Development Bank	12	4
Sub-total 1	**82**	**24**
2-Loans granted directly to SNIM:		
-World Bank (IBRD)	60	18
-Caisse centrale de coopération économique (CCCE)	50	15
-European Investment Bank (EIB)	30	9
-Kuwait Funds for Arab Economic Development	45	13
-Arab Economic and Social Development Fund (AESDF)	35	10
-Abu Dhabi Fund for Arab Economic Development	20	6
-Overseas Economic Cooperation Fund (Japan) (OECF)	16	5
Sub-total 2	**256**	**76**
TOTAL 1+2	**338**	**100**

Source : confidential

Loan and repayment conditions :

Lender	Grace period (years)	Repayment period (years)	Rate of interest (per cent)
IBRD[6]	5	10	Libor+ 2.1 %
EIB	5	10	6 %
CCCE[7]	3	9	9 %
AESOF	3	12	4 %
Abu Dhabi	7	18	3 %
OECF	7	18	4 %
ADB	5	10	8.75 %
OPEC	4	16	0.5 %
Saudi fund	4	16	3 %

Source : confidential

The agreement provided that this bank account credit first of all each month a trust account in London with one-sixth of the value of the debt servicing scheduled for the semester to come and maintain a deposit equal to the debt servicing for the following semester. It was only after this operation that part of the product of sale would be paid directly to a SNIM account in Paris to enable the payment of foreign currency operating expenditure, these sums being paid in accordance with a monthly operating provision established on the basis of forecast foreign exchange requirements drawn up each year by SNIM, approved by the Mauritanian Central Bank and communicated to the lenders[8]. Lastly, the remainder of the product of sale would be repatriated to a SNIM account with the Mauritanian Central Bank. No fraction of the product of sale could be attributed without the authorisation of the World Bank, intervening in the name of all the backers. Furthermore, SNIM coud not get involved in any new project without World Bank authorisation. For its part, the Mauritanian government guaranteed:

-- To accept responsibility, for and on behalf of SNIM, for the remainder of the compensation to be paid for the nationalization of Miferma, as well as for the whole of the debts of SOMIMA[9], of which $30 million owed to SNIM;

-- That the marketing of the iron ore should be exclusively reserved to SNIM, except with special authorization from the World Bank;

-- That SNIM should be able to import fuel oil directly at the international market price.

The first orders were placed in 1979, after completion of the financing package. Various difficulties, technical and financial, delayed the work on Guelbs, but the apparent cost was nevertheless kept under control, and even reduced under the combined effect of good financial management of markets and the rise of the dollar with respect to the European currencies in which most of the epuipment supply contracts were drawn up.

The Guelb El Rhein unit was inaugurated in July 1984, somewhat prematurely as construction was scarcely completed and tests were still in progress.

SNIM's financial difficulties, connected with the increased costs of the Kédia mine and the launching of the Guelbs project, led to the drawing up of a restructuring plan in 1984. This plan included rationalisation and cost reduction measures on the part of SNIM, associated with financial aid from the backers: reallocation of sundry sums remaining from loans not used for the Guelbs project and complementary loans from the CCCE and the World Bank. On the fiscal side, the Mauritanian government agreed to reduce the 10 per cent export levy in force up to 1986 to 5 per cent[10]. The implementation of this restructuring plan nevertheless came up against further difficulties which will be discussed below.

However, as from 1986, the difficulties with the Guelbs plant made SNIM actively prospect for deposits of rich ores around the indications of low-grade ore. This led to the discovery, in June 1987, of the M'Haoudat hematite deposits,

55 kilometres northeast of Zouérate. According to the pre-feasibility study submitted to the backers in September 1988, the exploitable reserves amounted to about 80 million tonnes, of which 70 per cent rich ore (64 per cent Fe) and 30 per cent silicious ore (55 per cent Fe). The envisaged output would be 4.7 million tonnes a year of low-phosphorus ore (0.045 per cent P) and 0.9 million tonnes of phosphorus ore (0.27 per cent P). The study envisages the build up of production starting in 1992 after an investment of $130 million. The investment should pay for itself within 8 years of this date. It is not the least of the paradoxes in this operation that a richer deposit should be discovered after the implementation of the Guelbs project.

SNIM'S POSITION IN THE MAURITANIAN ECONOMY

Before going any further in the analysis of the company's recent evolution it is appropriate to point out the central role it has played in the economic dynamic of the country since independence. First, a few figures.

Mauritania's GDP was estimated at $850 million in 1986, about 30 per cent of which corresponded to the remuneration of services (including the administration). The state budget[11] is in the order of $300 million, of which one-third corresponds to foreign gifts (the Gulf States). SNIM's turnover fell from almost $180 million in 1980 to $110 million in 1987. SNIM's net foreign currency earnings (exports-imports, excluding financial transfers) are now about $40 million a year. Before 1985, SNIM directly contributed about $14 million to the state budget (excluding income taxes and social insurance contributions). Since 1986, the company has paid virtually no more taxes. Its tax arrears payable to the Mauritanian treasury amounted to $10 million in 1987. The Guelbs investment, $500 million, is comparable to the country's GDP. Mauritania's outstanding debt is roughly double the GDP.

Mauritania is what is known as a "mining country", i.e. a country in which the overall economic dynamic has been based on an exporting mining sector for the last 25 years. Simplifying, it can be said that iron ore exports have made it possible to finance a disarticulated development of the economy in which:

-- Marginalised agriculture has been replaced by policies of importing foodstuffs;

-- The rural exodus and the increased population of the towns has been accompanied by the creation of an enlarged system of income redistribution through the proliferation of parasitic administrative jobs.

In other words, the financial surpluses of the mining sector, far from being reinvested in other productive sectors oriented towards domestic demand, have for the most part circulated in a redistributive fashion, notably through the administrative apparatus, to finally pay for imported goods. As from the late 1970s, the mining surpluses had become insufficient to finance this dynamic, and to make matters worse the Mauritanian ore deposits were threatened with

77

exhaustion. Furthermore, redistribution through unproductive jobs, without direct consequences when it affected the apparatus of the state (whose vocation is not that of production), became more worrying when it affected SNIM itself. In 1978, the company, which covered all the economic activities of the country, was in its turn in danger of becoming completely paralysed by the redistribution logic described above. It was this threat that led to the restructuring imposed by the backers when the financing package for the Guelbs project was being set up.

However, the development of the Guelbs project, despite the control over SNIM exercised by the backers, did not resolve the management problems associated with the economic contradictions within the country. On the contrary, this control led to the mistakes being compounded. Not only, as we shall see, did the Guelbs operation turn out to be hazardous, but SNIM's management, in particular as regards personnel and plant maintenance, got worse. Without going into detail, it can be stated that it was this situation that led to the "readjustment plan" of 1984.

Under this plan, the organisation of SNIM was rationalised and simplified. The number of departments was reduced from 22 to 10, and then to 9 with the abolition of the Administrative Department in 1986. The reorganisation of SNIM also resulted in the company's withdrawal from secondary activities: the Nouadhibou steelworks was made into a subsidiary, [Société Arabe du Fer et de l'Acier (SAFA)] in July 1985; the air transport activity between Nouadhibou and Zouérate was hived off in 1986; the accommodation, catering and leisure activities

The following graph shows how the fishing sector is tending to replace SNIM as Mauritania's biggest foreign exchange earner. According to our estimates, SNIM's balance of payments probably became negative in 1987.

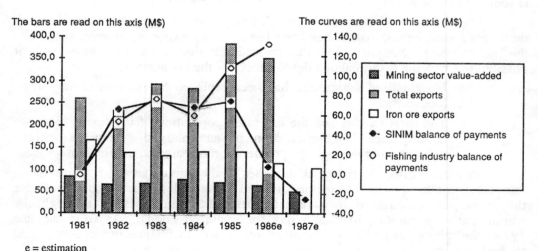

e = estimation

were turned into a subsidiary in 1987. The explosives manufacturing activity (SNIMEX) was suspended. SNIM was now able to devote itself exclusively to the extraction, rail transport and shipping of iron ore. On the other hand, the considerable numbers of excess staff accumulated in the period up to 1983 were still not significantly reduced, even though this was part of the readjustment plan. In 1987, SNIM still employed about 5 660 people, of whom 1 660 in administrative departments. The country's biggest employer after the administration, SNIM was able to stop recruitment, did not succeed in raising productivity.

At the same time, under the impetus of private Arab capital, the fishing industry has been developed considerably since the beginning of the 1980s, with its share of total exports rising from 18 per cent in 1981 to over 40 per cent in 1986. The net foreign exchange earnings of the fishing industry was $135 million in 1986, while SNIM, having benefitted from capital inputs connected with the Guelbs project in the preceding years, saw the transfers connected with its activity reverse direction (see graph below). The great expansion of the fisheries has brought about a significant reorientation of the Mauritanian economy: simplifying, the country is in the process of replacing the ailing iron ore sector by a new and more profitable exporting sector. It would nevertheless appear that the fishing sector is fairly fragile. The investments made in 1986 and 1987 (purchase of boats and refrigerating equipment) caused a considerable deterioration in the invisibles balance, and hence the overall balance of payments of the sector. What is more, it seems that the halieutic resources have been rapidly run down due to over-fishing. This phenomenon could well become worse.

While it may seem appropriate to develop fishing in order to diversify the country's exports, it also constitutes a danger for SNIM. There is in fact reason to fear that the rise of the fishing industry compromises the revival of the iron ore sector. SNIM, which during its expansion period offered the best jobs in the country to young Mauritanian graduates, has lost some of its experienced managers to the fishing sector which now offers better opportunities. In the late 1980s, the qualified Mauritanians who choose SNIM do so more out of a sense of duty towards the country than because of the career prospects.

The following graph shows how the fishing sector is tending to replace SNIM as Mauritania's biggest foreign exchange earner. According to our estimates, SNIM's balance of payments probably became negative in 1987.

THE DIFFICULTIES ENCOUNTERED

Difficulties encountered in setting up the financing package

The negotiations concerned with the restructuring of the company, the enlargement of its capital and the financing contract occupied a team of World

Bank legal experts for 30 months. For the bankers, the restructuring was aimed at constituting a profit-making company capable of bearing a heavy debt over a long period. As we have seen, this meant that SNIM had to abandon its loss-making activities, SOMIMA in particular. In addition, the bankers tried to isolate the project from the Mauritanian state budget. In fact, in its earlier structure, SNIM had represented the market economy of the country to such an extent (iron ore, copper, importing and marketing of oil products, steel, etc.) that the company could be confused with the state apparatus.

The more marked dissociation between SNIM and the state ran into political obstacles which hampered the negotiations. The same difficulties appeared in the discussions concerning the opening of the company's capital structure to new shareholders, an operation which apart from making the contribution of equity capital possible had the added advantage for the lenders of further accentuating the separation between SNIM and the state.

On top of these difficulties there were other obstacles connected with the evolution of the political context, notably:

-- The overthrow of the Mauritanian government during the negotiations was another factor that slowed down the reaching of an agreement;

-- The repeated attacks by the Polisario Front on the railway between the iron ore mines and the port almost paralyzed SNIM's production just before work began on the project site. They also constituted a major risk for the construction and operation of the project.

Technical difficulties

a)   **In the Guelbs project**

The Guelbs project is an enormous operation in relation to SNIM's size. It consists of extracting 12 million tonnes a year of mainly magnetic ore with a 36 per cent Fe content and an overburden to ore ratio of 1:1. The magnetite is encased in a very hard quartzite. The blocks are crushed, screened, passed through an impact breaker, ground, sorted according to oxide content and sent to the concentrator.

Innumerable technical problems were encountered in these operations. Some examples:

-- At the mine: the drilling tools and explosives had to be adapted to the hardness of the ore;

-- On the primary crusher: the hardness of the blocks caused excessively rapid wear of the cams; a repair shop was set up on the site; the lubrication pumps were of the wrong size and the lubricant injection holes were badly placed, causing poor circulation of the fluids. The crusher motor can only be started off load. The metal apron extractor had to be replaced by a chute;

-- The discharge stackers all slipped, so that the belts and tension had to be modified;

-- The ore sampler at the head of the circuit worked for only half an hour.

-- The drum of the impact breaker is not suited to the hardness of the blocks emerging from the primary crusher. Teeth and plates are regularly broken. Another secondary crushing system should be envisaged;

-- In the grinder, the casing lasted 600 hours instead of 3 000. Modification of the profile should improve its functioning;

-- However, it is above all the circulation of dust-laden air at the grinder outlet that must be avoided. The initial system of extracting the unfiltered air coming from the crushers was corroded in record time. Tests were first made with protecting the corrodable parts of the extractor fan with ceramic coatings, but this was unsuccessful. A covering of small magnets seemed more effective as this caused the rubbing of ore on ore, but this was not enough in itself. The circuit had to be modified to filter the air from the grinder using electrostatic pressure filters.

-- The conveyors (there are 84 in the plant) turned out to be usuitable for transporting the crushed ore. This point is vital, for the very nature of the plant is such that it involves transporting fine, dry products from one treatment station to another. Not only are the quartz and ultra fine particles very abrasive for the conveyor belts and drums, but above all, the very dusty product does not adhere to the belts. A redesign of the conveyor system (although supplied by Krupp) is planned, as its gradients were incorrectly calculated, but it is still not certain that this will solve all the handling problems.

-- In the magnetic separator, the moving parts are constantly breaking down.

All these mechanical breakdowns obviously require the availability of many spare parts, hence a lot of working capital. Having the purchasing department centralised in Nouadhibou causes the additional problem of cumbersome procedures for ordering and delivering spares. Furthermore, in addition to the mechanical and electrical problems, there are difficulties with the separation process. Among the short-term solutions envisaged is a possible redefinition of product quality, such as dropping to 63 per cent Fe. Another option would be to extract the magnetic ore only (two-thirds of the deposit). In any event, even assuming that it will be possible to return to the original flow sheet, it will take years to regulate the process.

To resolve the difficulties and ensure that the sub-systems delivered by the 200 suppliers not only meet specifications but actually work, SNIM has only 13 engineers and 40 technicians. In view of the number of markets to be watched over and the scale of the technical difficulties, this structure seems very inadequate.

Generally speaking, it would appear that the plant was poorly designed and badly built. It consists of a large number of sub-systems, each of which taken separately works more or less satisfactorily, but the overall system is incoherent. The worst thing is that there were so many actors involved in implementing the project that each one of them can make himself appear not to be responsible for the malfunctions observed. Thus SNIM claims to have strictly followed the engineering design endorsed by the bankers, to which the suppliers retort that their products met specifications, and the engineering consultants that they were improperly used. As for the bankers, they say nothing but are worried about the increasing cost of the operation. In order to demonstrate its good will and its technical ability to manage the operation, and thus obtain an extension of credit, SNIM is trying to increase production despite the obvious inadequacy of the plant. This carries the risk of the degradation in series of a number of items of equipment which otherwise work reasonably well.

b) Maintenance of the Kédia infrastructures

The ore is carried by rail over a distance of about 650 kilometres to Nouadhibou where the storage areas, treatment installations and loaders are located, as well as the railway workshops. Since 1985, the central services of SNIM have also been located in Nouadhibou. There are two trains a day carrying 15 000 tonnes of ore and consisting of 4 locomotives, 200 ore wagons and sundry other wagons and passenger stock over what is the main and virtually only link between Zouérate and the outside world. This railway requires a great deal of maintenance because of the difficult local conditions and the obsolescence of most of the locomotives, a situation aggravated by the effects of the war in the western Sahara. The locomotive stock was partly renewed for the Guelbs project, six locomotijes being bought in 1982 and a further four in 1987.

The wind and the sand of the Sahara cause an enormous amount of abrasion of tracks and wheels, and there are many accidents, generally three or four a year; there were four in the last seven months of 1988. It would appear that SNIM's policy is aimed more at being able to quickly re-establish traffic after an accident than at avoiding accidents. The large number of wagons available to SNIM seems to favour this attitude, and in fact comparison with other iron ore mines indicates that SNIM could no doubt transport its 10 million tonnes a year using only 900 wagons. It is clear that systematic inspection of the track and early replacement of faulty sections would improve the safety and efficiency of the railway. The restriction on SNIM's foreign exchange expenditure works against systematic track maintenance (new rails have to be imported), thus compromising the maintenance of the ore removal capacity in the longer term.

The survey work on the M'Haoudat deposit and the start-up of the Guelbs plant have occupied a substantial part of SNIM's technical potential. This partly explains the low productivity increases at the Kédia mine since 1986.

Financial difficulties

In June 1988, SNIM was in a position where it could not meet its financial obligations. With over $20 million owing to suppliers, a bank overdraft of the same order of magnitude and tax arrears of almost $12 million, it was virtually impossible for the company to continue its operations. The primary objective of the meeting of backers in July 1988 was to resolve this short-term situation.

SNIM's longer term financial situation seems seriously compromised.

The total investment for the Guelbs project inscribed in the balance sheets between 1981 and 1985 amounted to UM 26.9 billion. Applying the annual average rates of exchange to the investments of each year, this amounts to a total of $413 million, excluding interim interest and sundry pre-operational expenditure. Taking the interim interest as to the end of 1986 (in the order of $45 million) and the pre-operational expenditure into account, the total cost of the project as at the end of 1986 was in the order of $490 million. In 1987, in accordance with the financing contract, the debt servicing figure increased from $30 million to $50 million ($20 million being interest and $30 million repayment of the principal, or almost half SNIM's turnover. From the accounting standpoint, the Guelbs project, inaugurated in 1984, was still considered in financial 1987 to be in the "pre-operational" phase, and was thus entered in the accounts under fixed assets and not subject to depreciation. This meant that the operating losses were very much understated in the presentation of SNIM's accounts and in particular the disastrous cash flow situation discussed above was hidden. The Caisse Centrale de Coopération Economique and the World Bank undertook a technical and financial audit in mid-1988 with the aim of evaluating the company's accounting situation, and the Guelbs assets were shifted into the operating accounts.

The outstanding question in this analysis is: at what level of output does the Guelbs operation become economic? In 1989, ten years after construction began, this is still very much a moot point. According to the World Bank experts, it would appear that the break-even point, disregarding the financial costs, could be reached with an output of 2 million tonnes, while the CCCE experts are not even sure that equilibrium would be reached with 4 million tonnes. In our opinion, it is clear that the operating costs of the Guelbs operation cannot be covered unless the plant works, if not at full capacity, at least without the constant breakdowns caused by the poor design of the operating sequence. In view of the Mauritanian context described above, the technical difficulties of the Guelbs plant make it unlikely that the plant will be able to work continuously at full capacity, so that financial equilibrium cannot be achieved unless the project's debt is purely and simply cancelled.

The World Bank has studied the possibility of gradually abandoning Guelbs as from 1991, when the new M'Haoudat mine could take over from it. All the projections (whether production at Guelbs continues or not, whether M'Haoudat is developed or not) show that the burden of debt servicing brings about an annual shortfall of around $20 million[12]. There is no scenario conserving the debt that would enable the company to right its financial situation.

In 1988, the envisaged financial reorganization was aimed at correcting SNIM's cash flow situation by increasing the company's equity capital through the granting by the Mauritanian government of an IDA loan transmissible to SNIM. This amounts to reconstituting the capital of the company to enable it to go on financing its losses out of own funds. In our opinion this is a very short-term solution which will cease to have any positive effect before the loan is even handed over.

CONCLUSION

The realization of the Guelbs project came at a time when the social and political context was characterised by the following factors:

-- At the time the decision to proceed with the project was taken, Mauritania was at war with the Polisario Front;

-- The drought beginning in the Sahara further aggravated the domestic economic difficulties of one of the poorest countries in the world;

-- The country's economy was very dependant on an iron ore industry threatened by the exhaustion of reserves in the longer term. In addition, the towns of Zouérate and Nouadhibou, each with 30 000 inhabitants, live directly on the circulation of incomes created by the mining industry. The World Bank stated in 1979 that it would be difficult to exaggerate the effects that closing down the iron ore mines would have on the situation of the country;

-- Mauritania's internal political situation was unstable because of the factors cited above.

In this context, it was mainly the macroeconomic and political factors that led the financial partners, all emanating from bilateral or multilateral development aid bodies, to support the realisation of the project. Among these factors, we would mention in particular:

-- The desire of the European, and to a lesser extent the Japanese, steelmakers to diversify their sources of supply at a time when most of the experts were forecasting considerable tension on the iron ore market by about 1985;

-- The existence of transport infrastructures to evacuate the product, limiting the unit cost of the investment and the financing requirements of the project;

-- The desire of the Middle East oil states to develop their own steel industries on the basis of ore supplies from the Arab world[13];

-- The possibility for European exporters to sell services and capital goods;

-- The political will of the Middle East oil states to invest in Muslim African countries;

-- The desire of the industrialised countries as a whole to preserve the fiscal resources and export capacity of the Mauritanian state in order to prevent the possible destabilization of the country resulting from the exhaustion of the reserves being exploited.

This position based on principle made the lenders look for a contractual arrangement that would make it possible to reduce to a minimum the economic risks run by the project. However, while these arrangements have so far been able to ensure the relative stability of the agreements, the technical and economic parameters of the operation, the actual evolution of the iron ore market and the political constraints within Mauritania have turned out in such a way that the most far-sighted contract could not protect the project from traditional industrial risk. Whether in the end the Guelbs project will enable Mauritania to preserve its iron ore industry and its share of the international market still remains an open question.

At the moment of writing (May 1989), SNIM is in a very unstable situation, the outcome of which will determine its survival in the medium and longer term. The company's financial situation has seriously deteriorated since the beginning of the 1980s. Despite the Guelbs project, production has fallen, productivity is not increasing, SNIM's debt is equivalent to over half the GDP of the country and its working capital is exhausted. The conclusion of our analysis is that it would appear impossible for SNIM to be able to survive after the exhaustion of the Kédia mine (1995) on the basis of the Guelbs deposit alone. The company therefore has to meet three challenges:

-- Maintain and modernise the Kédia mine in order not to waste the economic rent of the project and to preserve the infrastructures;

-- Develop the exploitation of the M'Haoudat deposits, which are likely to be able to take over from those at Kédia. As this involves an investment of $130 million, SNIM will have to be very careful with the implementation of this project, even though the mining operation appears simpler and more conventional than Guelbs;

-- Modify the technical layout of the Guelbs plant, implement the modifications and step up production.

Even supposing that the financial problem were resolved, it appears unlikely that the human resources available would enable SNIM to fight on all three fronts simultaneously. From the industrial standpoint, it would appear most reasonable to envisage the temporary shut-down of the Guelbs complex in order to concentrate all SNIM's technical and human resources on the first two objectives, which determine the company's ability to survive beyond the year 2000.

The Guelbs operation has turned out to be a technical and economic disaster. The logic of its implementation led the SNIM management, who had only just taken over technical responsibility for the operation of the Kédia mine, to sacrifice the financial independence of the company. This situation affects the industrial logic of the entire enterprise. It means that the management is now more concerned with denying their responsibility to the lenders than with taking the necessary strategic decisions as a function of the company's own resources. In our opinion this is why the optimisation of operations at Kédia is currently being neglected while at the same time SNIM is trying to prematurely increase production at Guelbs. In this situation it is relations between the lenders and the company that are imposing a very short-term logic, whereas in actual fact it is illusory to imagine that the debt can ever be repaid. There is reason to fear that the perversity of this state of affairs may in the longer term cause a certain demotivation of supervisory staff and workers, many of whom regard their work for SNIM as a duty towards their country.

It is possible to envisage another scenario in which the rehabilitation of the Kédia mine, the realisation of the M'Haoudat project and the start up of the Guelbs operation could be presented as three separate investments among which SNIM, endowed with greater financial autonomy, would have to chose according to its own priorities. The corresponding financial restructuring would consist of isolating and freezing the Guelbs debt -- conversion of the debt into capital -- and giving SNIM the resources to partly finance M'Haoudat, it being understood that the relaxation of supervision by the banks would mean that the company could not afford to make any mistakes in its industrial decisions, the penalty being its disappearance. This scenario may appear more risky than the present one, because it does imply that SNIM really could go under. But actually it may not be more risky, for the instability of the present short-sighted management policy, timidly supported by the banks, is beginning to be seriously felt by all the observers.

Inset 1: Technical description

The aim of the Guelbs project was to exploit the Guelb El Rhein iron ore deposit, situated about 20 kilometres northeast of the mining town of Zouérate, to be followed in 1990 by the exploitation of the Guelb Oum Arwagen deposit situated about 40 kilometres northeast of Zouérate. These mines are in the eastern Guelbs, El Rhein and Oum Arwagen, where development work began in 1980 and where production was to proceed in two phases:

-- The exploitation of Guelb El Rhein as from January 1984, the proven reserves here amounting to 250 million tonnes of magnetite assaying between 35 and 40 per cent iron. The annual output of the mine was to be 13.8 million tonnes of crude ore, crushed and concentrated on site using a dry magnetic separation process. The nominal capacity is 6 million tonnes of crushed ore concentrated to 65 per cent iron;

-- Exploitation of the Oum Arwagen deposit, 12 kilometres from El Rhein, was programmed for 1990. The proven reserves are in the order of 150 million tonnes and annual output was planned to be 9 million tonnes of crushed ore concentrated to 65 per cent iron, thus giving SNIM an annual production capacity of 15 million tonnes. It is now very unlikely that this phase will be implemented before the year 2000.

A 650 kilometre railway links the Kédia mine and Zouérate to the bulk ore port of Nouadhibou. The railway was extended by some 15 kilometres to be able to carry the output from the new mines. Two trains of 191 wagons and each carrying 15 000 tonnes of ore leave the Kédia mine each day, thus giving a rail transport capacity of 10 million tonnes a year. SNIM plans to bring an additional train into service to give a capacity of 15 million tonnes a year.

The ore carrier terminal at Nouadhibou enables the port to stock 2 million tonnes of ore separated into 9 grades corresponding to the qualities marketed by SNIM. SNIM at present has a loading capacity of 100 000 tonnes in 30 hours for a single grade of ore. The company intends to increase the capacity of the port to be able to handle 14 million tonnes of ore a year and to increase the loading capacity by installing a new loader with a capacity of 7 500 tonnes an hour. However, the port cannot take ore carriers of over 150 000 dwt.

Inset 2: Marketing

SNIM is a veritable shop for the European steel industry, which accounts for over 95 per cent of the company's sales. Italy, France and Belgium together have accounted for almost 80 per cent of sales since 1986. SNIM is not well-established in the German market and the share sold on the United Kingdom market fell sharply in 1986.

Sales on other markets are limited. The Japanese share in particular has been falling for some years. After a spectacular upturn in sales in 1983 and 1984, they are now stagnant in both volume and value terms. However, SNIM managed to maintain a constant average price ($16.3 per tonne) in 1985 and 1986 despite a general tendency for prices to fall.

The magnetite concentrates from the El Rhein plant seem to be appreciated by the consumers, but SNIM sold scarcely 1 million tonnes of them in 1987. The gap of over 1.5 million tonnes between the total sales forecast of 10.5 million tonnes in 1986 and the actual figure of 8.93 million, and the stagnation of 1987, resulted from the limitation of production in the Guelbs plant, which was the basis for sales promotion on new markets, and which it was not possible to compensate for by the sale of fines from the Kédia mine.

Inset 3: Cost of the Guelbs project

The overall investment cost for the two phases of the Guelbs El Rhein and Oum Arwagen project was estimated in 1979 at $937 million. The cost evaluation carried out by the World Bank in 1979 was based on the establishment of a mine and an ore enrichment plant at El Rhein in Phase 1 and another mine and another enrichment plant at Oum Arwagen in Phase 2. The breakdown of the investment costs of Phase 1, in foreign and local currency, is summarized in Table 3.2. It can be seen that the local currency expenditure amounts to less than 10 per cent of the total investment.

Table 3.2. : Investment cost of the Guelbs project (Phase 1)
(million 1977 dollars)

	Total	Foreign currency	Local currency
Mines and concentration plant	89.0	87.2	1.8
Infrastructures :	161.5	140.3	21.2
- Port and railway	(35.7)	(35.0)	(0.7)
- Power station	(34.9)	(34.3)	(0.6)
- Housing and administrative buildings	(57.6)	(48.6)	(9.0)
- Construction	(33.3)	(22.4)	(10.9)
Project study, management, preparation	31.1	27.4	3.8
Cost of physical investment	**281.7**	**254.9**	**26.8**
Provisions :			
- Contingencies	27.6	24.9	2.7
- Inflation	110.1	99.7	10.4
Total investment cost	**419.4**	**379.5**	**39.9**
Working capital	33.5	30.0	3.5
Interest during construction	27.8	26.6	1.2
Special provision	20.0	20.0	0.0
Total financing	**500.7**	**456.1**	**44.6**

Source confidential

89

NOTES AND REFERENCES

1. Bureau de Recherches Géologiques et Minières.

2. The forecast poor return on the project and the political risks made the commercial banks refuse to get involved in the financing of this project. All the more so because neither the Mauritanian government nor SNIM were at that time in a position to contribute equity capital to the extent of the 30 per cent of the total cost of the operation generally necessary for traditional project financing.

3. Among the first restructuring measures was the closing of the Akjoujt copper mine.

4. These data correspond to the realisation of what the feasibility study considered to be the first phase. For the financing of Phase 2 it was envisaged that SNIM would contribute $187 million of equity capital and borrow $250 million.

5. In October 1988, $US 1 = UM 74.14.

6. The state gave its guarantee for the loan for an additional charge of 2.1 per cent. In other words, SNIM received a loan from the World Bank at the Libor rate and paid interest of 2.1 per cent per annum to the Mauritanian state as payment for its guarantee.

7. The Caisse Centrale de Coopération Economique granted SNIM a $30 million loan and provided an advance of $20 million on the purchase of equipment guaranteed by the French government.

8. The aim of this procedure was to ensure that the Mauritanian state's short-term foreign exchange requirements would not affect SNIM's capacity to pay its operating expenses in foreign currency. The system set up provided that SNIM would present its planned budget to the Mauritanian state six weeks before the beginning of the financial year. If the state objected to the proposed budget, it had then to make a counter-proposal which must have the lenders' backing. The difficulty of this task and the very short period of time allowed meant that this procedure was not very workable, so in order to avoid it, the SNIM management generally preferred to propose a budget plan that already had the backing of the state.

9. The company operating the Akjoujt copper mine.

10. SNIM paid nothing to the state in 1987 and 1988 however.

11. Consolidated financial operations of the public administrations (source: confidential IMF report).

12. It should be noted that for once the World Bank chose somewhat pessimistic hypotheses based on a dollar at FF 5.50 and an iron ore price constant at the 1988 level. In fact, SNIM's results could be improved by a rise in the dollar (currency of its earnings) as against the European currencies (in which it pays for its imports of intermediates and its financial charges), and a rise in iron ore prices. But the positive effects to be hoped from favourable variations in these parameters would not be able to compensate for the company's structural imbalances.

13. Thus, for example, the Kuwait Foreign Trading, Contracting and Investment Company envisaged the construction of a pelletisation plant in Mauritania, integrated with the Guelbs iron ore operation and exporting its products to the direct reduction plants in Qatar, Irak and, in the longer term, Saudi Arabia.

Chapter IV

PT INCO*

INTRODUCTION

The PT Inco operation in Indonesia is illustrative of what the growth mode of an oligopolistic leader used to be. The principal role here is played by the Canadian company Inco, world leader on the nickel market.

After the nickel boom of the late 1960s, Inco tried to increase its production capacity in order to retain its position as leader and its control over price formation. In particular, Inco was trying to increase its penetration of the Japanese market where the annual average growth rate during the 1950s and 1960s was over 20 per cent. However, the company had to overcome three constraints:

    a)   The Japanese nickel industry was made up of smelters importing high nickel content matte or oxidised ores. This industry was protected by customs tariffs that placed heavy duties on imports of refined nickel;

    b)   The Canadian legislation prevented Inco, whose mines were in Canada, from exporting non-refined nickeliferous products;

    c)   The company's technical experience was based on the exploitation of sulphurous Canadian ores, whereas the majority of the known deposits elsewhere in the world (apart from Australia and Botswana) contain oxidised ores, generally with a low nickel content (laterites). At the end of the 1960s, the treatment process for these ores was still experimental.

---

* Chapter prepared by Paulo de Sa.

93

Inco's desire to develop its sales on the Japanese market and thus resist the tendency for its share of the world market to fall was to outweigh the dissuasive nature of the constraints. Until that time not very internationalised[1], Inco launched itself into the adventure of a vast laterite mining and ore treatment operation in Indonesia.

HISTORY OF THE PROJECT

-- As from 1945, when Indonesia became independent, the government undertook geological surveys in the Soroako region -- in the northwest of the archipelago -- before deciding to put a huge perimeter in this area up for auction.

-- In 1967, the Indonesian government issued a call for tenders for the evaluation of the deposits found, and received tenders from four big groups and consortiums: the French company Le Nickel; Kaiser Aluminium and Chemical Corp.; a consortium of Japanese companies; and the Canadian group Inco Ltd.

-- In 1968, Inco, who obtained the concession, undertook the exploration of the deposit that covers 25 000 km. A new company was formed, PT International Nickel Indonesia (PT Inco), a 75 per cent subsidiary of Inco, the rest of the capital being contributed by Japanese companies: three refiners and three traders. The state insisted on the right to take a stake of up to 20 per cent in the company by means of gradually buying shares during the first ten years of operation.

-- In mid-1971, the results of the exploration campaign showed that the lateritic deposit contained enough nickel to justify setting up a mine and a smelting plant in the Soroako region. The Japanese metallurgical industry was at that time to be the main market for the product. Inco ordered the feasibility study from the Japanese company Tokyo Engineering Co., and planned to later rely on Japanese enterprises for the engineering design, construction and bank financing of the project.

-- The complementary exploration carried out up to 1972 confirmed that the reserves of the Soroako region were sufficient to support the exploitation of a mine with a capacity of 45 million tonnes a year of ore containing 2.5 per cent nickel for a period of 30 years. The initial project envisaged a smelter, supplied by a thermal power station, producing 15 000 tonnes a year of nickel matte, and in the longer term a second phase in which the capacity would be increased to 45 000 tonnes a year.

-- In 1972, a technical assistance and management contract was signed between PT Inco and Inco Canada. The technical studies and tests were carried out in Inco's laboratories in Canada.

-- The first oil crisis considerably modified the economics of the project, a very big consumer of fuel oil. In 1974, Inco decided to extend the project to 45 000 tonnes of nickel matte a year, through adding two new smelting lines and building a dam for a hydroelectric power station in order to take advantage of economies of scale and reduce the energy dependence of the project. *The extension was in fact the anticipated implementation of Phase 2 of the project, initially programmed for long after the completion of Phase 1. The global cost of the two phases was estimated at $578 million.* The Japanese refused to participate in Phase 2 and their shareholding in PT Inco was to gradually fall to 2 per cent. Site preparation at Soroaka and construction of surface installations were completed in 1974. Completion of the construction of Phase 1 was planned for 1976 and that of Phase 2 was reprogrammed for 1979.

-- In 1975, construction fell behind the planned schedule. In November 1975, the physical investment cost of the project was re-estimated at $820 million, or a total cost (including working capital) of over $900 million. Phase 1 of the plant came on stream at the end of 1977.

-- In 1978, the delays in building up the level of production of Phase 2 caused financial difficulties which forced Inco to increase its equity capital contribution to PT Inco and reschedule its long-term debt. The second stage came on stream in November 1979.

-- In 1980, PT Inco offered shares to the Indonesia government, who refused them.

-- In 1981 there was a further restructuring of the long-term debt.

-- In 1982, the accumulation of technical and commercial difficulties led to the prolonged shut-down of two of the three furnaces at the Soroako smelter.

-- In 1983 there was yet another restructuring of the debt and Inco was forced to take over all the financial guarantees required by the banks: the bank loans granted to PT Inco, originally contracted to finance the project (off balance sheet), were posted to the liabilities in Inco's consolidated balance sheet.

-- In 1983 PT Inco repeated its offer to sell shares to the Indonesian government, this time at a 50 per cent discount, but the offer was again refused.

--   In 1984, the market conditions made it possible to bring the second and third furnaces back into operation and the complex reached 80 per cent of its nominal production capacity for the first time. Unfortunately, technical problems all too soon slowed production again.

DIFFICULTIES ENCOUNTERED

Technical difficulties

When the plant first came on stream in 1977, technical difficulties immediately appeared and considerably delayed the production programme. The studies and preliminary tests had not revealed the technical implications of the acidity of the high-grade ores to be treated in the early years of the project. This ore seriously damaged the refractory linings of two of the smelter's three furnaces, necessitating major repairs. To overcome this problem, PT Inco started exploiting the eastern block of the zone, whose less acid but lower grade ore was to be mixed with that of the western block. This reduced the average nickel content of the ores treated from 2.4 to about 2.1 per cent. This change caused not only a linear increase in the cost of extracting the ore (more ore to be extracted to obtain the same amount of nickel) but also an exponential increase in energy consumption for the treatment processes, to say nothing of the cost of relining the furnaces. Needless to say, the economic impact of these technical problems was aggravated by the second oil crisis of 1979.

In addition, the global production capacity of the complex was reduced. In 1980, a special Inco and PT Inco committee reviewed the situation and decided to reduce the capacity to a maximum of 36 000 tonnes of nickel content a year.

Commercial difficulties

The marketing of PT Inco's entire output was guaranteed by three long-term purchase contracts expiring in 1990, whose prices in the initial formulation were indexed on the producer price set by Inco. Two of these contracts were concluded with Japanese nickel refiners who had a holding in PT Inco (including Shimura Kako Company Ltd, in which Inco had acquired 34.7 per cent of the capital, and Tokyo Nickel Company, in which Inco held 45 per cent). These contracts covered the purchase of 15 000 tonnes of nickel a year, corresponding to the output of Phase 1 of the project. The third contract concluded with Inco concerned the purchase of output over and above this (Phase 2).

The overproduction crisis in the world nickel industry in the early 1980s resulted in two complementary phenomena appearing as regards prices:

-- Spot prices dropped dramatically to reach $1.60 a pound in 1982;

-- A producer price announced by Inco was maintained until 1983, with the gap between this and the spot price constantly increasing. Thus in 1982, while average spot prices did not exceed $2 a pound, the Inco price remained at about $3.20 a pound.

This crisis had two consequences for PT Inco:

1. The contracts concluded between PT Inco and the Japanese refiners provided for the removal of the output at a price based on the Inco price, refining of the metal, and repurchase of the metal by Inco at the Inco producer price. Inco then sold the metal on the Japanese market, this time at the free market price. This system enabled PT Inco to sell part of its output at a price very much higher than the free market price. But since Inco remained the owner of the metal refined by the Japanese, it was the parent company who directly financed this commercial bonus. It is estimated that on this part of the output, Inco transferred about $1 per pound of nickel -- or $30 million a year -- to its Indonesian subsidiary.

2. In order to limit the sums transferred from the parent company to Indonesia, Inco imposed production restrictions on its subsidiary. Under normal circumstances, once the contracts with the Japanese had been honoured, the excess production should amount to less than 15 000 tonnes that Inco could send to Japan or to its refinery in the United Kingdom. In 1982, in view of its increasing stocks of the metal, Inco ordered the shutdown of the production lines for which it was supposed to market the output. PT Inco's output was thus reduced by two-thirds, which very significantly increased the unit cost of production.

In 1983, the disappearance of Inco's producer price caused PT Inco to renegotiate its marketing contracts, and its prices are now indexed on the spot market price for nickel.

Financial difficulties

Eight separate credit agreements for a total of $125 million were negotiated to finance Phase 1 of the project, whose investment cost was initially estimated at $170 million. Eighty per cent of these loans were obtained from government agencies, 64 per cent of them being at fixed rates of interest. The Japanese refiners lent $36 million, repayable on the sale of the output. The rest of the financing corresponded to a loan of $25 million by a commercial bank syndicate headed by the Bank of Montreal, and financed on the Eurodollar market. The repayment period for these loans was in the order of 10 years.

The conditions under which loans were obtained for Phase 2 were much more severe (cf. Tables 4.1 and 4.2). Only 44 per cent of the total sum borrowed was obtained from government agencies, 30 per cent of which were at fixed rates of interest[2]. The biggest loan -- $200 million borrowed on the Eurodollar market -- came from a syndicate of commercial banks headed by Citycorp. The suppliers' credits from the United States, Canada, Australia, the United Kingdom, France, Norway and Japan totalled $190 million. By the end of 1975, total financing of $500 million had thus been obtained.

Table 4.1. : Financing of the PT Inco project (Million dollars)

	Phase I	Phase II	I + II
Commercial loans			
- Variable rates	25	340	365
Government loans			
- Fixed rates	78	168	246
- Variable rates	18	16	34
TOTAL	121	524	645

Source : Grave (1979)

Table 4.2. : Rates of interest on loans (per cent)

	Phase I	Phase II	I + II
Purchaser credits :			
- Fixed rates	6.81	9.45	8.86
- Variable rates	10.0	10.50	10.25
Supplier credits :			
- Fixed rates	7.8	8.34	8.32
Eurodollar loans :			
- Variable rates	9.94	10.10	10.09
Japanese loans			
- Fixed rates	8.6125	-	8.6125
Average	8.48	9.85	9.58

Source : Grave (1979)

In 1976, however, the overshooting of the investment cost obliged PT Inco to apply for more commercial credits from the same consortium of banks, to the tune of $140 million. The conditions for this complementary loan were even less favourable (Libor + 2.25 per cent). The establishment of the financing package was complicated by the need to implement Phase 2 of the project before the completion of Phase 1. The withdrawal of the Japanese, who had contributed a substantial share of the equity capital and the bank financing of Phase 1, forced PT Inco to find new backers. What is more, as from 1974, the change in the export financing policies of the industrialised countries had the effect of increasing the cost of outside financing and shortening the repayment periods[3]. The average rate of interest on supplier credits, which had been 6.8 per cent for Phase 1, went up to 9.5 per cent for Phase 2. The average rate for bank financing, which had been 8.5 per cent for Phase 1, went up to 9.9 per cent for Phase 2, or a global rate in 1977 of 9.6 per cent for the whole of the two phases.

To make matters worse, the high proportion of variable interest rate loans in the financing of Phase 2 (68 per cent) made the project very sensitive to interest rate increases. This was why in 1978 Inco requested a rescheduling of the $200 million loan granted by Citycorp in 1973 and the anticipated repayment in 1976 of a $65 million loan obtained from the same bank in 1976. Citycorp accepted this proposal on condition that Inco increase its equity capital contribution to bring the debt/equity ratio down to 60:40[4].

The system of guarantees associated with the financing of the PT Inco complex was characteristic of "project financing". In fact, Inco was never willing to give a guarantee on its industrial assets, limiting its liability to completion of the construction of the complex. The system of guarantees was therefore as follows:

-- *Completion guarantee:* Inco, as prime contractor, had to complete the construction of the project, except in the case of *force majeure* (natural catastrophe, civil war, nationalisation, etc.);

-- *During the construction stage, Inco had to service the PT Inco debt and could not allow the PT Inco debt/equity ratio to exceed 2:1.* This provision nevertheless allowed PT Inco to go further into debt in the case of cost overrun, provided that Inco took one-third of the burden. The project was to be considered completed once it could produce at 80 per cent of nominal capacity for a period of three months and service the bank debts itself;

-- *Establishment of a trustee account* with the Morgan Guaranty Trust in New York, where the product of PT Inco's sales is systematically deposited. The debt servicing is automatically debited to this account;

-- *Marketing guarantee* on the basis of the contracts described above.

In the event, all these guarantees worked against Inco. As the threshold of 80 per cent of nominal production capacity was never reached, the completion guarantee forced Inco to go on servicing the PT Inco debt until the financial restructuring of 1983. Inco thus had to bear not only the technical risk associated with the completion guarantee, but also the effects of the fall in nickel prices on PT Inco's results while production was being built up. The trustee account also caused additional financial charges through freezing a substantial part of PT Inco's income. As for the commercial guarantees, they have already been discussed above.

To explain the situation more precisely, when the complex came on stream, the cash flow was negative, so the debt could not be serviced. In 1981, the bankers, worried about this situation, imposed a first financial restructuring which led Inco to repay $100 million of the rescheduled loan ahead of time and to increase the capital to bring the debt/equity ratio down to 50:50, or invest a further $127 million. Inco received certain concessions in return: reduction of the rate of interest over and above the Libor, reduction of the deposit frozen in the trustee account.

In 1983, a further restructuring of the debt meant that Inco took over all PT Inco's debts: Inco lent $300 million to PT Inco who used this to pay off all the bank loans. The debt structure was now no longer a matter of project financing, but a financial commitment in the balance sheet of the parent company. There was therefore no longer any reason to keep the trustee account. This restructuring reduced PT Inco's financial charges by 65 per cent, making the cash flow positive.

As long as the operation was losing money -- i.e. until 1988 -- the Indonesian government, which had insisted on the option of taking up to a 20 per cent share of PT Inco's capital, refused all offers to participate.

CONCLUSION

Until 1986, the PT Inco mining and metallurgical project appeared to be a failure. Since 1987, the substantial efforts made to reduce operating costs[5] and the spectacular rise in nickel prices have enabled the company to achieve a favourable balance on the operating account. The Indonesian government and the Japanese metallurgists who had earlier kept out of or withdrawn from the project now want to come in. However, does this mean that the PT Inco investment has been a success after all? We think not.

It seems to us that in the initial stages (before 1974), all the actors involved in the project proceeded very carefully:

- For Inco, the development of a small project aimed at gradually penetrating the Japanese market was intended to:
  -- Limit the equity capital commitment without losing control of the operation;
  -- Provide technical experience in the treatment of oxidised ores;

-- Provide experience in project development in the Third World, the company having previously exploited mainly deposits in Canada;

• For the Japanese refiners, the project gave a guaranteed supply under an agreement with a reliable partner in a part of the world close to their market;

• For the Indonesian government, the type of contract proposed offered an advantageous share in the profits, without being involved in any industrial risk and with the guarantee of being able to maintain control over the company's activities.

The first oil crisis was to very seriously upset the technical and economic parameters of the operation. The need to achieve economies of scale essential to compensate for the higher cost price of the product was to radically change the scale of the project. In view of this situation, the Japanese decided to pull out, while Inco, feeling its position on the world market under threat, decided to commit itself much further than originally intended. The Indonesian government stood aloof. This strategic choice was to prove very costly for Inco.

The world's biggest nickel producer thus embarked alone on a project costing almost a billion dollars, without having full mastery of either the technical or the financial parameters. The second oil crisis was to penalise the operation even further. The final blow was to be the overcapacity crisis in the nickel industry at the very time when production was being built up in the complex. This deprived Inco of its only trump card: mastery of the marketing side, i.e. the company's ability to fix the price of the product. What appeared in 1973 to be a small project intended to give Inco entry to a rapidly-growing regional market turned into a financial nightmare. *By 1986, the cumulative cost of the operation to Inco -- i.e. Inco's equity capital immobilised in the project -- amounted to $850 million.*

It could be that in the longer term, if nickel demand should go on growing, it may be possible to amortize PT Inco, and even make a profit. But the fact remains that:

1. The project that was intended to make it possible for Inco to keep control of the prices on the market has had precisely the opposite effect;

2. The financial consequences of implementing the project deprived Inco of resources at a time when it had most need of them.

Inset 1: Technical and economic description

The Soroako nickel deposit is situated on the island of Sulawesi in Indonesia. The site is near Lake Matano, in a thinly populated area. The project consists of an open cast mine and a metallurgical complex comprising a concentration plant and three smelting lines. The electricity for the complex is supplied by a 165 MW hydroelectric power station and a 56 MW thermal power station. It also includes the associated installations such as the township, roads, airport and port. The Soroako open cast mine exploits a lateritic nickel ore deposit. The ore is extracted by hydraulic shovels and carried by truck to the screening stations where it goes through a series of screens and classifiers to separate the sterile rock. The ore is then dried to 18 per cent and mixed with ore from other sites. The resulting mixture is fed to the furnace where the nickel and iron are reduced. The matte from the furnace containing about 30 to 35 per cent Ni is transferred to a rotary converter where the iron is oxidised. The matte from this converter, containing 75 to 80 per cent Ni and traces of cobalt, is granulated and prepared for transport.

The 1973 feasibility study envisaged the realisation of the project in two stages:

-- Phase 1, based on the thermal power station, with a nominal capacity of 15 000 tonnes of nickel matte a year, was planned to be implemented by 1976;

-- Phase 2, involving the construction of a hydroelectric power station and bringing the production capacity up to 45 000 tonnes of nickel matte a year was to be envisaged after completion of Phase 1.

Inset 2: Forecast costs and returns

The cost of Phase 1 was estimated in 1973 at $170 million, the physical investment amounting to $105 million. In 1974, following the decision to implement Phase 2, the total cost of the project was estimated at $580 million. By the end of 1982, even though the production capacity had been reduced to 38 000 tonnes of nickel matte, the effective cost of the project had risen to over $900 million, including the working capital. The unit cost of the project with the complex working at full capacity is about $11 per pound of nickel per year.

The 1973 feasibility study estimated a rate of return of 15 per cent on equity capital for Phase 1. The extension of the project envisaged in 1976 forecast a rate of return of 12.2 per cent on the whole of the invested capital and 15.6 per cent on equity capital.

In 1976, with a nickel price estimated at $2.40 per pound, the forecast rate of return was 6 per cent on the total investment and 13.3 per cent on equity capital. This optimistic projection was based on the hypothesis that the complex would have reached full production capacity by 1979. *Between 1979 and 1984 production never exceeded 20 000 tonnes of nickel content, very far from the 40 000 tonnes initially planned.*

NOTES AND REFERENCES

1. About the same time, Inco also launched another laterite mining and treatment project in Guatemala (Exmibal), which the company abandoned after its realisation in 1983, writing off $350 million.

2. See GRAVE (1979).

3. Thus, for example, the United States Eximbank decided in 1974 to participate in the financing of the project only in association up to a maximum of 50 per cent with commercial banks generally offering less favourable loan conditions.

4. This ratio was previously fixed at 67:33.

5. At the end of 1986, thanks to the devaluation of the Indonesian rupiah, the project was able to balance its operating costs with a nickel price of about $2 a pound. The actual price was then in the order of $1.70 a pound.

Chapter V

CERRO MATOSO*

INTRODUCTION

The Cerro Matoso operation illustrates how new forms of investment enabled the risks involved in a project to be shared between the actors during the period in which the oligopolies were losing their power. The fact is that after 25 years of studies and negotiations this Colombian ferro-nickel complex came on stream at the very time when the nickel market was escaping from the control of the producers, revealing a hitherto unsuspected price risk. As will be seen, through combining their equity participation with the sale of services, the foreign investors (Hanna Mining and Billiton) managed to reduce their exposure to the price risk, while because it wanted to take a share in the capital and the financing of the project in order to encourage its realisation, the Colombian government, supported by the World Bank, took the maximum risk.

HISTORY OF THE PROJECT

-- The Cerro Matoso deposit was discovered in 1955 by Richmond Oil, a subsidiary of SOCAL, prospecting for oil. Richmond Oil immediately began negotiations with the Colombian government to obtain an iron ore mining concession. To explore the deposit, SOCAL formed a joint venture with Hanna Mining, one of the foremost mining companies in the United States, specialised in iron ore and nickel mining.

---

* Chapter prepared with the aid of Paulo de Sa.

105

--	Between 1960 and 1963, Hanna Mining and SOCAL stepped up their exploration of the region, confirming the existence of the deposit and coming to the conclusion that it would be more profitable to exploit the nickel than the iron ore.

--	In March 1963, Richmond Oil signed a exploration contract to evaluate the deposit. Hanna Mining was designated operator, but the project advanced only slowly. The Colombian government for its part was looking for a new form of association involving its equity participation in the project.

--	As from 1969 the nickel market appeared very tight, with the free market price reaching $20 a pound or six times the producer price. In July 1970 the SOCAL-Hanna Mining joint venture had to be modified to include the Colombian government. Furthermore, SOCAL wanted to withdraw from the project while Hanna Mining was aiming to consolidate its position on the nickel market. An agreement was signed allocating one-third of the shares to a government-owned subsidiary, and two-thirds to Conicol (Compania de Niquel Colombiano SA), a company emerging from the SOCAL-Hanna Mining joint venture. Hanna held 87.5 per cent of Conicol and SOCAL 12.5 per cent. The government's stake was held by Empresa Colombiana de Niquel Limitada (Econiquel), a subsidiary of the Instituto de Fomento Industrial (IFI). Hanna Mining, now the majority shareholder, was the adminstrator of the new joint venture and represented the foreign shareholders in the negotiation of all subsequent agreements.

--	Up to 1971, Hanna Mining was carrying out laboratory tests but there was little progress on the project proper.

--	In 1975 and 1976, Hanna built a pilot plant in its installations at Riddle (Oregon). The project still appeared to be suspended. This delay can be explained by the effects of the first oil shock on the structure of laterite nickel refining costs, which threatened the profitability of the operation. The technical problems also remained serious.

--	In 1977, nickel prices fell in a worrying fashion for the first time. Hanna then seemed to favour the development of the rival Exmibal project in Guatemala, in which it was associated with Inco, the world's biggest nickel producer[1]. In order to revive the Cerro Matoso project, Econiquel decided to step up its investment and increase its shareholding to 40 per cent.

--	In 1979, when the nickel market picked up again, Billiton Overseas Ltd offered to take a share in the operation to the tune of 35 per cent. Billiton, a company hitherto oriented more towards trading, was looking for minority holdings in projects under study or in the development stage, aiming to increase its commercial activity in this way. In this context, a new company was created in March 1979 under the name of Cerro Matoso SA (CMSA) with which Billiton signed a purchase contract for the entire production over a period of 13 years. This contract included the following clauses:

a) Payment to the Colombian government of a royalty of 8 per cent in foreign currency calculated on the basis of an fob ex-works price based on the price realized by Billiton;

b) Obligation for CMSA to make its nickel production available to the local market or Latin American consumers at the international market price.

Billiton's taking over the commercial risk appeared advantageous to Hanna Mining for two reasons:

1) By and large, non-integrated producers who negociate long-term contracts with buyers run a commercial risk to the extent that a temporary surplus or a price collapse on the spot market can cause the non-respect of contracts, either through a reduction in the volume of purchases or the granting of substantial discounts. When the buyer is involved in the joint venture this commercial risk appears to be reduced.

2) The buyer's presence in the operation limits the risk of expropriation by the government, who would then lose most of its market outlets.

Under the terms of the contract, the price paid by Billiton to CMSA was calculated on the basis of the average prices for the quarter in Europe, Japan and the United States for products comparable to those sold by CMSA, after deduction of freight and insurance (fob Colombia). In addition, the prices were to be adjusted at the end of every year to reflect the conditions on the market on which Billiton had sold its ferro-nickel. This adjustment was made by the deduction of a commission paid to Billiton corresponding to the marketing costs -- between 3 per cent of the international average price for the year when prices were high and 6 per cent when they fell below $2 a pound. In view of the guarantee of outlets for the product through the London Metal Exchange, the commercial risks run by Billiton were thus very limited. What is more, it is generally admitted among traders that in a depressed market, realisation of a price corresponding to the average LME price constitutes a fairly poor commercial performance.

-- CMSA also signed a series of contracts for the construction of the complex, the supply of fuel oil and electricity, project management and technical assistance. This last contract concluded with Hanna Mining provided that during the construction phase Hanna would receive payment for its services equal to the direct and indirect costs of its work. Until the completion of the project and for the first seven years, Hanna Mining was to receive a payment of $0.011 per pound of nickel for project management and $0.0165 per pound for technical assistance. For an output of between 16 000 and 22 000 tonnes of nickel, Hanna Mining would receive between $1 million and $1.4 million a year. This contract was renegotiable after seven years. As the Colombian government demanded some control over management and decision-making structures, it obtained representation on a five-member board: 2 from Billiton, 2 from Econiquel and 1 from Conicol.

-- The financing of the project could now be finalised. Three groups of banks agreed to contribute $227 million of project financing. The agreement signed in 1979 provided that in the case of a total cost of $425 million, 47 per cent would be equity capital and 53 per cent, or $225 million in the form of loans. There was a clause providing that Conicol would in no circumstance increase its shareholding, in particular in the case of investment cost overrun. Conicol thus tried to limit its financial contribution and hence the risks it ran in the project, an attitude which led it to gradually withdraw from the operation. The initial financing package for the Cerro Matoso project is shown in Table 5.1.

Loans were granted to CMSA by three groups of banks:

a)   The Chase Manhattan Bank group;

b)   The World Bank (IBRD);

c)   The US Eximbank in association with a group of commercial banks.

These institutions contributed between $200 million and $225 million. Table 5.2 summarises the terms of the loans granted to CMSA.

The banks imposed a system of decreasing debt:own-funds ratio in the case of investment cost overruns. This ratio varied between 66:33 for the initial estimated cost and 47:53 for the maximum overrun envisaged. This maximum was in fact reached. The World Bank required a guarantee from the Colombian government. Earnings were to be paid into a trustee account.

Table 5.1. : Initial financing package

A/ Shareholdings	US$ Million	Per cent
1. Old[2]		
-Econiquel	10.0	3.1
- Conicol	15.0	4.7
Sub-total 1	25.0	7.8
2. New		
- Econiquel	41.3	12.9
- Billiton	39.9	12.5
- Conicol	7.8	2.4
Sub-total 2	89.0	27.8
TOTAL 1+2	114.0	35.6
B/ Long-term loans		
- World Bank	80.0	25.0
- US Eximbank[3]	26.5	8.0
- Chase Manhattan	100.0	31.4
Sub-total	206.5	64.4
Total financing for 1982	320.5	100.0
C/ Working capital		
for 1983-84[4]	19.5	
TOTAL financing	340.0	

Table 5.2. : Terms of the loans granted to CMSA

Source	Amount ($ dollars)	Repayment period	Grace period	Interest rate	Conditions
Chase	94.4-120.0	6.5	4	LIBOR+1.25	
B.M.	80	11	4	7.9+2.0	import of goods and services from Member countries
EXIM	12.8	5	4	$8^{5/8}$	importt of goods and services from the United States
Commercial banks	12.8	5	4	$1^{1/8}$	

Source : Zinser (1982)

-- In 1981, Hanna Mining, who refused to contribute to the increase in own-funds, now held only 13.7 per cent of the shares but remained the operator. The breakdown of shareholdings was now as follows[5]:

Shareholder	Per cent
Conicol	15.6
SOCAL	1.9
Hanna Mining	13.7
Econiquel	45.0
Billiton	39.0
Total	99.6

-- In 1983, the technical assistance contract was renegotiated: the payments made to Hanna Mining being reduced by half. CMSA was becoming technically independent while Hanna was gradually withdrawing from the project.

DIFFICULTIES ENCOUNTERED

Technical difficulties

According to World Bank analyses, the project as a whole involved little risk from the technical standpoint. The deposit was well-known and of exceptional quality. The choice of the operating methods and the equipment was guided by the desire for mobility and the maintenance of flexibility in the operating programme. From the technical standpoint only the rotary electric kiln gave any cause for concern at the beginning of the project, this on account of its size and despite the tests carried out by Hanna Mining.

In fact, since 1982 technical difficulties encountered in treating the ore have constantly slowed production. Before 1984 the kiln was never able to operate at full capacity. It was shut down in June 1985 and started up again towards the end of the year. This caused lost production of about 12 million pounds of nickel and the 1985 targets were not met, any more than those for 1983 and 1984.

Financial and commercial difficulties

According to initial forecasts, the project should have begun to show a profit as from the second year, but between start-up in 1982 and the end of 1985,

CMSA had suffered accumulated losses of $145 million. The forecasts had been too optimistic with respect to the sales price of the nickel. While the market forecasts indicated a price of $3.61 a pound in 1984, the actual price virtually never exceeded $2.50 after 1981, sometimes reaching historic lows below $1.60 a pound.

Despite the technical difficulties, CMSA succeeded in covering its operating costs in 1982, 1983 and 1984. However, it was unable to make margins big enough to be able to service its long-term debt. In 1984, the Colombian government had to honour its guarantee by servicing the CMSA debt to the World Bank. In June 1985, CMSA negotiated a rescheduling of its debt with the commercial banks[6] and obtained a grace period of three years which delayed the payment of $43 million that the company should have paid over the period 1985-87. This meant that during this period CMSA serviced only the World Bank debt, involving a payment of $8 million a year.

In addition, in 1983 and 1984, CMSA signed a series of agreements with the Instituto de Fomento Industrial (IFI), Empresa Colombiana de Niquel (Econiquel) and Billiton Overseas Limited (Billiton) aimed at increasing the company's capital. IFI and Econiquel on the one hand and Billiton on the other agreed to bring in additional funds of $16 million in 1983 and $46 million in 1984. A similar agreement was signed on 14th February 1985 between IFI and Econiquel on the one hand and Billiton on the other to bring in $8.7 million which was to be converted into shares between 1985 and 1988. In practice, IFI gradually took the place of Econiquel in CMSA. In addition, in 1982 CMSA contracted a further loan of $45 million with Billiton and Econiquel, who, though this solution seemed to them to be better than contributing additional capital (they would in theory receive interest), actually became CMSA's last-line creditors.

Lastly, in 1987, CMSA restructured its debt with the World Bank. Under the terms of this original agreement, CMSA pays the interest normally, but repayment of the principal depends on the nickel price. Despite the burden of its external debt, CMSA is protected in this way against the more violent fluctuations in the price of its product.

CONCLUSION: LOGIC OF THE ACTORS' INTERVENTION

Compared with the majority of mining projects developed in the Third World during the 1970s, Cerro Matoso enjoyed a certain number of advantages. The fact is that the geological characteristics of the deposit were very favourable and in view of the transport possibilities the investment costs were relatively modest. However, the financial results of this operation turned out to be very negative, at least during the first five years of operation. In what follows we shall try to briefly summarise the reasons and show how the risks of this project were shared among the different actors.

The reasons for the difficulties

Poor market analysis was a major factor. Twenty-seven years elapsed between the discovery of the first indications and the coming on stream of the plant. As from the 1970s there were periodical tensions on the nickel market, when the producers interpreted temporary sudden revivals as reversals of the long-term trend. None of the traditional producers had foreseen the extent of the structural break in the trend of the rate of increase of world nickel consumption. The end of oligopolistic regulation of the nickel market caused an unprecedented collapse in prices. *The Cerro Matoso project came on stream at the worst possible time.*

The poor quality of the preparatory technical evaluations caused an underestimation of the investment expenditure and modification of the financial parameters of the project. As a result the overhead cost burden per tonne of output became one of the highest in the world for this industry. This burden was made even worse by the plant's operating below capacity, for technical reasons, during the early years of operation.

This combination of higher fixed costs and the lasting depressed state of the market turned a project with relatively favourable operating costs into a financial nightmare. From this standpoint, Cerro Matoso illustrates how mining and metallurgical operations appear much more risky once prices can no longer be controlled. Even operations rather well situated on the cost scale can suffer when the price trend is against them.

How the risks were shared

The financial risks of the operation were appreciated and accepted in different ways by each of the actors involved.

Hanna Mining: a typical new form of investment: Hanna's overall strategy was influenced by the crisis on the iron ore market and the failure of the Guatemala project in which it was associated with Inco, a project simply abandoned after its construction in 1981. From this time on, Hanna Mining was therefore trying to diversify its investments and limit its risk in each operation. The clause in the contract limiting the company's overall engagement in the project was very advantageous. It also enabled the company to benefit from its technical experience in mining and ore treatment through selling its services. Hanna Mining, who put a total of about $19 million into the project received on average about $2 million a year in payment for its services until 1983, while CMSA was making substantial losses.

Billiton: a new form of investment oriented towards selling a marketing service: Billiton's joining the project was to largely determine its realisation.

However, this investment, in which there was no limitation of the company's financial engagement in the project, led Billiton to spend over $100 million. This sizeable amount, which the company had no doubt initially underestimated, is far from being compensated by the marketing service for the output which brings Billiton about $6 million a year. This sale of services should be analysed as a limitation of risk which insures an income for Billiton regardless of the market situation.

The Colombian government: aiming to promote a foreign currency earner: the different interventions of the Colombian government had contradictory effects. The fact is that the first intervention, aimed at involving the state in the project at the time of the 1970 nickel market boom, no doubt tended to frighten off the foreign investors and delayed the start of the operation. On the other hand, the increase of the state's share to 40 per cent in 1977 reflected its desire to promote a foreign currency earning investment at a time when the operation was already appearing much more risky. This strategy led the state to assume the greater part of the financial risk of the project, despite its minority holding.

This lack of prudence on the part of the Colombian government was nevertheless encouraged by the intervention of the other actors in the project, whether they be nickel producers who failed to see the structural changes on the market in time, or banks, and in particular the World Bank, who tried to promote this financial service consuming project, which would theoretically be a foreign exchange earner for Colombia. At first, the Colombian state serviced the project's external debt. The upturn in nickel prices since 1987 and the original way in which the debt was restructured, now being indexed on the nickel price, has put the Colombian government in a more favourable situation. In the longer term, this new financial structure should enable CMSA, which enjoys advantageous production costs due to the quality of the deposit, to cope with price falls. Under these circumstances, this project, through which the Colombians are gradually acquiring technical know-how, could become a more prosperous industrial operation after its very shakey start.

Inset 1: Technical and economic description

The Cerro Matoso nickel deposit is situated in northwest Colombia, in the department of Cordoba, 430 kilometres south of the port of Cartagena. The project site is near the town of Montelibano, where the workers' accommodation was built. The Cerro Matoso industrial complex consists of an open cast mine and a nickel concentrating plant.

The mine is on a lateritic deposit similar to the Falcondo deposit in the Dominican Republic. The reserves are estimated at 25 billion tonnes with an average Ni content of 2.89 per cent (and a minimum of 1.5 per cent). The proven reserves are estimated at 0.9 million tonnes of nickel metal, or a little less than 1 per cent of world reserves. The annual output of the mine was planned to be between 16 000 and 22 000 tonnes of Ni content. Under these conditions, the deposit would allow 25 years of operation. The deposit also contains 41 billion tonnes of lower grade ore with an average Ni content of between 1 and 1.5 per cent.

The Cerro Matoso concentrating plant is one of the most advanced for the treatment of lateritic nickel ores. The product is conditioned in the form of granules. Operating at full capacity, the plant can produce 55 000 to 65 000 tonnes of ferro-nickel a year, with an average Ni content of 37.5 per cent. The plant came on stream in 1982.

The output is taken away on a road that involved little infrastructure cost: 12 kilometres of unmetalled road leading from Montelibano to the motorway linking, from south to north, the industrial centre of Medellin (333 kilometres) to the ports of Cartagena and Barranquilla (538 kilometres). Furthermore, during the construction phase it was possible to discharge heavy equipment at the river port of Caucasia, 30 kilometres southeast of the site. The river now constitutes a back-up mode of transport for the output if the road should be blocked.

The cost of the project was estimated in 1979 at $340 million, or the equivalent of 14 billion Colombian pesos. Sixty-four per cent of the financing, or $216.2 million corresponded to foreign exchange expenditure. Investment expenditure was broken down as shown in Table 5.3.

114

Table 5.3. : Forecast investment cost
(Million dollars)

	Local	Foreign	Total	Per cent
	Currencies			
Mine	9.6	14.6	24.2	10.3
Concentrating plant	34.8	53.8	88.6	38.0
Pre-operational expenditure	14.4	29.1	43.5	18.6
Pipeline	1.0	2.0	3.0	1.3
Civil engineering, installations	24.1	5.0	29.1	12.5
Engineering and project studies	16.4	28.8	45.2	19
Physical investment cost	100.3	133.3	233.6	100.0
Provisions	19.9	23.3	43.2	
Working capital	3.6	32.2	35.8	
Project cost	123.8	188.8	312.6	
Interest payment during construction	-	27.4	27.4	
Financing requirement	123.8	216.2	**340.0**	

As can be seen, the expenditure in local currency corresponded essentially to the civil engineering work, materials and construction. Provision was made for contingency expenditure esimated at about 18 per cent of the total initial cost of the project. The unit investment cost estimated in 1979, excluding inflation, working capital and interest payments during the construction phase, was about $6 per pound of nickel per year. In 1979, the pre-tax rate of return on the investment was estimated at 17 per cent in real terms and the return on equity capital at about 19.4 per cent.

In 1982, the cumulative cost of the project had reached $500 million, or almost 50 per cent above the original budget.

Since then, a number of repairs of defective equipment have brought additional expenditure of over $100 million. The investment cost overrun means that the actual unit investment cost is now between $8.5 and $10 per pound of nickel producing capacity[7].

NOTES AND REFERENCES

1. This project was nevertheless to be definitively abandoned after its construction in 1983.

2. Non-discounted assets at the end of 1978.

3. Half this sum, or $12.8 million came from commercial banks, the rest being contributed by the United States Eximbank.

4. The working capital in 1982 ($16.3 million) was financed by loans and shares as if forming part of the physical investment cost of the project.

5. Source: ZINSER (1982).

6. Cf. *Metal Bulletin* of 4th June 1985.

7. The financial risk run by such a capital-intensive investment can be judged by calculating the unit cost per pound of nickel. In 1986, nickel was traded on the LME at between $1.55 and $2.10 a pound. In 1988, the nickel price reached $10 a pound. In other words, depending on whether it starts up in a period of low or high prices, the period over which an investment of this type can pay for itself can range from 2 to 20 years.

Chapter VI

SELEBI-PHIKWE*

INTRODUCTION

The Selebi-Phikwe operation, a copper/nickel mining and smelting complex in Botswana, shows how the participation of numerous actors in the realisation of an industrial project largely financed by bank loans can lead to a mug's game in which each player tries to take advantage of the implication of the others to reduce his own responsibility and reap the benefits.

As will be seen, this operation which took nearly ten years to set up (from 1963 to 1973) came into being in a context marked by:

-- The independence of the countries of southern Africa and the restructuring of the assets of mining enterprises in this region;

-- The progressive destabilization of the nickel market after the boom of the late 1960s.

In this context, the Selebi-Phikwe project was to give rise to what became known as new forms of investment, involving enterprises with complementary but contradictory objectives, consumers looking for sources of supply and commercial profits, commercial and development banks, and a government anxious to benefit from a foreign investment on its territory.

---

* Chapter prepared with the aid of Djibril Ndiaye.

HISTORY OF THE PROJECT

-- On 2nd June 1959, an exploration concession was granted to Rhodesian Selection Trust (RST), a 51 per cent subsidiary of Amax, by the Bamangwato tribe. In November 1959, an exploration company was created, Bamangwato Concession Ltd (BCL), controlled 15 per cent by the tribe and 85 per cent by the following mining companies:

RST Exploration Ltd (Rhoselex, subsidiary of Amax and AAC)	51%
Mond Nickel Exploration Ltd (subsidiary of Inco)	32.7%
Mineral Separation Ltd	16.3%

-- From 1960 to 1968, exploration was directed by RST Exploration Ltd (Rhoselex) under a management contract with BCL. The capital of Rhoselex was then shared between Rhodesian Selection Trust (RST) and Roan Antelope Copper Mines controlled by Amax and Mufulira Copper Mines in which Anglo-American Corporation (AAC) held a 32 per cent interest.

-- In 1963, the Selebi copper/nickel deposit was discovered. The nickel-rich Phikwe deposit was discovered in 1966. After Zambian independence in 1964, all the Rhoselex assets outside Zambia were brought under RST Bechuanaland Holding Ltd. Similarly, after Botswana's independence in 1966, a new subsidiary, RST Botswana Holding Ltd, took over the Botswanan assets of the former Rhoselex.

-- In 1967, RST Botswana Holding Ltd was liquidated. The holdings in BCL were split between Mufulira Copper Mines Ltd, who redistributed them to its shareholders[1], and the RST group. Amax and Anglo-American Corporation (AAC) set up a new company, Botswana RST Ltd (BRST), which covered certain of their activities in Botswana and in particular a 61 per cent holding in BCL. AAC also had a direct holding of 10.5 per cent in BCL. At the same time, Mineral Separation Ltd increased its holding to 23.1 per cent, while Mond Nickel Exploration Ltd (subsidiary of Inco), refusing to increase its own-funds contribution, saw its share fall to 5.4 per cent.

-- By mid-1967, Amax had an indirect holding of 31 per cent in BCL.

-- In 1968, the nickel/copper reserves at Selebi were estimated at 13 million tonnes (1.57 per cent copper, 0.66 per cent nickel and 0.23 oz/tonne silver), the Phikwe reserves at 15 million tonnes (1.2 per cent copper, 1.5 per cent nickel and 0.09 oz/tonne silver) and finally the Matsitama reserves at 6.4 million tonnes containing 2.2 per cent copper. The large tonnages and the nickel price, rising strongly at the time, focussed the interest of the operators on the Selebi and Phikwe deposits.

-- In order to raise the funds necessary for financing the feasibility study, BRST floated a share issue in the United States, which reduced RST's holding to 30 per cent. Amax then took a direct holding of 30 per cent in BRST, the rest of the shares being held by small shareholders. The BRST capital was then held as follows:

RST (51 per cent controlled by Amax)	30%
Amax	30%
Minerals Separation Ltd	6%
Small shareholders (a thousand)	34%

-- In 1969, the Zambian government took 51 per cent control of the national copper industry. RST's Zambian assests (excluding those of Amax -- 42.3 per cent) were nationalised, the other shareholders receiving in addition to the compensation a share in RST's assets outside Zambia (including 17.8 per cent in BRST). Amax then created RST International to unite its Zambian and Botswanan holdings in BRST.

-- In 1969, Amax decided to buy the Port Nickel refinery in Louisiana, built in the early 1960s and intended at the time to refine nickel matte coming from Cuba.

-- From 1968 to 1970, BCL directed the metallurgical treatment tests and the feasibility study. The technical studies for the non-mining infrastructures began in 1967, following a request from the Botswana government to the World Bank and the United Nations Development Programme (UNDP).

-- In July 1971, the plan for exploiting the Selebi-Phikwe mine complex was defined.

-- In 1972, the legal and financing packages were set up. It was the principal shareholders in BRST (which held 85 per cent of BCL), Amax and AAC/Charter, who provided the lenders with a completion guarantee and the loan guarantees. In the joint venture then set up, the Botswana state took a free 15 per cent holding, as provided for in the mining concession. The capital of the company was then held as follows:

119

Government of Botswana	15%
BRST	85%

BRST's capital was increased and restructured: AAC bought Inco's share and converted its holding in BCL into BRST shares. In return AAC obtained the management of the project. A marketing agreement stipulated that part of the output of the complex would be sold to Metallgesellschaft (MG) after contract refining by Amax at Port Nickel. The rest was to be marketed directly by BCL, after refining by Amax.

-- After completion of the feasibility study in June 1971, the project financing was quickly settled. The negotiations on the financing of any cost overrun continued until March 1972. *Equity made up only 21 per cent of the total project financing:*

	$ Million (1971)
Equity funding	43.9
Total loans	169.4
Total investment cost	213.3
Debt/equity ratio	21:79

Source: MIKESELL 1982.

If the infrastructure expenditure born by the Botswana state is deducted, the debt/equity ratio becomes 31:69.

Table 6.1. : ECL's financing package[2]

Source	$ Million (1971)	Percentage of total
KFW Consortium	68.9	48
IDC : Industrial Develop- ment Corporation of South Africa	18	13
Subordinate loans[3]	11.2	8
Own funds	43.9	31
Total BCL	**142**	**100**
Infrastructures	71.3	
Total Phase 1	**214**	

The sum of $ 71.3 made available to the Botswana government to finance the non-mining infrastructures is broken down in Table 6.2:

Table 6.2. : Sources and conditions of the loans granted to the State
to finance infrastructures[4]

Source	$ Million (1969)	Percentage of total	Conditions
World Bank	32	45	7.5 per cent interest
CIDA : Canadian International Development Agency	30	42	50 year interest-free loan converted to a gift
USAID : US Agency for International Development	6.5	9	Low rate of interest
Other sources	2.8	4	Soft loans and gifts
Total	71.3	100	

The financing for Phase 1 of the project was for the most part provided by the development banks, whose loans were guaranteed by the principal shareholders, Amax and AAC/Charter Group (cf. Inset 4).

-- In December 1973, operations began at the Phikwe mine, 33 months after construction started. The cost of the non-mining infrastructures was estimated at $82 million.

-- In February 1974, the ore treatment plant and smelter came on stream, but technical problems appeared immediately. The copper and nickel contents of the matte produced were not as planned.

-- In September 1974, the estimated total cost was increased to $290 million. Expenditure to date amounted to $244 million.

-- In December 1975, the technical problems were being gradually overcome and the production of matte reached 70 per cent of the planned monthly output. However, BCL recorded a net loss of $62 million in 1975, because of the high cost of production aggravated by the oil price rise, the inadequate level of production and an unprofitable price level. The total funds invested in the project now amounted to $300 million, taking into account the installation costs, working capital and the operating losses suffered.

-- 1976 saw the start of negotiations on the first financial restructuring, which was completed in 1978. BCL made an operating profit, but suffered a net loss of $33.8 million after payment of interest and other financial charges.

121

-- In 1977, the Amax board, having lost all hope of the investment proving profitable, approved the writing down by $50 million of Amax's holding in BRST, which then appeared in the balance sheet at $94.4 million.

-- The first restructuring was completed in March 1978, ratifying the financial agreements and the revision of the marketing contract. Under the terms of the new agreement, BCL's entire output was to be bought and refined by Amax, before being re-exported to Germany. BCL's position is scarcely any better than it was before. Net losses were slightly lower than in 1977 ($52 million as against $62 million). Phase 1 of the project was considered completed.

-- In 1979, sales of BCL matte plunged to 29 000 tonnes because of a strike at the Port Nickel refinery from September 1979 to 25th January 1980. Amax invoked the *force majeure* clause so as not to have to honour its purchasing engagements. Despite this, an improvement in prices enabled net losses to be reduced.

-- In January 1980 the Selebi mine started production and was operating at full capacity by the month of May. Net losses were brought down to $19 million thanks to the increased volume of sales and a relative improvement in metal prices.

-- In May 1980 an agreement on the restructuring of the principal debt was concluded, repayment being deferred for a period of four years ending on 31st December 1983, after which this debt was to be paid off over three and a half years.

-- In October 1981, Amax entered into negotiations with BCL for a 25 per cent reduction in the volume of its purchases and the indexation of the matte price on the price realised on the sale of its copper and nickel content.

-- In December 1981, Amax wrote off the group's holding in BRST ($22.1 million). Discussions were opened on a restructuring that would make it possible to reduce the financial pressure on Amax and the AAC/Charter Group.

-- In 1982, Amax obtained the reduction in its matte purchases and the desired changes in the pricing system. The restructuring of BCL's debt, completed in June 1982, resulted in the conversion of a substantial part of the priority debt into subordinate debt. This part included the debts guaranteed by Amax.

-- In 1983, Amax put $4.7 million into BCL, as against $2.7 million in 1982, and undertook to cofinance until December 1985, together with the Botswana government and AAC, an emergency fund of $24 million. However, Amax set a maximum of $9 million for its contribution. *At the end of December 1983, the total debt accumulated by BCL amounted to $622 million.*

-- In 1984, two new marketing contracts were negotiated: one for period of 15 years with Falconbridge International Ltd (FIL) and the other for 10 years with Rio Tinto Zimbabwe.

-- In 1985, these contracts, whose terms were considered more favourable to BCL than those of the earlier contract, were ratified by the principal shareholders, the lenders and the government of Botswana. Amax received compensation of $30 million. In July 1985, Amax announced the shut-down of the Port Nickel refinery.

DIFFICULTIES ENCOUNTERED

Technical difficulties

There were many technical difficulties, but it may be considered, without trying to put anyone in the dock, that they were foreseeable. Most of the problems encountered can be attributed to the choice of risky techniques, either because of insufficient funds or induced by a very imperfect knowledge of the properties of the ore:

-- The lack of experience of the workforce and the premature departure of the LED[5] staff after the ore treatment plant came on stream caused minor difficulties during start-up;

-- In order to try to curb rapidly escalating costs, changes to the original operating system were decided despite warnings from the equipment suppliers and the designers, who stressed the potential risk. Thus, for example, the modification of the operating sequence initially planned for the flotation of sulphides made the pulp acid, so that an additional lime circuit had to be built to raise the pH;

-- An explosion in the concentrate storage and drying silos, caused by the pyrophoric properties of the marcasite in the oxidised part of the deposit, and the inappropriate crushing of the concentrate, seriously damaged the drying system and temporarily halted production. The silos had to be rebuilt;

-- The use of a magnetic separation process ill-suited to only slightly magnetic ores such as pyrrhotite was a cause of low productivity in the concentrator;

-- The high proportion of fines in the ore lowered the efficiency of the enrichment plant. This problem was solved only at the price of installing a preconcentrator unit to rid the ore of fines;

123

-- Lastly, the malfunctions of the smelter and sulphur reduction unit can be attributed to the use of process that had not been tried and tested on such a large scale. The company was obliged to abandon the production of sulphur, even though there was a sulphur marketing contract with Triomf Fertilizer Ltd (RSA). The non-respect of this contract cost BCL $4 million in damages and interest in 1977. What is more, since the sulphur dioxide was now no longer reduced but released into the atmosphere, the Botswana government forced the company to install a pollution control facility. In 1978 this expenditure amounted to $13 million.

Commercial difficulties

The nickel boom of the late 1960s made Amax want to enter this market. The purchase of the Port Nickel refinery, the moderate price and renovation costs of which appeared to promise good profits, fitted into this logic. However, the vertical integration of the nickel industry, to which Amax did not yet belong, obliged Amax to associate itself with a matte producer with no downstream integration. This was the logic behind the successive marketing agreements involving Amax and BCL.

In the initial plan, BCL remained the owner of the entire matte output and of the metal, for which Amax had an exclusive refining contract. The first marketing contract (1973), covering a period of 15 years, bound Metallgesellschaft (MG) to buy two-thirds of the nickel production and the entire copper and cobalt production, i.e., 9 300 tonnes of nickel and 18 600 tonnes of copper a year for the first ten years, and 7 300 tonnes of nickel and 14 300 tonnes of copper a year for the following five years. Any surplus production could be sold on the free market on BCL's behalf. Under the terms of the contract, the nickel was to be bought by MG at the Inco producer price and the copper at the price realised by the big German producers, less 3 and 2 per cent respectively, representing the marketing margins granted to MG. For other BCL sales realised by MG outside the contract quotas, the margins were between 2 and 2.75 per cent of the sales price. MG was also to receive a commission on the product of all nickel sales[6] effected at a price higher than $1.50 per pound (8 per cent of the margin between this floor price and the sales price). This marketing contract was largely instrumental in BCL's obtaining a $70 million loan from KFW, the German development bank. It should be noted however that in this arrangement MG took no investment risk, the KFW loan being guaranteed by the German government and the shareholders, but received far from negligible commissions in return for taking a virtually zero commercial risk. The conditions of this contract show that *already in the late 1970s, it was the partner capable of guaranteeing outlets for the product who enjoyed the most favourable situation.*

This contract was soon to prove unfavourable to Amax when, after the first oil shock, its refining margin became less profitable. In 1978, during the first restructuring of BCL, the Botswana government and the foreign partners wanted to put an end to this system of marketing. In agreement with the lenders, a new contract gave Amax exclusive purchasing rights to the BCL matte, with Amax using MG as marketing agent in Germany for 6 600 tonnes of nickel a year. At the same time, Amax managed to increase the refining charges.

In 1981, the financing of its stocks caused a net loss for Amax-Nickel, despite an operating profit. Amax then began negotiations with its matte suppliers to modify the method of fixing the purchase price and proposed a 25 per cent reduction in its purchases from BCL. In 1982, the 1978 marketing contract was amended to allow the matte price to be indexed on the nickel metal price realised by Amax. This new contract, together with the overproduction crisis on the world nickel market, caused BCL's income to tumble from $90.6 million to $59 million between 1981 and 1983, even though output and sales increased throughout this period. In fact, Amax was able to take advantage of the new arrangement to get rid of all its nickel stocks, making BCL bear the brunt of the price collapse caused by this decision. BCL's losses being financed by Amax and the AAC/Charter Group (on a fifty-fifty basis), *Amax thus chose to share with its principal partner the losses resulting from the liquidation of its position on the international nickel market.* These massive sales also greatly aggravated the disequilibrium on the market and hastened the loss of control over it by the big traditional producers.

One may well ask why the other partners in the project signed a marketing contract with Amax that involved such a risk to the joint venture. The fact is that *by 1981, Amax considered it had nothing more to lose and envisaged shutting the Botswana operations down completely if its demands were not met. In other words, Amax squarely confronted AAC[7] with the obligations it had accepted with regard to the financial risks of the project. It would appear that when it came to the crunch AAC preferred the commercial risk associated with Amax's demands and the development of a joint strategy vis-à-vis the lenders to the rapid liquidation of the company.*

This period saw the beginning of Amax's withdrawal from the project. The company continued to lend to BCL and BRST, but in December 1981 wrote off the BCL assets in its balance sheet and set a limit of $9 million as its contribution up to December 1985 for priority debts or supplier advances.

In 1984, BCL was to negotiate a more favourable marketing contract with Falconbridge International Ltd (FIL) and Rio Tinto Zimbabwe. This new contract had the blessing of the lenders, the principal shareholders and the Botswana government even though it involved a $30 million compensation payment to Amax for breach of the previous contract and the resultant closure of the Port Nickel refinery.

Financial difficulties

From start-up in December 1973 and up to 1988, BCL made a net loss every single financial year. In 1984 the cumulated losses amounted to $746.5 million, $183 million of which appeared in the shareholders' balance sheets. The initial investment cost overrun was considerable, notably because of the technical difficulties which necessitated supplementary investment. The company, deprived of working capital, was forced to go further into debt. In December 1983, BCL's cumulated debt amounted to $622 million. On the face of it, the Selebi-Phikwe complex was not too bad a project, since it generally showed a gross operating profit, but right from the outset BCL ran into constant difficulties resulting from the inadequate financing of the enterprise, the direct consequence of the pussyfooting approach by the industrial partners. The financial package had to be restructured several times.

Tied by the completion guarantee, Amax and AAC were obliged at first to finance the cost of BCL's financial restructuring, which the lenders wanted to see guaranteed to the maximum by the shareholders. Under the terms of the restructuring of 1978, Amax and AAC obtained from BCL's creditors:

-- A reduction of the foreign exchange risk -- the strong appreciation of the mark throughout the 1970s had caused substantial financial losses -- through anticipated repayment of 25 per cent of the loans contracted with the KFW and 20 per cent of those obtained from the IDC. This payment was effected thanks to a fresh loan of $25 million granted by the Chase Manhattan Bank and guaranteed by the two principal shareholders.

-- An increase in BCL's endebtment capacity, enabling a loan of $30 million to be subscribed with Barclay's Bank International Ltd and Barclay's Bank Botswana, guaranteed by the matte in transit to the port and by the product of sales effected but not yet settled.

On the other hand, the two shareholders had to accept:

-- The conversion of $90 million of loans advanced to BCL into preference shares;

-- The granting of additional credits[8], including $50 million for the working capital requirements and $13 million for the purchase of pollution control equipment.

-- To guarantee the development of Phase 2 of the project and the injection of $8 million in equity to finance this expansion.

Long before the negotiations on this first restructuring of BCL's debt were completed, it was clear that it would not suffice to resolve all the financial problems of the enterprise. It should be noted however that after the construction of Phase 2 of the project (completed in 1980), the completion guarantee clause having been met, Amax and AAC were no longer solely responsible for servicing BCL'S debt, this responsibility now being shared by all the shareholders.

In 1979, Amax and AAC contributed a further $60 million in the form of loans to BCL. In 1980 however, they were able to obtain more advantageous conditions in the negotiations for the second financial restructuring of BCL. At the end of these negotiations, BCL obtained the rescheduling of repayment of the principal of its loans from the KFW, IDC, and Chase Manhattan Bank, payment now being due in seven half-yearly instalments beginning in June 1984, i.e. after a grace period of four years. At the same time, the taxes on production, due to the Botswana government, and the loans granted by the shareholders were rescheduled on the same basis.

The nickel market crisis as from mid-1981 again affected BCL's ability to repay. The company was not able to honour its commitments under the second restructuring of its debt, in 1980, so a third restructuring was decided upon in 1983, with the agreement of the bankers:

-- BCL's entire principal debt (with the exception of the part contracted by the Botswana government with the World Bank) was restructured in such a way that only 30 per cent of the total sum retained the status of priority debt. This debt was to be repaid over a period of ten years (1986-1995), after a grace period of four years. The balance was converted into subsidiary debt, the repayment period not being specified. The taxes due to the Botswana government were subject to the same conditions;

-- BCL's subordinate debts owed to BRST (in fact Amax and AAC) were converted into preference shares in BCL, giving the right to an annual dividend of 12 per cent, payable only after the repayment of the entire debt;

-- Between 1982 and 1985 (grace period for repayments) BCL was not authorised to make repayments of any sort of any part of its debt. Payment of the interest and taxes due was dependent on the state of the company's cash flow;

-- After 1986, when BCL no longer had the cash flow necessary for payment in full of the taxes due to the Botswana government, the latter was forced to accept part payment in the form of a subordinate debt of $2.8 million a year;

-- The subordinate debt cannot be paid until after 1990, and depending on BCL's cash flow, after the servicing on the principal debt, payment of short-term loan commitments, and the taxes due to the government. The rate of interest on the subordinate debt was fixed at 12 per cent per annum;

-- During the grace period, the BCL shareholders (i.e. Amax, AAC and the Botswana government) were obliged to find the funds necessary for the normal course of operations, either through the injection of own-funds, or through emergency credit lines, guaranteed by the three shareholders. Since BCL continued to make losses between 1982 and 1984, short-term credits with priority over the whole of the debt had to be contracted as from 1982, at a rate of 6 per cent above Libor (or 17 per cent in 1983).

BCL can use its cash flow to pay ordinary creditors only after servicing the emergency loans and the priority debt, the constitution of the necessary working capital and operating expenses. BCL's difficulties in honouring its engagements when the market is depressed together with the unpredictable nature of nickel and copper price fluctuations, have led to consideration of the possibility of converting the whole of the debt into subordinate debt, with no explicit repayment period.

CONCLUSION: A CASINO LOGIC

The difficulties experienced by the Selebi-Phikwe project reveal the fragility of the economic rationale in this type of project in which the number of actors and the intervention of development banks made it possible to implement the wrong choice, wrong even from the standpoint of each of the actors involved. In fact:

-- For Amax, the project provided the opportunity for a lasting incursion into the nickel industry, but made sense only insofar as it made another investment, one made in the United States, profitable;

-- For AAC/Charter Group, the project provided the opportunity to join with an *a priori* reliable partner in an operation opening up diversification into the very closed nickel market. But in addition, the investment in Botswana where AAC was already mining diamonds enabled the company to stabilize its interests in this country. AAC has in fact always tried to be on good terms with the countries neighbouring South Africa. Lastly, control of the project management appeared to be a favourable position for being able to profit from the technological know-how;

-- For the Botswana government, the project appeared to be a potential source of foreign currency and also provided the opportunity to have the construction of infrastructures financed by the development banks;

-- For Metallgesellschaft (MG), the marketing contracts appeared very advantageous for a completely covered involvement in the project;

-- For the German government, the project was a reliable and stable source of supply for the metallurgical and processing industries, the financing of which would lead to the sale of equipment to Botswana, not only for Selebi-Phikwe, but also for other mining projects envisaged by Botswana in the 1970s;

-- Lastly, for the development banks, the project perfectly symbolised the existence of a community of interest between the numerous actors of North and South, which their general policy of the 1970s was trying to promote.

This complex system of motivations made it possible to limit the commitment of each one, so the risk, though very real, appeared greatly diluted when the financing package was being set up. Rarely has it been possible to see in a project so much skill exercised in the passing of financial responsibilities from one player to another, as in a game of mistigris:

-- BCL, with the blessing of the development banks, passed on to the state the construction of the infrastructures essential to the project;

-- The banks accepted an extremely high debt:equity ratio, compensating for the minimal contribution of the shareholders by a very strict right of control over the management of the company (completion guarantee for both phases, revenue paid into a trustee account, etc.);

-- The significant contribution of small shareholders in BRST further reduced the initial equity contribution of the big firms, Amax and AAC;

-- MG gave financial guarantees almost entirely covered by the German government, Amax and AAC;

-- BCL was always "too far from the market". The company subcontracted the marketing to MG when the commercial risk was low, at that time overpaying for this service, then assumed the risk, covering also that of Amax -- whose sales policy consisted of taking maximum advantage of this cover -- when it became greater at the beginning of the 1980s;

-- When Amax realized at the end of the 1970s that the guarantees given to the bankers kept it locked into the project with AAC, it tricked AAC in its turn, making all the actors in the project pay for its unsuccessful foray into the nickel market.

In this affair, which would have looked more like a casino table than an industrial operation had there not actually been a mine in Botswana, the main beneficiaries were without doubt the providers of goods and services (constructors, engineering consultants, equipment suppliers, MG, Inco), who were able to pull out of the operation without any financial obligations. The other players left a few hundred million dollars on the gaming table. The very sharp rise in nickel prices as from 1987 will perhaps enable them to recoup their losses. To cap it all, the Botswana government ignored Amax's offer to sell its share just before the dramatic price rise of 1987.

Inset 1: Technical description

Bamangwato Concessions Ltd (BCL) exploits two sulphurated deposits of nickel, copper and iron, 15 kilometres apart, at Selebi and Phikwe in the northeast of the Republic of Botswana. The ore is enriched and smelted on site. The product exported is matte with a combined copper and nickel content of 78 per cent. Until 1985, this matte was supplied to the Amax refinery at Port Nickel in the United States (Louisiana).

The Selebi-Phikwe complex is about 55 kilometres east of the railway linking South Africa, Zimbabwe, Zambia and Zaïre. Theoretically the branch line to the site should have made it possible to transport the output by rail to the port of Maputo in Mozambique, from where it could be carried by sea to the refineries. In practice, the rail service to the port of Maputo is very bad because the route passes through areas of guerilla operations in Mozambique. Like the majority of producers in southern Africa, it is probable even if not officially confirmed, that BCL exports its output via a South African port.

The Phikwe mine was worked by open cast and underground methods between 1973 and 1980, and underground only since then. The underground Selebi mine was opened in 1980 to take over from the open cast Phikwe mine. The mining output of about 3 million tonnes a year has been rising ever since 1982 even though technical problems bedevilled the early years of operation. The ore reserves were estimated in December 1984 at 68.5 million tonnes, or about 20 years of exploitation at the present rate. The treatment plant produces a concentrate containing 3.70 per cent nickel and 3.72 per cent copper from a raw ore containing 1.10 per cent of nickel, 0.9 per cent copper and traces of cobalt. The recovery rate for nickel and copper is 77.5 and 95.2 per cent respectively. The treatment capacity is 6 000 tonnes of ore a day.

The ores richest in nickel were exploited first. The present nickel and copper content is in the order of 0.8 and 0.85 per cent respectively. The metal content of the output from the concentrator has also fallen and has now settled at about 2.6 per cent nickel and 3.3 per cent copper.

The smelter uses the Outokumpu flash-smelting process. Its treatment capacity is about 1.08 million tonnes of concentrate a year. The capacity utilisation rate was over 95 per cent in 1983 and 1984. The metals marketed in the form of matte are nickel (39 per cent), copper (39 per cent) and cobalt (0.5 per cent).

Until 1980, the output capacity of the smelter was 42 000 tonnes of matte (or 17 000 tonnes of nickel and 15 000 tonnes of copper) a year. This capacity has since been increased to 52 000 tonnes (22 000 tonnes Ni and 20 000 tonnes Cu).

131

Since September 1976, pulverised coal has replaced fuel oil in the furnaces. Despite the low calorific value of the local coal, this substitition has made it possible to divide unit energy costs by ten: light fuel oil costs $5.95/GJ while the coal costs $0.59/GJ.

Table 6.3. : Production trends 1981-1985[9]
(Thousand tonnes)

Product	1981	1982	1983	1984	1985
Ore	2.46	2.46	2.84	3.11	3.26
Concentrate	687.04	691.32	755.81	754.02	793.2
Matte (78 % Ni, Cu, Co)	45.56	45.68	48.08	51.84	53.18

The mining operation, the Phikwe beneficiation plan and the BCL smelter are entirely integrated. The matte produced was treated by the Amax refinery at Port Nickel until its closure in 1985. It is now sent either to Falconbridge's refinery at Kristiansund in Norway or Rio Tinto Zimbabwe's at Eiffel Flats.

Inset 2: Cost factors

The plan for working the Selebi-Phikwe mining complex, decided in July 1971, was in two phases:

-- Phase 1 covered the development of the Phikwe mine, both open cast and underground, and the construction of a concentrator and smelter;

-- Phase 2, much less costly and planned for 1980, covered the opening of the Selebi underground mine and extension of the concentrator and smelter capacities.

The total cost of Phase I was estimated at $142.7 million in 1971.

The infrastructures, i.e. electricity and water supplies, connecting the site to the railway and construction of the township, roads and hospital were to be paid for by the Botswana government.

The forecast cost of Phase 1 of the project is shown in Table 6.4.

Table 6.4. : Estimated cost of the project in December 1971

	Million 1971 dollars	Per cent
Mine, concentration plant and smelter equipment	142.7	55.1
Exploration and development before December 71	43.2	16.68
Infrastructure (railway + roads + township)	73.1	28.22
Total	**259.00**	**100.0**

Source : R. Mikesell (1982)

At the end of 1973, the infrastructure cost (initially $73.1 million) had to be revised upwards to $82 million. The Phase 1 capital equipment and start-up costs were calculated at $325 million in December 1976.

133

In March 1978, Phase 1 was considered to be completed and the total investment cost of the project (Phase 1 + Phase 2) was estimated at about $360 million.

A loan of $20 million was obtained in March 1978 to enable Phase 2 to be completed, together with a complementary loan of $13 million to reduce SO2 emissions.

The final total cost of the project, including infrastructures, amounted to $442.5 million. The provision of the non-mining infrastructures by the state was the subject of a long-term contract for the use of the installations containing a "take or pay" clause.

Several financial projections were made in 1971 to forecast the rate of return on BCL's Selebi-Phikwe investment. Table 6.5 shows two BCL estimates and a World Bank projection[10].

Table 6.5. : Forecast rate of return on the project (per cent)

Internal rate of return on investment	Before taxes, royalties and interest	Including exploration and preparatory work	Excluding
BCL feb. 1971		12.5	19.9
BCL 1971		13.5	21.4
World Bank, June1971	11.2	7.7	12.8

Source : R. Mikesell (1982)

To compensate for this rather low internal rate of return, the promotors resorted to extensive outside borrowing (80 per cent of the investment). On the basis of this financing hypothesis, BCL was able in February 1971 to estimate the rate of return on own-funds (taking into account exploration expenditure and the granting of a free 15 per cent share to the Bostwana state) at 17.8 per cent. The subsequent falls in nickel and copper prices and the unexpected increase in investment costs as the result of various technical problems greatly reduced the profitability of the project and made the leverage effect work in the opposite direction to that hoped for.

Inset 3: Taxation of the project

Taxes on production

The tax regime established when the concession was granted was based on taxing the gross operating profit. The tax rate was 15 per cent of the gross operating profit, with a minimum of $8 400. It was to be applied as soon as production began.

In 1972, the new mining lease provided for a tax of 7.5 per cent on pre-tax net operating profit (after deduction of marketing expenses, rents and sums payable to the government, interest, administrative costs and depreciation). The mimimum level was $975 000 a year.

The technical difficulties encountered caused the company to be restructured between 1976 and 1980 and many contracts had to be renegotiated. The state had the earlier tax regime replaced by an ad valorem tax of 3 per cent of the product of the sales of nickel, copper and cobalt. Because of BCL's financial difficulties, the state of Botswana never received these taxes, which were transformed into debts.

Taxes on profits

On 5th March 1970, an agreement between the government of Botswana and BCL established the tax regime for BCL, BCL Sales and BRST. Stability of the tax regime was guaranteed for 25 years from the start of production.

The basic rate of this corporation tax is 40 per cent of the net profit.

BCL's tax rate increases with the net operating profit when this is above 41.5 per cent, the maximum tax rate being 65 per cent. The net profit is defined as the difference between the product of sales and the cost of production, the latter including operating costs, depreciation, taxes on production, rents and other payments to the state, including BCL's contribution to the construction of the township.

BCL may deduct investments from its taxable income including investment made before production started. Expenditure on exploration in Botswana can also be deducted from taxable income. Lastly, this deduction may not exceed 25 per cent of taxable income and may extend over a period of five years.

BCL may apply as a tax credit any foreign taxes paid which are superior to 50 per cent of its taxable income in Botswana.

The dividends paid by BRST and BCL are not subject to any taxation except where dividends are paid to residents other than the companies.

Inset 4: The financial guarantees

The financing of BCL was through a typical project financing package.

A trustee account was opened at Barclay's Bank in London to receive the entire receipts of BCL and its subsidiary BCL Sales. This account is used to credit in order of priority: debt servicing for the World Bank, KFW and IDC, the taxes on production, BCL's contribution to the construction of the township, and payment of BCL's electricity and water consumption to Botswana Power Corporation and Botswana Utilities Corporation. It also credits a provision intended to make up for any shortfall in BCL's receipts[11].

In addition, BCL can neither contract any debts nor guarantee loans. BCL can subscribe debts only with its principal shareholders in the form of non-priority loans, coming in last place before the associates.

BCL's loans from the World Bank, KFW and IDC are guaranteed by a mortgage on the mining lease and the associated assets, and by mortgage debentures secured on the properties owned by BCL.

The $32 million World Bank loan to the government is guaranteed 40 per cent by MG, 30 per cent by Amax and 30 per cent by AAC/Charter group. The MG guarantee covers a maximum of $12 million, the excess being covered by Amax and AAC/Charter Group. Lastly, the MG guarantee is itself covered to 90 per cent by the German government[12]. Furthermore, Amex, BRST and BCL have undertaken to cover 90 per cent of the MG guarantee in the case of non-intervention by the German government.

In addition, the principal shareholders gave a completion guarantee, undertaking to directly or indirectly (by guaranteeing loans to BCL or BRST) meet any additional investment cost. Amax and the AAC/Charter Group thus each had to contribute 50 per cent to the coverage of any cost overrun. This completion guarantee given to KFW and IDC (not forgetting the World Bank[13] meant that the development banks participated in the various restructurings of BCL, requiring in particular that Amax and the AAC/Charter Group provide the funds necessary for restoring BCL's cash flow and financing the expansion investments.

The completion guarantee, the undertaking by the shareholders not to reduce their holding in BCL without the agreement of the lenders, together with the mortgage taken out on the mining lease and installations, were to force Amax and AAC/Charter Group to go on keeping BCL afloat, despite the uncertainty of the return on this investment.

136

NOTES AND REFERENCES

1. AAC thus became the owner of 10.5 per cent of BCL.

2. Source MIKESELL (1982).

3. Loans from or guaranteed by Amax and AAC.

4. Source MIKESELL (*ibid*).

5. Selection Trust subsidiary responsible for the construction and start-up of the treatment plant.

6. Including sales not realized by MG.

7. Cf. *Metal Bulletin* of 23rd October 1981.

8. This also applied to the state as a shareholder.

9. Source: Botswana RST Limited, Annual Accounts 1981-1985.

10. These forecasts apply to an annual output of 42 000 tonnes of matte and are based on slightly different hypotheses regarding prices and production costs. The prices forecast by BCL for nickel and copper were $1.36 and $0.50 a pound respectively, while the World Bank took prices of $1.20 and $0.43 a pound. BCL's estimates for operating costs were 10 per cent higher than the World Bank's. The internal rate of return is more sensitive to variations in price than to operating costs.

11. This trustee account system nevertheless enabled the seizure of the company's earnings, thus depriving BCL of working capital.

12. The German government guaranteed MG against "economic risk", not political risk.

13. The World Bank granted an additional loan of $5.5 million to the government to cover the infrastructure cost overrun.

Chapter VII

BOUGAINVILLE COPPER*

INTRODUCTION

The Bougainville operation in Papua-New Guinea was no doubt the last big Third World mining investment success before the crisis. It was also the last mining project implemented in the context of a country obtaining its independence. However, the inevitable nature of this development led the backers of the project to associate the future leaders of the country with its implementation through introducing new forms of investment. As we shall see, the timing of the operation turned out to be particularly favourable as regards both the evolution of market conditions and the geopolitical framework.

HISTORY OF THE PROJECT

-- In 1929 a copper and gold deposit was discovered at Kupei, not far from Panguna, and from 1930 to 1951 the deposit was mined for gold.

-- In 1961, a report by the Australian Bureau of Mineral Resources raised the possibility of exploiting the Panguna deposit on a large scale.

-- In 1963, CRA[1,] a subsidiary of RTZ (itself resulting from a merger in 1963 between the British firm Rio Tinto Company and the Australian Zinc Corporation), launched a mining diversification programme and started looking for big deposits. Copper was a major target for CRA because of Rio Tinto's solid position on the international market.

---

* Chapter prepared with the aid of Djibril Ndiaye

--   The Panguna zone was prospected by CRA and NBHC[2], who in June 1967 created the Bougainville Copper Proprietary Limited (BCL), a company domiciled in Papua-New Guinea, to exploit the deposit. BCL's capital was held as follows:

Conzinc Rio Tinto of Australia Ltd (CRA)	2/3
New Broken Hill Consolidated Ltd (NBHC)	1/3

The Australian government, then responsible for the territory, signed the mining contract which was ratified in August by the Territorial Assembly of Papua-New Guinea. This contract carried a guarantee against any repudiation by the Papua-New Guinea government after independence. The guarantee was given by the Australian government, the elected parliament of Papua-New Guinea and local notables. Partial revision of certain clauses by the new government after independence remained possible however. The tax regime set out in this contract was relatively favourable to BCL. The main provisions were:

--   An *ad valorem* tax of 1.25 per cent of the fob value of the ore and a rent of $2 per hectare per annum;

--   A right of occupation fee of $4 per hectare per annum payable to the owners of the land, and compensation for the loss of agricultural crops occasioned in most cases;

--   A progressive tax on company profits.

BCL was exempt from the tax on profits for the first three years of commercial operation, then followed a period of four years of accelerated depreciation where the operating profit would make it possible to reconstitute the original investment. The effective rate of tax was to be introduced on a graduated scale after the three-year grace period, with an initial rate of 20 per cent rising by annual increments of 5 percentage points to reach 40 per cent after five years. As from the twenty-sixth year the rate of tax is to rise by 1 percentage point a year up to a maximum of 58.2 per cent

--   By July 1968, over 65 kilometers of drilling had been completed since the start of exploration. Development underground was begun. The pilot plant started up in October.

--   In March 1969, Bechtel-Western Knapp Engineering was engaged to build the washing plant and the ore port.

--   In February 1969, seven Japanese smelters signed purchase options covering 965 000 tonnes of copper over 15 years. BCL's desire to limit the commercial risks associated with the production of concentrates in a market where the majority of the producers are integrated, together with the demands of the lenders, made the negotiation of long-term sales contracts an essential factor in BCL's

policy.   These contracts, negotiated between 1967 and 1969,
associated BCL with the Norddeutsche Affinerie (NA) refinery in
Germany, Rio Tinto Minera (RTM) in Spain and a group of Japanese
metallurgists and traders for a period of 15 years.   The contracts
covered virtually the entire output of the complex.

Table 7.1. : Long-term sales contracts negotiated by BCL
(Thousand tonnes of metal content in the concentrate)

Period of contract	Volume of metal sold per contract and per year				
	Japan	*N.A.*	*R T M.*	*Options*	*Total*
1-5 years	96.5	53.3	15.2		**165.0**
5-10 years	81.3	53.3	15.2	16.8	**166.6**
10-15 years	30.5	53.3	6.1		89.9
TOTAL (15 years)	**1025.0**	**787.5**	**180**	**82.5**	2075

Source : BCL, Annual Report 1972

The sales price of the metals[3] was fixed on the basis of the London Metal
Exchange (LME) price for copper, London Gold Market for gold and London
Silver Market for silver:

-- The Japanese metallurgists and traders buy on the basis of the average
   LME price in the month following delivery;

-- The European metallurgists (NA and RTM) enjoy a more flexible
   system.   They can chose as reference price any daily LME quotations
   established in the 60 days following delivery.   The only restriction is
   that a daily quotation can index no more than 10 per cent of the
   delivery, and the quotations of a given week no more than 25 per
   cent.   In addition there is a floor price for copper of 30 cents a
   pound[4.]

-- The signing of these long-term sales contracts for a very substantial
   part of the output of concentrate was the vital factor for securing the
   bank financing agreements.

-- October 1969 saw the start of the construction of the port, washing
   plant, priority installations and access roads.

-- In March 1970, the Papua-New Guinea government, which had only
   just been constituted, decided to take a 20 per cent stake in BCL,
   which resulted in a reorganisation of the capital structure:

141

| Bougainville Mining Limited | 80% |
| The government and Investment Corp of PNG | 20% |

Bougainville Mining Limited is an Australian company whose capital is held as follows:

CRA	56.3%
NBHC Holdings	28.2%
Public	15.5%
Total	100.0%

The financing package was completed on 28th July 1970. The total financing was estimated in 1971 at $436 million, of which $160 million own-funds and $269 million long-term loans. These loans included in particular a Eurodollar loan of $122 million granted by a group of banks led by the Bank of America.

The debt:equity ratio was therefore 63:37.

The lenders required CRA to give a completion guarantee and to maintain its position as majority shareholder until all the loans had been paid off. The banks obtained a guarantee on the whole of the capital of the company held by CRA, NBHC and the Papua-New Guinea government, or 87.6 per cent of the shares initially issued. The loan of $12.5 million for the construction of the township was guaranteed by mortgages on the houses. Lastly, a ceiling of 20 per cent was put on the state's holding in the capital of BCL during the repayment period.

-- In December 1970, the investment made reached $170 million.

-- By the end of 1971, the installations were operational and tests of the crushing and flotation systems were already under way. A foundation sponsored by the BCL mining company was set up to encourage the natives to invest in BCL. Thus among the 9 007 shareholders resident in Papua-New Guinea there are now a few natives.

-- In December 1971, before the start of commercial production, because of the increased refining costs resulting from the anti-pollution standards and the devaluation of the dollar, the Japanese metallurgists, Norddeutsche Affinerie (Germany) and Rio Tinto Minera (Spain) proposed an upward revision of the refining margins, invoking the "fair play" clause in the marketing contract, which provided for a renegotiation when the economic situation seriously disadvantaged one of the parties[5].

Table 7.2 : Loan sources and conditions

Source	Amount ($ Million)	Percentage of total	Conditions
Mitsubishi Shoji Kaicha Ltd and Mitsui and Co Ltd	30	9.7	Cash loan at 8.2 per cent interest repayable between 1973 and 1979. Provision for pre-payments and deferred payments.
Commonwealth Savings Bank of Australia	12.5	4.1	Cash loan at 8 per cent interest repayable between 1974 and 1978
US Eximbank	46.8	15.7	6 per cent interest on half the loan, the rest variable. Repayable between 1973 and 1978. For the purchase of goods and services in the United States.
Mitsubishi Shoji Kaisha Ltd and Mitsui and Co. Ltd	30	9.7	6.85 per cent interest. Repayable between 1973 and 1982. For the purchase of equipment in Japan.
Commonwealth Trading Bank of Australia	67.4	21.8	10.6 per cent interest. Repayable in 1978.
Bank of America	122	39.5	Rate of interest adjustable on the LIBOR every six months.
Total	308.7	100	

Source : BCL, Annual Report 1972

-- In April 1972 commercial production began, slightly exceeding the forecasts. It was noted that from the monetary standpoint, the level of income was going to depend on the trend in gold prices, the pound sterling in which the base price of the concentrate was denominated, and the US dollar for the repayment of the loans.

-- In 1972, the Papua-New Guinea government instituted a tax of 15 per cent on dividends paid to foreign companies (withholding tax), which applied to the shareholders, resident or otherwise, of Bougainville Mining.

--   In October 1973, the Bougainville Mining holdings were converted into a direct holding in BCL, in order to avoid having the withholding tax affect resident and non-resident shareholders in Bougainville Mining indiscriminately. The company made anticipated repayment of some of the loans, the amount still outstanding being $164.2 million.

NBHC Holding Limited was consolidated into CRA, causing its holding in BCL to be redistributed to its shareholders. The breakdown of the shareholdings in Bougainville Copper Proprietary Limited (BCL) thus became:

Conzinc Rio Tinto Australia Ltd (CRA)	53.6%
Public	26.2%
Government and Investment Corporation of PNG	20.2%
Total	100.0%

Source: BCL Annual Report 1972.

Between June and December 1974, the Papua-New Guinea government and BCL negotiated a modification of the 1967 mining contract, redefining the depreciation plan for the original investment and cancelling the exemption from taxes. In the new contract there was no longer a three year exemption from corporation tax or accelerated depreciation, but the new arrangements did nevertheless allow for adjustments in the rate of tax if the real rate of return on own-funds should be eroded away by inflation or if the exchange value of the Papua-New Guinea currency should be overvalued by more than 15 per cent. These adjustments were to be determined jointly by the company and the Papua-New Guinea government. The new tax rate was set at 33.3 per cent of profits up to $87 million and 70 per cent above this figure. BCL's tax rate could in no case be less than 25 per cent, which was the standard rate for corporation tax in Papua-New Guinea.

--   In December 1974 and January 1975, 15 per cent of the deliveries to Japanese metallurgists were deferred because of the large stocks on the Japanese market. This situation recurred at the end of the 1970s.

--   In September 1975 Papua-New Guinea became independent.

--   In 1976, the signing of a convention on electricity distribution between the central government and the North Solomons province marked a truce in the conflict opposing the two administrations and reassured the BCL shareholders. The company nevertheless remained the hostage of the province in negotiations with the central government.

144

-- In 1975, 1976 and 1977, part of the company's tax payments were deferred to permit investments required to maintain the level of production.

-- In January 1978, the rate of tax was increased from 33.3 to 36 per cent. Copper prices were very low, but the company's income was maintained by its gold output, for which prices were constantly rising. In addition, the falling metal content of the ore required further investment to maintain the level of output. However, as repayment of the loans was completed, the company was able to distribute exceptional dividends.

-- The price of gold doubled during 1978 and 1979, so that as from 1979 almost half the turnover came from gold sales. BCL undertook metallurgical research with the aim of improving gold recovery.

-- As from 1979, the treatment and refining charges were renegotiated between BCL and the Japanese, allowing the refiners to make an annual provision for increasing charges. A similar arrangement exists between BCL and RTM since 1982[6].

-- In 1980, the introduction of a law regulating the employment of foreign staff reduced the efficiency of BCL's operations, the company being in the habit of hiring highly-qualified foreign staff very quickly whenever the need arose.

-- The Bougainville Copper Proprietary Limited (BCL) mining contract of 1967, amended in 1974, provided for a negotiated revision of its terms every seven years. Discussions began in 1981 and continued in 1982. BCL proposed amendments concerning taxation, the taking into account of inflation in the calculation of profits, and lastly the possibility for the company to explore outside the perimeter covered by the mining concession. However, the North Solomons provincial government clashed with the central government over the sharing of revenue from BCL's operations. The conflict between the local and central governments halted production for a while, the roads linking the mining town and the Panguna site being blocked by the provincial government. Negotiations were not completed until 1982.

-- In 1983, the Papua-New Guinea government decided, with the aim of stimulating the private sector, to reduce the corporation tax from 36 to 35 per cent and to increase the withholding tax on dividends from 15 to 17 per cent.

-- BCL agreed to take a 12.5 per cent share in a joint venture with Bougainville Limestone Mining Proprietary Ltd, which was to produce hydrated lime as from 1985, this being used as a reagent in the sulphide flotation plant.

-- Lastly, in 1984, the central government, the North Solomons provincial government and BCL jointly undertook the pre-feasibility study for a hydroelectric power station in order to reduce the company's dependence on foreign oil. The energy cost at that time amounted to 27 per cent of the total operating cost. This project is still being studied.

DIFFICULTIES ENCOUNTERED

Bougainville Copper Proprietary Limited (BCL) is often considered to be a project that enjoyed exceptionally favourable conditions for success. The fact is however that the backers of the project encountered various types of difficulties, but were always able to adjust very quickly, sometimes going as far as to be able to turn to their advantage what at first appeared to be an obstacle to the planned course of operations.

The main technical difficulty was having to regularly compensate for the falling metal content of the ore, this being made necessary by the long-term marketing contracts covering 90 per cent of the production. The capacities of the crushing and flotation units were steadily expanded to compensate for the falling quality of the ore. Further capacity expansion is now limited by the size of the valley which, as from 1986, allowed the installation of only three more crushing units, i.e. an increase in the tonnage treated of about 30 per cent. What is more, the hardness of the rock is increasing, so that crushing is constantly becoming more costly.

The falling metal content and the increases in oil product prices caused rising production costs. However, rising gold prices largely cancelled out the detrimental effects on BCL's profits.

The overvaluation of the Kina affected BCL's profits more than the increased production costs because it had a direct effect on the company's receipts. Thus, between 1977 and 1978, the London metal prices rose from 59.3 to 61.3 cents a pound for copper and by 31 per cent for gold. These increases led to a fall in the prices denominated in Kina from 47 to 44 toea[7] a pound for copper and an increase of only 17 per cent for gold (cf. Figure 1). BCL was nevertheless able to take advantage of these monetary distortions through the anticipated repayment of part of its foreign currency debt.

Lastly, the differences between the central and provincial governments over the sharing of the economic rents have sometimes made BCL the hostage of the provincial government. Thus the blocking of the mine access roads by the latter in October 1981 caused a gross loss of 4 million Kinas. The political troubles on the island seem to have intensified since 1988, though the company has recorded good results. The landowners on the island are demanding compensation of almost $4 billion for the despoilment due to the mining activities. A curfew was instituted in January 1989 and the army was stationed near the mine. As of April 1989 there had been 12 people killed since the beginning of the year[8].

CONCLUSION

Among all the metal mining projects of the 1970s, the successful Bougainville operation stands out as an exception. We can see three main factors behind this success:

-- The industrial logic of the project;
-- The technical, legal and financial skill of the operators;
-- The fortunate timing of the operation.

The industrial logic of the project

The Bougainville project fitted into the strategy developed by RTZ in the mining sector since the late 1960s, i.e. to get involved only in projects lying in the lowest third of world production costs, and not to dilute the mining profits by transforming the ores on site. This strategy, which may look obvious today, was not yet so at a time when the big mining and metallurgical companies were more concerned with maintaining their market shares on rapidly growing markets than with their costs of production. In the early 1970s, when RTZ was orienting its strategy towards earning differential rents, Inco in Indonesia was trying above all to preserve its market share in order to be able to control prices. From this standpoint, Bougainville's economic rationale based on costs rather than prices was in advance on what we have called the end of the oligopolies.

However, this example shows that the concept of differential rents is not associated solely with the natural advantages of the deposit. The fact is that at first sight Bougainville did not appear to be a particularly profitable project. The comparative advantage of the operation stemmed from RTZ's technical and financial skills in working large, low-grade deposits (see below). *In RTZ's strategy, the creation of differential rents corresponded to the search for the proper fit between the configuration of a deposit and the know-how of the mine operator.*

In addition, producing copper concentrates cheaply at a time when the Japanese non-ferrous metallurgical industry was investing in the construction of smelters and refineries that were not integrated upstream gave protection from the risk of not finding a ready market, all the more so as RTZ's traditional customers in Europe were also buyers. Furthermore, by giving control of the project to its Australian subsidiary CRA, RTZ gave this company an opportunity to diversify in the copper industry and internationalise outside Australia.

The Japanese metallurgists have always considered BCL to be a source of supply essential to the development of their industry, relatively close and sure. The signing of long-term sales contracts was a precondition for the development of the operation. In accordance with the practice to which Japanese industry has been able to accustom its partners, the financing of this project exporting its output to Japan enabled Japan to export equipment through the granting of tied credits.

The technical, legal and financial skill of the operators

An original feature of the Bougainville project is that right from the beginning of the 1970s it was planned as an evolving project, with a steady fall in the metal content of the ore being taken into account as a vital operating parameter. The priority exploitation of the best ores with high copper and gold contents made it possible to achieve exceptional cash flows in the initial years of operation (almost two-thirds of the turnover in 1973 and 1974). The company was thus able to take maximum advantage of the very favourable tax regime in the early years and pay off the loans in a very short period (five years after starting production). It is probable that the capital investment was recovered even more quickly, for in 1974, thanks to a rise in copper prices, BCL's net profit amounted to 50 per cent of the turnover. In 1975, before the withholding tax on the repatriation of dividends was instituted[9], BCL had paid out a total of almost $400 million in dividends to its shareholders since 1972, or two-and-a-half times the equity invested.

These very short repayment periods facilitated the gradual adjustment to falling metal contents, for the necessary increases in mining and ore treatment capacities were able to be achieved through marginal additional investments maintaining the overall profitability of the installations.

The fortunate timing of the operation

The implementation of the Bougainville project took place in a specially favourable constellation of circumstances. We would mention in particular:

-- The fact of finding a deposit in the 1960s in a country that had not yet achieved independence and whose government did not claim from the outset a substantial share of the mining rents (it will be seen that this was already no longer the case with the realisation of the Ok Tedi project, which, though it was in the same country, came two years later);

-- The soaring copper prices is 1973 and 1974, just as commercial operation began and when the fiscal conditions described above were still favourable;

-- The doubling of gold prices and the revival of the copper price in 1979, enabled the mine to double its turnover with a constant tonnage, precisely at the time when costs were rising because of falling metal contents and the second oil shock. It was practically a new operation that began at this time.

This is illustrated by the graph below, which shows what the Bougainville turnover would have been as a function of the gold and copper prices, in constant dollars with a fixed level of production. It can be seen that between 1965 and 1972, the turnover would not have exceeded $150 million, but then definitively passed the $200 million level as from 1974 and the $400 million level as from 1979.

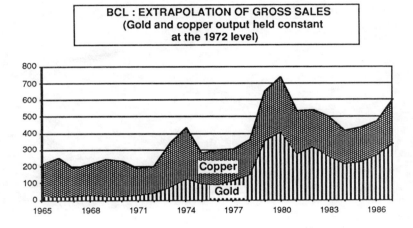

BCL : EXTRAPOLATION OF GROSS SALES
(Gold and copper output held constant at the 1972 level)

It should be added that the bankers were not put off by the size of the project[10], because of the existence of market outlets and the completion guarantee given by CRA. Their contribution also provided a guarantee against the Papua-New Guinea state taking more than a 20 per cent share or even nationalising the company. The financial success of the Bougainville project was to constitute a precedent contributing to the development of project financing.

As for the Australian government, who had undertaken to provide financial aid to Papua-New Guinea after independence in the case of a budget deficit, it considered BCL to be a source of public revenue capable of helping the country towards greater economic independence.

Lastly, the state that had emerged from independence was to constantly exercise pressure to increase its share of BCL's profits. The initial mining contract, very favourable to the operators, was quickly modified. However, the development of the project and in particular the circulation of mining rents in the Papua-New Guinea economy, hitherto very little monetarised, was to cause significant economic imbalances. Thus for example, the overvaluation of the Kina with respect to the United States and Australian dollars fitted into the framework of an economic policy of redistribution in which the import of consumer goods, financed thanks to the mining revenues, was given priority over the development of national production. The structural instability of the Papua-New Guinea economy and the political tensions between the central and provincial governments are at present the major question marks hanging over the operation.

Inset 1: Technical description

Bougainville Copper Ltd (BCL) is the world's biggest non-integrated producer of copper concentrates. Since 1972 the company has been mining a porphyry copper deposit in Papua-New Guinea[11]. The exploitation of this deposit required considerable infrastructures (construction of an ore port, road, township, etc.).

The operation is an open cast mine from which BCL produces an average of 175 000 tonnes of copper a year in the form of concentrates also containing substantial quantities of gold and silver. The output is sold mainly through long-term contracts with customers in Germany, Spain and Japan.

When the operation began, the reserves were estimated at 915 million tonnes of ore containing on average 0.48 per cent copper and 0.56 g/tonne of gold. In 1984, the reserves were re-evaluated at 675 million tonnes with an average content of 0.40 per cent copper and 0.46 g/tonne of gold.

The very considerable preparatory work[12] began in mid-1969. The operating plan for the mine was for operations to begin with the exploitation of the richest zone, then gradually to expand towards the lower grade zones. The cut-off point for copper was fixed at 0.25 per cent, the fall in copper content being estimated at between 0.01 and 0.02 per cent a year[13]. Since the start of operations in April 1972, the metal content has constantly declined, the output of concentrates being maintained stable by steadily increasing the tonnage of ore mined[14]. The resulting increase in the operating costs of the washing plant amounted, in 1984, to 22 per cent of the 4 per cent increase in total operating costs over the year-earlier figure. After the first oil shock, energy became an important cost factor, amounting respectively to 25 and 27 per cent of total operating costs in 1982 and 1984.

151

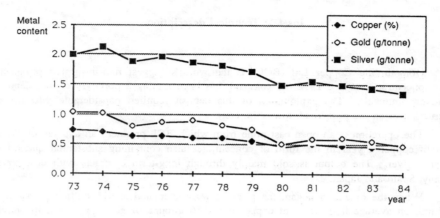

Figure 1: BCL- Trends in the metal content of the ore mined

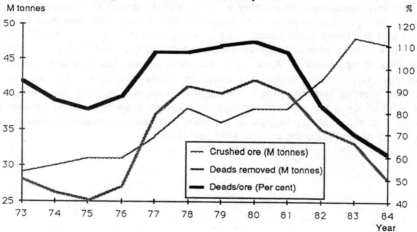

Figure 2 : BCL - Trends in production

The cumulated production over 12 years of operation -- 7.21 million tonnes of concentrates, but above all 852 million tonnes of rock removed -- since the beginning of commercial production in April 1972, gives an idea of the scale of the operation and the efficiency of its implementation despite the difficult geographical conditions (tropical rain forest, high altitude -- 2 600 metres above sea level --, frequent earth tremors, proximity of an active volcano). This success is largely due to the quality of the team who stayed with the project right from the beginning of the exploration.

Table 7.3. : Cumulated production (April 1972-December 1984)

Mining production	459.73 (million tonnes)
Concentrate	7.21 (million tonnes)
Copper content	2.30 (million tonnes)
Gold	239.00 (tonnes)
Silver	568.00 (tonnes)

Source : BCL, Annual Reports 1972-1984.

The ore port in Anewa Bay is equipped with covered warehouses capable of storing 60 000 tonnes of dried concentrate, and enables the company to load about 25 cargos a year for the different markets in Europe, Japan, etc. The company's own 25 000 tonne vessel is used.

Inset 2: Cost and profitability of the project

Total cost of the project

The estimated total cost in 1972 was $400 million, broken down as follows:

-- $21 million expenditure by Conzinc Rio Tinto Australia Ltd (CRA) and New Broken Hill Consolidated Ltd (NBHC) on exploration and feasibility study before the decision to implement the project;

-- $69 million for financing preparatory work, the purchase of mining equipment, start-up costs, staff training, and finally the constitution of a contingency reserve;

-- $310 million for the construction of port infrastructures and the ore treatment plant.

The actual cost of the project, $436.2 million, was as follows:

	$ Million (1971)
Preparatory work, acquisition costs	55.44
Construction and equipment of the mine, washing plant and port	282.36
Administration, project management, general expenses	90.48
Working capital, other costs	7.92
Total cost of the project	436.2

Source : BCL, Annual Report 1972.

Forecast profitability of the project

In 1969, CRA estimated the internal rate of return on the project at between 5 and 20 per cent[15], and considered that a minimum of 15 per cent was necessary to justify an investment in Bougainville in view of the political uncertainties.

In 1967[16], when the mining contract was being negotiated with the Australian government, the copper price varied between 30 and 40 cents a pound. According to the estimates, the project would scarcely be able to service its debt with a copper price of 30 cents a pound, whereas it became very attractive with a price of 40 cents if it could benefit from accelerated depreciation and exemption from taxes. The project's sensitivity to copper prices[17] thus considerably influenced the preliminary negotiations which covered, among other things, the tax regime for the project. In particular, the lenders were able to obtain tax conditions that made it possible to have a cash flow that would enable the debt to be repaid quickly.

NOTES AND REFERENCES

1.   CRA was then the Australian subsidiary of RTZ. In 1970, RTZ controlled 80.6 per cent of the capital of CRA. The programme of "Australianising" the economy launched by the Australian government in 1979 forced RTZ to gradually reduce its holding in CRA to 49 per cent.

2.   NBHC was a 32.2 per cent subsidiary of CRA until its consolidation.

3.   BCL's concentrate contains copper, gold and silver, the approximate content of which is respectively 29 per cent, 20 grammes per tonne and 70-80 grammes per tonne. The prices paid for these principal metals correspond to 96.7 per cent of the copper content, 97-98 per cent of the gold content and 90 per cent of the silver content.

4.   The freight and insurance are at the expense of the Japanese, who buy the concentrate fob, while BCL pays for the freight and insurance on the concentrate sold cif in Europe.

5.   The ore treatment and refining charges were fixed in US dollars at the beginning of the contract, but there was a provision that these charges could be increased if the operating costs of the smelters and refineries should rise significantly -- according to measurement criteria agreed by both parties -- or in the case of large variations in the exchange rates.

6.   In fact, as we have seen, certain deliveries of concentrate appearing in the contract had to be deferred, often at the request of the Japanese parties and sometimes at the request of European metallurgists and refiners. Short-term contracts made it possible to sell the surplus production in South East Asia, China, the United States and the Soviet Union and other Eastern Bloc countries. Only a small percentage of the output was sold on the spot market. Conversely, BCL was not always in a position to supply the quantities laid down in the contracts, notably when substantially lower metal contents reduced the volume of output.

7.   100 toea = 1 Kina.

8.   *Mining Journal*, 14th April 1989.

9.   It was not until after the introduction of the withholding tax that the balance of the initial external loans was finally repaid in 1977.

10.   The scale of the project should be regarded more as an advantage, since it enabled the bankers, remunerated in proportion to the size of the sums lent, to recycle a very sizeable amount of capital in a single operation.

11.   The mine is situated in the centre-east of the mountainous island of Bougainville (in the Solomon Islands), at Panguna, a seismic area with very dense vegetation and high rainfall (5 metres a year).

12.   The very dense vegetation of the rain forest was felled, transported and burned in ravines and the oxidised part of the deposit was completely exposed. A layer of an average thickness of 60 cm of volcanic ash and large blocks was removed and deposited along the Kawerong River.

13.   What is more, the deads:ore ratio was between 0.68:1 and 1:1, which is fairly low for an open cast copper mine.

14.   The daily output depends on the capacity of the crushing unit. Initially planned for 80 000 tonnes a day, it is now 130 000 tonnes a day. Its future extension is limited to 130 per cent of present capacity because of the size of the valley.

15.   The CRA estimates are confidential and take account of all the capital invested in the project, including the working capital. Dr. B. R. Stewardson of the Department of Economics at Trobe University (Australia) has estimated the rate of return on CRA's and NBHC's own-funds ($A 84 million) at around 7.7 per cent, 15.2 per cent and 27.2 per cent for copper prices of 30, 40 and 55 cents/lb. The lifetime considered is 20 years, but this estimate does not take account of the tax on dividends paid to foreign companies (15 per cent).

16.   After the Second World War, Papua-New Guinea was under the protection of Australia. It became independent in 1975, after having an intermediate status between 1970 and 1975, during which period it was administered jointly by the Australian government and a local government.

17.   According to the estimates, a 10 per cent increase in operating costs would have a less serious impact than the one-fifth reduction in cash flow that would result from a 10 per cent fall in prices.

Chapter VIII

OK TEDI

INTRODUCTION

Ok Tedi is a gold and copper mine in Papua-New Guinea. Its realisation was the result of negotiations extending over more than 15 years. Never have so many consultants and experts of all sorts been called in to advise a government during the implementation of a mining project. Even before the build-up of production in 1984, there were already no less than three books devoted to the history of its realisation.

The duration and exemplary nature of the negotiations are illustrative of the tensions that had grown up between the foreign mining and metal industry operators engaged in the project and the government of Papua-New Guinea, one of the last countries in the world to have achieved independence (1975). At the centre of these negotiations was the question of the distribution of the economic rent of the mining operation:

-- In a country where an earlier project, Bougainville, had initially obtained a deal favourable to the foreign operator, this subsequently was being renegotiated;

-- At a time when the raw materials crisis was threatening the very existence of these economic rents.

HISTORY OF THE PROJECT[1]

The history of the project can be analysed in two periods: the first, in which the principal actor was the American company Kennecott, came to an end in 1975 with Papua-New Guinea's accession to independence and the renegotiation of the Bougainville mining agreement; the second is illustrative of the difficulties encountered by foreign mining investment in the Third World in the post-colonial era.

The Kennecott period

Before the Second World War, gold prospectors had located copper deposits in the Star Mountains. However, the Ok Tedi project did not really begin until the geochemical sampling campaign carried out in the region at the beginning of the 1960s by the Kennecott Copper Corporation.

-- At the end of 1960, Kennecott began a large-scale prospecting programme in the region. This programme led in 1964 to the identification of a deposit located in the mountains of northwest Papua-New Guinea[2].

-- In 1967 and 1968, the exploration extended to the southern flanc of the central mountain range of Papua-New Guinea. In June 1968, Kennecott requested a propecting licence and began the official reconnaissance of this zone. This work led to the discovery of a rich mineralisation of copper associated with gold on the slopes of Mount Fubilan.

-- Prospecting continued in 1969 and the first test drillings encountered a high-grade ore containing 3.05 per cent copper at 46 metres. Evaluation of the mineralisation of the zone led to the conclusion that the find was a very large copper deposit. Furthermore, the overburden covering the copper ore contained gold, but at this stage the operators were interested only in the copper.

-- In 1971, the evaluation programme was stepped up. Proven reserves were 137 million tonnes of ore containing 0.88 per cent copper and 0.66 grammes/t of gold. Kennecott immediately proceeded to metallurgical tests, whose results were encouraging. Feasibility studies were undertaken with a view to exploiting the deposit[3]. The financial estimates did not take account of the gold, which was then at a relatively low price.

At this stage, the exporation programme had cost Kennecott about $15 million.

-- In November 1971, Kennecott began negotiations with the Australian Resident Administrator of Papua-New Guinea for the development of the mine. Its proposals were transmitted to the Australian Bureau of Mineral Resources (BMR) for an opinion. The BMR's conclusion was that the Ok Tedi reserves were underestimated as regards volume and overestimated as regards metal content. The Bureau estimated the deposit at 230 million tonnes of ore containing 0.76 per cent copper and requested the reformulation of the operating programme.

-- In April 1972, new proposals were submitted by Kennecott. In addition to the points concerning the exploitation programme, these proposals raised questions relating to the participation of the future Papua-New Guinea government[4] in the project and the tax regime. Kennecott, whose interests in Chile had just been nationalised, was trying to protect itself against a possible revision of the fiscal conditions, and requested:

-- To be able to discuss with the future government the fiscal reforms affecting its operations in Papua-New Guinea;
-- To be exempt from local taxes, customs duties and export taxes;
-- To be protected against any possibility of nationalisation or state intervention in the management of the mine.

Kennecott's proposals were then systematically analysed and compared article by article with the Bougainville mine contract.

-- In December 1972, Papua-New Guinea unofficially sought advice from Peru to help in negotiating the terms of the mining contract with Kennecott.

-- In March 1973, official contact was established with Peru.

-- On 14th June 1973, Peru designated a commission to analyse the situation of the Ok Tedi project. This commission recommended that the information provided by Kennecott should be verified and that the financing and cash flow plan should be modified, notably on the following points:

i) Downward revision of the exploration expenditure;
ii) Reduction of the taxes to the same level as the Bougainville mine;
iii) Raising of the debt:equity ratio from 1:1 to 2:1;
iv) Priority development of the richest part of the deposit.

In January 1974, the Peruvian experts' report was analysed by the Papua-New Guinea negotiating team, who came to the conclusion that the Kennecott proposals, assuming a mine lifetime of 15 years, guaranteed the government a return of scarcely 1 per cent on its shares. The cumulated taxes and dividends paid to Papua-New Guinea would amount to only $120 million.

The Papua-New Guinea government then hired a consultant, who suggested that in order to increase the return on the operation the capacity of the mine should be increased to 40 000 tonnes a day, taking into account additional reserves. Kennecott was then informed that negotiations could continue only on the basis of a new technical and economic evaluation.

Kennecott gave in and produced the new proposals. But resuming exploration required the construction of costly infrastructures. The company therefore proposed a programme of integrated development for the zone in which the new exploration campaign would take place. In this way Kennecott would be able to obtain financing through the government from international institutions (such as the World Bank) for the construction of the infrastructures. In the course of these negotiations, Kennecott therefore insisted on the government's official support for the Ok Tedi infrastructure programme. The government refused, arguing that the company itself should be responsible for the construction of the transport infrastructures required for shipping the output from the mine.

-- In September 1974, Papua-New Guinea completed the renegotiation of the Bougainville contract. The signing of this new contract, much more favourable to the state, encouraged the government to take a firm stance *vis-à-vis* Kennecott. It therefore stepped up the pressure on the company to undertake further exploration work. Kennecott refused to undertake any further investment without the signature of an agreement guaranteeing it the exploitation rights. The government refused.

-- In February 1975, Kennecott pulled out of the project. This decision may be seen as the result of Kennecott's fear of having to commit itself for a long period in a country where the government was becoming increasingly demanding.

The post-colonial period

The Papua-New Guinea government then took charge of promoting the project and created the Ok Tedi Development Company (OTDC) to this end. In order to increase the volume of proven reserves, OTDC resumed the exploration work on the deposit, bringing in outside consultants. OTDC also established contact with several companies interested in Ok Tedi: Broken Hill Proprietary Co. Ltd. (BHPC); Swiss Aluminium Ltd. (Aluswiss); Peñarroya; MIM Holdings Ltd. (MIM); Anglo-American Corporation of South Africa Ltd. (AAC) and Placer Development Ltd. (Placer).

-- In June 1975, negotiations opened with BHPC, who obtained tax deductions from the Australian government as compensation for its future exploration expenditure in Ok Tedi, up to 1978. This considerable incentive given by the Australian government is explained mainly by its desire to obtain tax income for Papua-New Guinea to take over in the longer term from the budgetary aid that Australia was going to have to provide[5].

-- In September 1975, Papua-New Guinea became officially independent.

Other negotiations begun with Alusuisse and Peñarroya came to nothing and these two companies withdrew in December.

-- At the beginning of 1976, the government and BHPC, associated by an initial agreement, started actively looking for new partners. BHPC first proposed to Kennecott that it should come back into the project, but the company apparently considered it had burnt its fingers enough and refused. In February, Amoco (Standard Oil of Indiana), Shell, Newmont and Kupfer Exploration Gesellschaft (KE)[6] still seemed likely to form a joint venture with BHPC.

The German government granted KE a loan corresponding to 60 per cent of the exploration expenditure of the group, repayable only if the project went ahead. Under these conditions, KE agreed to join BHPC.

In June 1976, Amoco, an oil company wishing to diversify into the copper industry[7], joined BHPC and KE. The task of the resulting joint venture -- BHPC (37.5 per cent), Amoco (37.5 per cent) and KE (25 per cent) -- was to continue the evaluation work and carry out feasibility studies. The German consortium undertook to buy 50 per cent of Ok Tedi's gold and copper production during the first phase.

The agreement between the joint venture and the state was ratified by the Papua-New Guinea parliament in 1976 under the Mining (Ok Tedi) Agreement Act. This provided that the joint venture should submit to the government an exploitation plan in which the government would have the right to take a stake.

Under the terms of this agreement, Papua-New Guinea had an option on 20 per cent of the capital of the operating company. However, the German consortium, wanting to limit its stake in the project to 20 per cent, then found itself penalised by a German fiscal regulation taxing the profits repatriated by companies holding less than 25 per cent of the capital of foreign companies. To get round this regulation, KE's partners sought to increase the consortium's share in OTML by bringing the other shareholders into their group. As BHPC and Amoco refused, the Papua-New Guinea government agreed to join KE with 5 per cent of the total OTML shares, reducing its direct holding to 15 per cent. The structure of OTML at the time of its formation was therefore as follows:

Shareholder		Percentage holding
Broken Hill Proprietary Co Ltd (BHPC)		30
Amoco Minerals (Papua-New Guinea) Co.		30
Papua-New Guinea (direct holding by the state)		15
Star Mountains Holding Co, of which:		25
-- Metallgesellschaft (MG)	7.5	
-- Degussa AG	7.5	
-- Deutsche Gesellschaft[8]	5.0	
-- Papua-New Guinea (state holding)	5.0	
Total		100

As regards taxation[9], the agreement provides for:

-- An *ad valorem* tax of 1.25 per cent on the fob value of the ore or concentrate, and a tax on the smelting costs if a smelter should be built;

-- Taxes on the import of the machinery, equipment, materials and supplies necessary for construction or mining activities, at the average customs duty rate in force for the country;

-- OTML's subjection to the general corporation tax regime applied to all companies established in Papua-New Guinea. However, during the period of investment repayment there would be a ceiling of 35 per cent of profits;

-- A withholding tax of 15 per cent on dividends repatriated outside Papua-New Guinea;

-- Prospecting expenditure incurred during the eleven years preceeding the issue of the mining licence was deductable from taxable income. The amount of the annual deduction was to be obtained by dividing the prospecting expenditure not yet amortized by the estimated lifetime of the project. A special clause provided for the possibility of more rapid amortization of the exploration expenditure if the post-tax profits during the early years of operation should not reach 25 per cent of the initial investment. This was in fact the case;

-- A surtax on profits applicable each year that the discounted cash flow was positive. This sum was to be calculated by deducting from the sum of the discounted profits of the mine, the discounted sum of the investments made by the foreign partners plus the taxes paid to the state. The discounting rate used was to be selected between a fixed value of 20 per cent and the United States bond rate increased by 10 points.

Following Amoco's recommendation, the partners decided to hire an outside consultant for the feasibility study. This study, carried out by the American firm Bechtel-Western Knapp Engineering, took 31 months. The fact is that in view of the operating difficulties due to the site and the uncertain profitability of the project, BHPC wanted to explore all the technical possibilities before making its choice.

-- In December 1977, Bechtel gave a first estimate of the overall investment cost, which amounted to almost $1 400 million. This was based on a conventional copper mine with the construction of a flotation plant in the first phase.

-- In June 1978, in order to reduce the investment cost, Bechtel proposed reducing the copper ore production to 30 000 tonnes a day, making up for the reduced revenue through intensive exploitation of the gold.

-- The feasibility study was completed in December 1979 and submitted to the government for assessment. In addition to the Ministry of Mineral Resources and Energy, the Ministries of Finance, Planning, and Justice were all involved in studying the proposals.

-- As from February 1980, the Papua-New Guinea government was ready to discuss the establishment of a mine. There then began fresh negotiations between the two parties, which lasted almost six months. The resulting agreement associated the state's participation with a condition allowing the limitation of its guarantee on loans if there should be a construction cost overrun (see Inset 2 on the financing package).

-- Ok Tedi Mining Ltd (OTML) was created in February 1981. The shareholders were the Papua-New Guinea government (20 per cent), BHPC (30 per cent), Amoco Minerals Co (30 per cent) and the consortium of German companies (20 per cent). BHPC was designated operator.

-- In mid-1981, Bechtel won the contract for the construction of the mine and work began immediately. They ran into many technical obstacles, which will be discussed below. The construction cost overrun amounted to one-third of the original estimate, even though not all the planned infrastructures were built. The cost overruns were financed mainly by the foreign partners in the joint venture, thus reducing the state holding to 16 per cent.

-- The mine came into production in May 1984. The first gold tonnages were then sold, but the receipts scarcely reached 65 per cent of those forecast by the feasibility study. OTML then considered abandoning Phases 2 and 3 of the project.

-- On 1st February 1985, the Papua-New Guinea government gave an ultimatum: it ordered the mine to be closed and gave the foreign partners 28 days to close down the operation and get out of the country, unless they gave a formal undertaking to develop the remaining two phases of the project. The OTML partners agreed to negotiate, and the ultimatum was postponed for four months.

-- In July 1985, a new agreement was signed, engaging all the partners to continue the development of the project. The financing of Phase 2 was completed a year later. The capital of OTML was now held as follows:

Broken Hill Proprietary Co Ltd (BHPC)	31.0%
Amoco Minerals Co.	31.0%
Papua-New Guinea	17.1%
Metallgesellschaft (MG)	7.8%
Degussa AG	7.8%
Deutsche Gesellschaft	5.2%

-- In January 1987, BHPC and KE published estimates announcing that as the result of measures to increase the productivity of the mine and the restructuring of the company's debt, the return on copper concentrate production could justify the investment under way. OTML was initially responsible for the sale of the entire output.

-- As from 1988, Ok Tedi's copper concentrate output was marketed by Metallgesellschaft (MG), in return for this company's participation in the development of Phase 2. The concentrates were mainly destined for non-integrated metallurgical companies in Europe and Japan, who obtained their feedstocks on the basis of long-term contracts. It was estimated that 20 per cent of the output would be sold on the spot market[10].

DIFFICULTIES ENCOUNTERED DURING THE CONSTRUCTION STAGE

In the course of the 15 years it took to get the project going many difficulties arose from the contradictions in the particular rationale of the different actors involved. We shall try to detail these in the conclusion, where we specifically analyse the logic of their intervention. We would like to first emphasize the difficulties encountered during construction as a result of technical problems.

Ok Tedi had the reputation of being "a pot of gold at the end of the rainbow". The construction of the mining complex in the equatorial rain forest of

Papua-New Guinea was a titanic undertaking however. Engineers and workers had to battle with mud, rain and jungle in a totally isolated site.

Phase 1 involved the bulk of the infrastructure work: the access roads between the mine and the river port of Kiunga, the construction of a new town of 3 500 inhabitants at Tabubil and the gold concentration plant at Folomian. The plans also included the start of a spoil heap and the construction of a dam on the Ok Nungi river for a hydroelectric power station.

The geographical and climatic conditions made the construction of the roads more difficult and more costly than expected. The treatment plant and the township were completed on schedule by the subcontractors, Bechtel and Morrison Knudsen International (MKI).

The site selected for the dam had given rise to a great deal of criticism on the part of the government, and its construction was fraught with such technical difficulties that the partners decided to abandon the work. So though situated in the wettest region in the world, the complex is still supplied with electricity from an oil-fired thermal power station. What is more, in January 1984, a spectacular landslide destroyed the site selected for the spoil heap shortly after work began. These two events caused considerable friction between Bechtel/MKI and OTML, between OTML and the government, and between the technical and economic advisors within the government.

The spoil heaps were therefore temporarily established on another site in order to allow production to begin, but over half the spoil fell into the Fly River basin. Any change in the course of this river, which marks the disputed frontier between Papua-New Guinea and the Indonesian province of Irian Jaya could not fail to cause diplomatic tensions between the two countries. Furthermore, while the Papua-New Guinea government had shown itself to be particularly concerned about environmental protection, the sinking of a barge loaded with drums containing 300 tonnes of sodium cyanide -- enough to wipe out the whole human race -- in the Fly River estuary made relations between the state and its partners even more strained[11].

The recent discovery of relatively high copper contents in the reserves identified as gold-bearing is forcing OTML to modify its ore treatment installations. It is necessary on the one hand to extend the raw ore storage capacity and on the other to further increase the consumption of cyanides, essential for separating the gold from the copper. The government is already worried about the environmental consequences of this development.

In total, the construction costs of the project overran the feasibility study estimates by one-third. At the same time, the fall in gold prices reduced operating income by about 35 per cent. In 1984/85, the company was not able to service its debt, which had to be restructured. The foreign partners then wanted to postpone the investments corresponding to the construction of the hydroelectric power station and the start of Phase 2, but the government then suspected them of trying to cream off the best of the deposit without honouring their commitments, and threatened to expropriate them. The foreign companies finally agreed to resume investment. We shall return in the conclusion to the conditions under which the foreign partners agreed to go on working the deposit.

CONCLUSION: MULTIPLICATION OF ACTORS AND OF INTERVENTION LOGICS

The Ok Tedi mine came into production 24 years after the discovery of the first shows. The accumulation of technical difficulties during the construction phase and the present financial failure of the project show that the exceptional length of its maturation period cannot be explained solely by the actors' desire to study all the risks in order to minimise them. Quite the contrary. This project crystallised the many contradictions which tend to show that with the multiplication of actors associated with the emergence of a sovereign state taking control of mineral resources, the investment logics become more heterogeneous and hence the balance more delicate. The fact is that this project is characteristic of the gradually increasing complexity of relations between actors that has come about in the post-colonial period. Initiated by an operator looking for a conventional investment in order to maintain its mining capacity, it continued as a search for a precarious community of interest between actors whose logics were very different. It is these logics that we intend to identify below.

The reasons for the failure of negotiations with Kennecott

Kennecott, a big American copper producer, got interested in the Ok Tedi project because it wanted to extend its production capacities upstream of the metallurgical industry. Two factors outside the process of negotiating the Ok Tedi project changed its strategy:

-- The nationalisation in July 1971 of its assests in the El Teniente copper mine in Chile;

-- The price controls in the United States imposed by President Nixon in August 1971, affecting the copper industry in particular. This decision prevented the United States producers from taking advantage of the sharp price increase in 1973-74, when the price of copper reached $1.40 a pound, as the price control kept the American domestic price below $0.68 a pound.

As a result, Kennecott's net profits plummetted from an average of 7.7 per cent of turnover for the period 1967-72 to less than 0.4 per cent in 1976. The reduction in the company's liquidity, essential to finance mining exploration, was no doubt what made Kennecott pull out of Ok Tedi.

But over and above this, Kennecott's experience in Chile -- where the nationalisation was but the final stage in a negotiation process that had been going on with the government for over 30 years -- had clearly already convinced the company of the difficulty, for a foreign operator, of obtaining a lasting share of the economic rents of mining in a country very much dependent on tax revenues from the mining sector. It is certain that the renegotiation of the Bougainville agreement helped to scare Kennecott off. Its refusal to come in again with BHPC in 1976 after the conclusion of the mining agreement bears witness to this mistrust.

The attitude of the Australian government

The Australian government was an important actor in the negotiations over the Ok Tedi project. Through this experience and that of Bougainville, it can be seen that the development of the mining industry in Papua-New Guinea was a vital component in decolonisation policy. The Australian government clearly tried to ensure that the mining rents resulting from the exploitation of the natural resources of the island would gradually come to replace its own support to the Papua-New Guinea budget. However, by blocking Kennecott's proposals while granting a very favourable concession to Conzinc Rio Tinto Australia at Bougainville, the Australian administration showed that it preferred that this process should be led by Australian operators. The tax incentives given to BHPC were significant in this respect. It would seem however that once Papua-New Guinea became effectively independent, the desire of the new state to negotiate mining rents for its own benefit deprived the Australian authorities of much of their control over the process of making Papua-New Guinea financially autonomous. The Australian government was not in fact able to ensure that BHPC obtained the same initial tax conditions at Ok Tedi that CRA had enjoyed at Bougainville.

The attitude of the Papua-New Guinea government

For the Papua-New Guinea government, the negotiation of the Ok Tedi agreement coincided with the renegotiation of the Bougainville agreement. It so happens that during the early years of its operation Bougainville had enjoyed a particularly favourable tax regime that had enabled the operator to repatriate its original investment in less than three years. It therefore appears that in the case of OTML, the government, as well as the consultants it employed, was trying to spread the company's benefits over a longer period and get agreement in advance on a division of economic rents that would be more to its own advantage. The tax clause that provided as early as 1976 for a surtax once the discounted sum of the cash flows of the operation became positive shows the government's determination to remain in the longer term the main recipient of the mining rents.

However, what it was possible to obtain *a posteriori* from a mining operation that had already paid back its capital was more difficult to demand *a priori* from a project not yet implemented, and this slowed down the negotiations. What is more, the government, more concerned with fixing the size of the rents it could hope to get out of the operation than with its technical and financial viability, blindly placed its confidence in its partners for the ways and means by which the mining complex should be realised. However, the conditions that had made Bougainville such a success, i.e. the technical skills of the operator and the good fortune of being able to start selling the output at the very time that prices started to soar on the international markets, were not present in the Ok Tedi project, far from it, so that the state now finds itself a shareholder in a heavily indebted mining operation. It can certainly hope to tax the profits, but it is unlikely that these will compensate for the heavy liabilities in the shorter term.

Lastly, it should be noted that the state, scarcely become independent, directed the process of discussions with foreign companies for the development of the project. It was able to ensure that the balance of strength was always in its favour during the negotiations, especially when it brandished the threat of expropriation to force the foreign partners to continue to invest. It was particularly clever here in reacting early enough for these companies to have more to lose by ceasing operations immediately than by accepting to go on investing.

The investment logic of the main partners, BHPC and Amoco

BHPC and Amoco thought they would be able to earn differential rents in this operation, as CRA did in Bougainville. These two companies, engaged in the extraction of hydrocarbons in their own countries, had considerable cash flows at the end of the 1970s and wanted to reinvest in activities that could still give rise to economic rents. BHPC's diversification in the mining sector also led to the takeover of Utah, a big coal producer, in 1983. Amoco's diversification[12] was mainly in the copper industry and resulted in particular in the failure of and abandonment of the partly completed Tenké Fungurumé project ($300 million 1976 dollars had already been invested) in Zaïre.

The essential fact is that neither BHPC nor Amoco, nor indeed their German partners, had industrial experience of a mining project like Ok Tedi and in such an environment. This explains on the one hand why they called in an outside consultant to design their project, and on the other why they came to so seriously underestimate the technical difficulties of the operation.

The decision by BHPCc and Amoco to continue investment for Phase 2 of Ok Tedi was not simply a case of backing down in the face of pressure from the state. In our opinion it resulted from a calculation showing that the investment in Phase 2, looked at as a separate operation, was likely to be very profitable, since it could use the infrastructures built during Phase 1 and also enjoy a relatively favourable tax regime in view of the sums already spent elsewhere. Between totally losing the initial investment and creating the possibility of recouping some of the losses by implementing an operation that was technically less risky and whose profitability looked attractive, the companies opted for the second solution. They are still hoping that the cash flows of Phase 2 of Ok Tedi will help them to repay the loans of Phase 1.

The attitude of the German investors

The downstream integration of Third World copper producers had the effect of making 75 per cent of world copper mining output captive. As a result, the market for copper concentrates destined for non-integrated smelters had been tight on several occasions in recent years, despite the recession on the copper metal market. The German metallurgists, not integrated upstream, therefore wanted to promote the development of new new mining capacities that were not integrated downstream. They were supported in this by the German government who, through the intermediary of the KFW, participated in the financing of the project. In this logic, it should be noted that the investment of about $200 million made by the German firms supported by their government, even if it was not recovered, was fairly modest compared with the economic consequences that a shortage of concentrate would have had for the maintenance of the competitiveness of copper metallurgy in Germany.

This explains why the German partners agreed to follow BHPC and Amoco in the subsequent phases of the operation. It should also be noted that in Phase 2, Metallgesellschaft (MG), who had obtained exclusive marketing rights for the copper concentrate, was able to sell a service at the same time as guaranteeing its own supplies.

The financial failure of Ok Tedi thus did not have the same significance for all the actors involved. Those who were looking for economic rents -- the Papua-New Guinea government, BHPC and Amoco -- invested and got into debt, so far without deriving any advantages. On the other hand, those who, like MG, wanted to promote the construction of the mine to satisfy their downstream industrial needs, no doubt succeeded in deriving some profit from their initial stake somewhere in the production chain, and maybe even found in the operation certain synergies with some of their associated activities.

Inset 1: Technical description of Ok Tedi

The Ok Tedi copper and gold mine is situated on Mount Fubilan, in the heart of the central jungle on the island of New Guinea, 20 kilometres from the border between Papua-New Guinea and Irian Jaya . The site is particularly difficult of access. In 1988, the Ok Tedi mine became the first single non-integrated producer of copper concentrates. The production of copper associated with the extraction of gold began in 1985 and was to rise to about 70 000 tonnes in 1987 before reaching 200 000 tonnes in 1988. The Ok Tedi reserves are made up of:

-- 41.3 million tonnes of oxidised ore containing on average 2.59 g/tonne of gold (cut-off content 1 g/tonne);

-- 25.7 million tonnes of ore (skarn) assaying on average 1.17 per cent copper and 1.55 g/tonne of gold;

-- 351 million tonnes of porphyric ore assaying on average O.7 per cent copper associated with molybdenum (cut-off 0.4 per cent).

The heterogeneity of these reserves made it possible to conceive a development plan in three successive phases, assuming the opening of an open cast mine capable of producing an average of 60 000 to 70 000 tonnes of ore a day, or 200 000 to 230 000 tonnes of metal content a year. According to this programme:

1. The first phase, extending over two years (1982-84)[13], was to be based on exploiting the ores richest in gold. This would build up an ore treatment capacity of 12 000 tonnes a day in the first year, increasing to 15 000 tonnes a day in the second, or an output of about 15.7 tonnes of gold a year.

2. The second phase of the operation was to begin in the third year and last three years. A treatment plant would be built during this period to be operational in 1987. This unit would produce about 60 000 tonnes of copper and 14.7 tonnes of gold a year. Gold production would continue at this level until 1989, the year in which exploitation of the reserves of gold combined with copper would cease to be economic.

3. The third and final phase was to begin in the sixth year with the exploitation of copper and recovery of the associated molybdenum. Modifications were to be made to the plant by converting the gold treatment installation into a second copper treatment installation to bring the capacity up to 45 000 tonnes a day, or a metal content output of 100 000 tonnes a year[14]. Gold production would then be running at 7.6 tonnes a year.

The original feature of this operating programme is that investment was extended over time, so that Phases 2 and 3 could be self-financing thanks to the results of Phases 1 and 2.

The River Fly, navigable for over 800 kilometers from Kiunga to the delta and considered to be the best means of shipping the output, was used in the construction stage to carry heavy equipment to the site. The treatment plant installed at Folomian is connected by road to the main urban centre, Tabubil. The mine output is transported to Folomian, where it is concentrated for treatment, then the gold is taken to Tabubil to be exported by air. The copper concentrates have be to shipped through the port of Kiunga, on the River Fly, 134 kilometres from Tabubil, before being transshipped to ore carriers at Port Moresby.

The gold recovery plant -- with a capacity of 1 000 tonnes of ore an hour -- came into production in 1984. In August 1985, the agreement for the construction of the copper ore treatment installations with a capacity of 60 000 tonnes a day, corresponding to Phase 2 of the project, was ratified between the government and the partners in Ok Tedi. These installations entered service in 1988[15].

Inset 2: Cost of the project and the financing package

The cost of Phase 1 was estimated in the feasibility study at $730 million ($850 million with the working capital), financed through $224 million of equity capital, the rest being in the form of export credits and long-term loans. In this phase, the Papua-New Guinea government was to pay for its 20 per cent share in cash.

The cost of Phase 2, estimated at $440 million, was to be financed out of the profits realised by Phase 1. The cost of Phase 3 was estimated at $150 million.

The total cost of the entire project was thus initially estimated at $1 320 million, but the actual cost of Phase 1 alone turned out to be about $1 200 million.

It took two years to set up the financing package for Phase 1. The basic financing agreement signed in London in January 1981 defined the equity contribution of the different partners and their respective commitments with regard to guarantees on the loans. The state of Papua-New Guinea made its partners accept limitation of its liability in the case of cost overrun. The debt/equity ratio was fixed at 70:30. Under the terms of this agreement, the financing of Phase 1 was to be as follows[16]:

Total cost of project (Million dollars)	Subscription of loans		Equity contribution	
	Foreign Partners	State	Foreign Partners	State
Up to 400	280	-	96	24[18]
400-700	+ 168	+ 42	+ 72	+ 18
700-928	+ 160	-	+ 54-65	+ 3-14[19]
Above 928	The State had the choice of participating in the raising of loans or not. If not, OTML was to pay 5 per cent of the commission to the guarantors of the loans.			

After having examined the possibilities of "gold-backed finance", or the issue of stock indexed on the gold produced by the company, the partners preferred to rely on a financing structure based on export credits. It seems in fact that in 1980 and early 1981, export credits were much more attractive than conventional commercial loans.

The construction cost overrun in Phase 1 meant that loans of almost $800 million had to be sought. The financing package assembled in 1982 was as follows:

Type and source of loan	Country	Amount
Tied credits:		($ million)
Export Finance and Insurance Corp.	Australia	242
Lloyds Bank International[19]	United Kingdom	100
Export Development Corp	Canada	88
Österreichische Kontrollbank	Austria	50
Total tied credits		*480*
Non-tied credits:		
Kreditanstalt für Wiederaufbau (KFW)	Germany	100
Overseas Private Investment Corp. (OPIC)[20]	United States	50
Commercial bank syndicate led by Citicorp International	United States	150
Total non-tied credits		*300*
TOTAL LOANS		780

The actual cost of Phase 1 amounted to almost $1 200 million even though it was not entirely completed. The foreign partners were therefore forced to finance a large part of the additional expenditure, even if they had to be prepared to write this investment off at the same time[21].

As regards the financing of Phase 2, the Japanese smelters were approached at the end of 1983 to see if they would grant loans to OTML in exchange for long-term supply contracts. These discussions were unsuccessful.

The OTML partners nevertheless succeeded in mid-1986 in raising $256 million of supplementary commercial loans to finance Phase 2 of the project.

NOTES AND REFERENCES

1. The chronology given in this section relies heavily on the work by William S. PINTZ (1984).

2. Kennecott was also developing a similar exploration programme in the Indonesian province of Irian Jaya.

3. Kennecott contracted out the engineering consultancy work to American Construction Company and McKee Pacific Ltd in particular.

4. During the period preceding independence in 1975, Papua-New Guinea was administered jointly by the Australian government and a local government. This government, headed by Prime Minister Somaré, gradually took over the administration of the country, in a process controlled by Australia. This was the government that took part in the negotiations, alongside the Australian administration, before independence.

5. In 1985, ten years after independence and one year after Ok Tedi came into production, the Australian government was still financing 25 per cent of the Papua-New Guinea budget.

6. The KE consortium intially comprised MG, Kabel und Metallwerke Gutehoffnungshütte AG and Siemens AG. Another German group, Degussa AG (chemicals and precious metals), traditionally associated with MG, was to join KE shortly afterwards.

7. Amoco was then also engaged in the Tenké Fungurumé copper mine project in Zaïre, which was halted a little later in 1978.

8. A holding company holding the Kabel und Metallwerke Gutehoffnungshütte AG and Siemens AG shares.

9. The main features of the mining contract reproduced here are taken from MIKESELL (1985).

10. Cf. *Metal Bulletin Monthly,* January 1987.

11. Cf. *Mining Journal,* 15th March 1985.

12. On this subject, see DE SA *et al.* (1986).

13. The project actually only became operational in May 1984, but the different stages of its development remained the same.

14. However, the capacity of the mine is now fixed at 200 000 tonnes a year of metal content. The operators now seem to be in favour of building a smelter which could be in service towards the end of the decade.

15. The 60 000 tonne a day ore treatment capacity now installed at Ok Tedi will nevertheless make it possible to produce 200 000 tonnes a year of metal content.

16. Cf. William S. PINTZ (1984), p.120.

17. Of which $19 million to be financed by loans subscribed by the state.

18. The state could refuse to contribute more than $45 million, but its holding would be reduced accordingly.

19. Loan guaranteed by the Export Credits Guarantee Department (ECGD).

20. American Overseas Private Investment Corp. (OPIC) agreed to give a guarantee for $50 million, which made it possible to issue stock to groups of investors in North America.

21. BHPC wrote off $A 97.5 million corresponding to part of its investment in Ok Tedi in 1984/85.

Chapter IX

ALBRAS/ALUNORTE*

INTRODUCTION

The Albras/Alunorte aluminium complex project in Amazonia is the scene for two categories of actor with complementary and contradictory logics:

-- The Brazilian state enterprises specialized in exploiting natural resources, the mining company CVRD and the electricity producer Eletrobras, responsible for developing the potential of the Amazon region, the priority axis for economic colonisation since the 1970s;

-- A consortium of Japanese aluminium producers and processors associated with *sogo-soshas* seeking new sources of supply.

Among the points of contradiction was that of integration in the aluminium production chain. The manufacture of aluminium in fact combines the transformation of two natural resources, bauxite and energy (see Inset 1). The processors' degree of involvement in the investment concerned with the stages upstream of electrolysis -- electricity production and the primary transformation of bauxite -- was one of the issues in the association of the two groups of actors.

What is more, this huge project, conceived in 1973, will probably not be entirely completed until 1995, and in the meantime the market trends obtaining when the project was planned have reversed several times, causing tensions between and within the two groups of actors.

---

* Chapter prepared by Isabel Marquès.

179

In its conception, as we shall show, this project contributed to what we call the end of the oligopolies, for on the one hand it allowed the appearance of a new actor on the aluminium market, and on the other it associated non-integrated consumers with the realisation of an upstream project. In the ups and downs of its realisation, the example of Albras/Alunorte illustrates how, in a period where the adjustment of global supply escaped the producers, the consumers adapted their strategies to try to achieve this adjustment.

HISTORY OF THE PROJECT

Between 1972 and 1989, the history of the project has been marked by three distinct periods:

1972-76: The Brazilian dream -- to become the "seventh sister"

As is also shown by the Carajas project, to which we shall return, the 1970s in Brazil marked the development of the colonisation of Amazonia through the exploitation of its natural resources. The integrated production of aluminium using the electricity and mineral potential of the region constituted one of the major axes of this policy.

-- In May 1972 Alcan suspended the construction of the Amazonian bauxite mine at Trombetas because of the poor rate of return on the project and the possibility of maintaining supplies for its alumina plant in Quebec from Guyana in spite of the nationalisation of 1971. CVRD which had, at the behest of the government[1,] started talks about taking a minority share in Trombetas in 1971, became the biggest shareholder in the project in July 1972. The Brazilians now held a majority share of the capital[2] through CVRD (47 per cent) and CBA (Cia Brasileira d'Aluminio) (10 per cent). While other bauxite deposits had just been discovered by CVRD in Amazonia, taking control of Trombetas -- whose reserves were already estimated at the time at 600 million tonnes of trihydrate bauxite -- marked the beginnings of Brazilian strategy in the field of aluminium.

-- In June 1973, a delegation of Japanese aluminium manufacturers and processors and representatives of trading companies, headed by the managing director of Mitsui Aluminium Co, visited Brazil at the invitation of the government. The possibility of the Albras/Alunorte project was envisaged.

-- In July 1973, Eletronorte (Centrais Eletricas do Norte do Brasil) was founded, as the northern subsidiary of the holding company Eletrobras, a state electricity generating and distributing undertaking.

180

Eletronorte was to develop the energy potential of Amazonia and in particular build the Tucurui hydroelectric power station.

-- In December 1973, the Brazilian government promulgated a "participation" law, according to which an enterprise consuming large quantities of electricity could, if it subscribed capital for a power station, obtain at cost price a quantity of electricity proportional to its share of the capital. This law was aimed at encouraging the promotors of Albras to provide part of the capital for the energy infrastructure[3].

-- The first oil shock revealed the lack of competitiveness of the Japanese aluminium industry, based essentially on oil-fired power stations. In January 1974, CVRD signed a protocol with the Japanese consortium of aluminium producers LMSA (Light Metals Smelters Association)[4] for carrying out a feasibility study for the construction of *Albras I*, the biggest alumina and aluminium producing complex in the world, with a capacity of 1 300 000 tonnes of alumina and 640 000 tonnes of aluminium a year. According to the protocol:

   i)   51 per cent of the capital of Albras was to be subscribed by CVRD, either alone or in association with other Brazilian investors. The Japanese enterprises belonging to LMSA were to subscribed the remaining 49 per cent, either alone or in association with other investors.

   ii) The Albras shareholders had obtain the outside financing necessary for the development of the project and were to share the production *pro rata* to their shareholding[5].

   iii) Albras SA, which covered the alumina and aluminium plants, could participate in the extension of the Trombetas mine, and at a later date in the development of the Paragominas bauxite deposit.

-- In February 1975, the Albras I feasibility study, carried out jointly by Brazilian firms and the Japanese partners, was completed. In this scenario the capital was to be held 51 per cent by CVRD and 49 per cent by LMSA, with production to be shared *pro rata* to the shareholding. CVRD's share of the output was destined for the domestic market and LMSA's for export to Japan.

The total volume of investment was estimated at almost $3 billion, 36.5 per cent of which was for the construction of the infrastructures, i.e.:

   i) $800 million for participation in the construction of the Tucurui hydroelectric power station, or 60 per cent of the investment cost of the power station, giving the right to take 60 per cent of its output at cost price;

ii) $270 million for the construction of the port, the road network and township.

The unit cost of the investment per tonne of annual aluminium capacity for the overall integrated project, including energy and infrastructures, mounted to $4 700, and since a tonne of aluminium was selling at the time for about $900, the shareholders decided not to go ahead with Albras I.

In May 1975, CVRD proposed relaunching the operation, separating the alumina and aluminium projects and reducing their size by half. In the *Albras II* project:

-- The capacity of Albras was reduced to 320 000 tonnes of aluminium metal a year;

-- The alumina plant became an independant operation baptized *Alunorte*, Albras now being the name of the aluminium smelter alone.

For CVRD this solution had the advantage of reducing the investment and financing requirements, and the separate development gave CVRD independence vis-à-vis the Japanese for the construction of the alumina plant, an important factor in its strategy of integration in the aluminium industry. The Japanese could in this way be kept aside from the alumina plant project, whose realisation did not really concern them. The fact is that while aluminium smelting in Japan was at a cost disadvantage, this did not in the least mean that the Japanese would be interested in building an alumina plant in Brazil. LMSA thus refused at first to be involved in the Alunorte alumina project, for which the pre-feasibility studies were carried out without Japanese participation.

For its part, the Brazilian government tried to revive Japanese interest through offering much more favourable conditions for the development of Albras, notably that the government would:

i) Build Tucurui without the financial participation of Albras. Albras was to be supplied with electricity by the Nordeste network (CHESF) from 1979 and then by the Tucurui power station as from 1982. The basic tariff proposed was 0.8 cents/kWh for an aluminium price of 40 cents/lb[6]. This tariff was indexed on the aluminium price.

ii) Take responsibility for the port, the road network and the urban development for the project.

iii) Guarantee all the international loans for the construction of the project, including those subscribed by the Japanese partner.

LMSA confirmed its interest in the realisation of Albras, but left it to CVRD and the government to build Alunorte and Tucurui. What is more, the Japanese banks refused to grant loans for the construction of the power station. The financing package for Tucurui was completed by export credits granted by French banks.

At the same time, the Japanese were actively looking elsewhere in the world for investment opportunities in aluminium metal. Thus LMSA, with the support of the Japanese government, participated in the realization of the Asahan aluminium smelter in Indonesia[7], the pre-feasibility studies for which began in 1975. This project, 75 per cent controlled by the Nippon Asahan Aluminium consortium, came on stream in 1982 with a capacity of 75 000 tonnes a year, increased by stages in 1983 and 1984 to reach its present capacity of 225 000 tonnes a year. In the meantime, the Japanese firms Sumitomo, Mitsubishi and Showa Denko were developing the Venalum project in Venezuela, which came on stream in 1979 with a capacity of 140 000 tonnes a year, increased to 280 000 tonnes in 1981. A 20 per cent shareholder in this project, the Japanese consortium obtained an annual quota of 60 per cent of the output until 1989.

For its part, CVRD's aim was to be involved in the aluminium sector through a strategy of vertical integration from bauxite to the production of primary aluminium:

--   After taking a share in the Trombetas mine, CVRD requested an annual quota of 3.4 million tonnes of the output in the context of a project extending annual capacity to 12 million tonnes;

--   CVRD requested Alcan[8] to carry out a pre-feasibility study for Alunorte, whose capacity was fixed at 800 000 tonnes a year with the possibility of extension to 1.6 million tonnes. Alcan's final report was presented in June 1976 and served as the basis for a revised report by the Brazilians presented to the Japanese government in August 1976[9]. This report estimated the total investment cost at $409 million, or $511 per tonne of annual capacity;

--   In November 1975, CVRD and LMSA decided to carry out the feasibility study for Albras II[10];

--   Also in 1975, CVRD undertook the feasibility study for the Valesul aluminium smelter intended to serve the domestic market.

CVRD's initiatives concerning taking bauxite tonnage from Trombetas, trying to come to an agreement with Alcan for the development of Alunorte and the commencement of Valesul show that CVRD felt ready to develop its strategy of integration in primary aluminium production regardless of the outcome of the discussions with the Japanese.

It is reasonable to think that it was this attitude that caused the Japanese, anxious not be be squeezed out of Albras, to assert in 1976 in the context of the co-operation agreements between the two governments, their interest, at least formal, in the development of Alunorte. Nippon Light Metals, a 50 per cent subsidiary of Alcan, initially considered as the supplier of the technology for the alumina plant, then took the lead in the negotiations and Alcan withdrew. The projects took on a national dimension, involving government-to-government relations between Brazil and Japan.

The intervention of the Brazilian and Japanese governments was aimed at providing soft loans for the projects. However, these credits were to be subordinate to the investment priorities of the two countries, so that the period 1977-79 was to be characterised by very sluggish progress in the Albras and Alunorte projects.

The involvement of the Japanese partners in other projects and the enormous investments of the Brazilian state (iron ore, steelmaking, petrochemicals, energy, creation of a capital goods industry, etc.) were the main factors explaining the accumulated delays in implementing the project.

In addition, on the Brazilian side the CVRD management changed twice, while on the Japanese side the structure of the consortium was modified. LMSA expanded to 33 participants, 32 private operators[11] and a State body, Overseas Economic Co-operation Fund (OECF), with a holding of over one-third of the capital. The consortium then took the name of NAAC (Nippon Aluminium Amazon Co), and Albras become the only aluminium smelter project supported by the Japanese involving at the same time producers, processors and traders.

-- In 1977, the details of the participation of the Japanese shareholder in Alunorte were decided: this participation was to be proportional to the alumina quota necessary to supply 49 per cent of the capacity of Albras. The Japanese thus took a 39.2 per cent share in Alunorte, corresponding to 314 000 tonnes of alumina a year, CVRD providing 60.8 per cent of the capital to cover 51 per cent of the supply of Albras, plus an additional 160 000 tonnes a year for its subsidiary Valesul.

-- In December 1977, the Brazilian government granted Alunorte exemption from the import taxes on capital goods.

-- In June 1978, CVRD and NAAC signed the establishment agreements for Albras and Alunorte. These agreements covered the clauses governing the financial contribution of shareholders and the decision-making procedures:

i)   Composition of the capital of Albras and Alunorte:

Albras: Aluminio Brasileiro SA:
Valenorte Aluminio Ltd.   51%
NAAC (Nippon Aluminium Amazon Co.)[12]   49%
Alunorte: Alumina do Norte SA:
Valenorte Aluminio Ltd.   60.8%
NAAC (Nippon Aluminium Amazon Co.)   39.2%

ii) NAAC took the chairmanship of Alunorte and the vice-chairmanship of Albras.   In both companies, NAAC controlled the technical and planning services, which gave it the right to examine the specifications for equipment and the choice of suppliers. CVRD for its part took the chairmanship of Albras and the vice-chairmanship of Alunorte, and control of the administrative, financial, commercial and construction departments.

iii) The shareholders had preference in subscribing for shares in the case of an increase in capital or in buying the shares of any shareholder who should decide to sell.

iv) The minority shareholder reserved the right to take "appropriate measures" to protect its interests in the case of disagreement with the proposals of the majority shareholder. Among these "appropriate measures" were:

--   exemption from the obligation to subscribe capital over and above the annual sum scheduled;

--   provison by the Brazilian state of the guarantees necessary to obtaining any loan whatever, even the financing obtained by the Japanese shareholder.

v)   A right of "contractual exit" for the minority shareholder if the "appropriate measures" should not suffice to protect its interests.

1979-1989: The second oil crisis and the relaunching of Albras/Alunorte

The second oil crisis was to be fatal to aluminium smelting in Japan, where the cost of electricity per tonne of metal produced rose to over $1 000. Within a few years a large proportion of Japan's domestic production had been replaced by imports controlled through new forms of investment.

At the end of 1979, the Japanese partners relaunched the project in order to activate the construction of the complex. The shareholders estimated the investment cost for the two projects so as to be able to start setting up the financing package: a total of $1,861 million, of which $1 289 million for Albras and $572 million for Alunorte.

Meanwhile, CVRD had become heavily involved in the development of Carajas (see Chapter 2), whose investment cost was $3.6 billion. CVRD's industrial experience and its desire to increase its share of the world iron ore market made Carajas a priority project as compared with its strategy of diversification into aluminium. CVRD went so far as to suggest that CBA (Cia Brasileira d'Aluminio) take its place in Albras, while CVRD kept its shares in Alunorte. This proposal was rejected by the Japanese partners, who threatened to withdraw from the project if CVRD did.

--   In May 1980, CVRD came to an agreement with the Japanese to develop Albras in two phases (each with two potlines producing a total of 160 000 tonnes a year), with the foreign shareholder undertaking to find the external financing for the first phase and CVRD for the second. CVRD's contribution to the financing of the first phase was thus limited to *51 per cent of the equity capital,* any contribution of additional financing being delayed until the beginning of the second phase.

--   During the last quarter of 1980, the partners revised the marketing and electricity supply agreements and embarked on the final design work prior to starting construction.

--   In November 1980 the Brazilian government launched the "Programme Grande Carajas" (PGC), aimed at promoting the implantation of mining, metallurgical and agricultural projects in Amazonia. Albras was thus able to enjoy new tax advantages:

    --   Exemption from corporation tax for a period of 10 years;
    --   Exemption from taxes on the purchase of domestically produced capital goods, applicable also to suppliers.

--   In July 1981, the definitive agreements between the Albras and Alunorte shareholders were signed, making it possible to proceed with the financing package. In August 1981, the Brazilian government granted Albras/Alunorte exemption from the taxes on industrial production and on profits.

--   Still in 1981, Portobras started building the port of Ponta Grossa, the investment cost of which, $90 million, was 20 per cent financed by Japanese credits.

--   In March 1982 the financing packages for the two projects were completed, the debt/equity ratio being 70:30[13].

About 60 per cent of the Japanese shareholder's loans were obtained from the Export-Import Bank of Japan, the Japan International Co-operation Agency (JICA) and other government institutions, the remaining 40 per cent coming from

Japanese commercial banks. As regards CVRD, the company obtained financing from the BNDES (National Economic and Social Development Bank) for the infrastructure expenditure, from its subsidiary FINAME for the acquisition of domestically produced equipment and from the Bank of Brazil for the working capital. CVRD also obtained tied credits from foreign banks to finance the purchase of imported equipment.

-- In 1983, the consortium received a proposal from Alcoa regarding the supply of Albras with alumina from plants in Australia and Surinam on the basis of prices very competitive with the forecast production costs of Alunorte. In view of this possibility of supplying Albras at a competitive cost, the shareholders signed a second agreement concerning Alunorte, delaying the construction of the alumina plant. The partners decided to slow down the construction work for the three year period from 1st January 1983 to 31st December 1985, which put back the date of coming on stream to January 1989. The shareholders nonetheless undertook to make an annual investment of $100 million during this period. This investment was for the building of alumina silos, payment for equipment already ordered, and payment of interest on the loans.

-- At the end of 1984 the first stage of the Tucurui hydroelectric power station started production.

-- In October 1985, the first Albras potline, with a capacity of 80 000 tonnes of aluminium a year, came on stream. The second 80 000 tonne module followed a few months later. The supply of alumina came from Venezuela and Surinam on the basis of contracts that expire in 1991.

-- At the end of 1986, the depressed state of the alumina market made the Japanese consortium decide to withdraw from the Alunorte project. The consortium's investment in Alunorte, which was now one-third completed, was converted into non-voting shares.

-- In mid-1988, work commenced on the second phase of Albras. A technical improvement made it possible to increase the capacity of the existing potlines from 160 000 to 180 000 tonnes a year. The capacity of this smelter should reach 340 000 tonnes a year in 1992.

-- With the reversal of the cycle on the alumina market (bringing about a tripling of spot prices), the Japanese again became interested in alumina, and at the end of 1988, CVRD reopened negotiations on Alunorte, not only with the Japanese consortium but also this time with Alcan, through its subsidiaries Alcan do Brasil and MRN. Alunorte was redimensioned to 1.1 million tonnes a year (as against the earlier 800 000) for a total cost of $740 million. About $500 million still remains to be invested. CVRD has announced its

187

determination to go ahead with construction regardless of whether an agreement is reached with the other possible partners, so that the plant can come on stream in 1992, the year in which the second phase of Albras comes into production.

DIFFICULTIES ENCOUNTERED

Difficulties in setting up the legal and financial packages

During the ten years in which the project matured, the industrial logic of Albras thus changed from that of an integrated complex to an aluminium smelter only, realised in the framework of a "joint venture with production sharing". This process was strewn with difficulties stemming from the nature and location of the project itself, the financing package and relations between the shareholders:

i) The delay in the construction of Tucurui -- connected with the financial problems of Eletrobras and difficulties encountered in the deforestation of the area to be flooded -- accentuated the lack of confidence of the Japanese shareholder in the ability of the Brazilians to respect their engagements regarding electricity supply;

ii) The delays in the project resulted in increased investment costs. The 1976 estimate of about $1.4 billion for the two projects -- $955 million for Albras and $445 million for Alunorte -- had increased to $1.8 billion in 1981 for Albras alone. The effective final cost of the Albras project alone is about $1.3 billion.

iii) Although the economic logic of a "production sharing" project is to supply the shareholders with a product at an advantageous price rather than realising a direct profit, and despite the state's taking responsibility for the infrastructure expenditure, the forecast rate of return was always insufficient. The financing package therefore had to be shored up by soft loans underwritten by the development banks. The Japanese OECF (Overseas Economic Co-operation Fund) obtained advantageous financing conditions from 84 Japanese banks and government institutions, notably interest rates of 8 per cent per annum (renegotiated to 6 and 4 per cent in 1986) and repayment delays of five years together with a grace period of five years.

iv) However, this involvement of public Japanese institutions in loans to private firms for a project in Brazil raised the problem of the state guarantee. In fact, with the Japanese government refusing to guarantee the industrial risks of a project realised outside Japan, and although the Japanese private banks generally require that the guarantees are given by the private investors themselves, the Brazilian

188

government guaranteed the whole of the Japanese financing. NAAC thus had no liability in the case of the insolvency of Albras.

The bilateral national interests of the project, involving government-to-government talks, certainly carried weight in obtaining particularly favourable financing conditions. However, the slowness and complexity of this process (negotiations lasted four years) slowed the development of the project.

v) At the same time, negotiations with the BNDES, the biggest lender to the Brazilian shareholder, also turned out to be long and delicate. The BNDES made much of the fact that Albras did not appear to it to be "under national control" because:

-- It was a production sharing project;
-- The terms of the establishment agreement, besides the right of veto, gave the minority partner considerable powers of decision in the case where a consensus could not be reached;
-- Virtually the entire output was destined for the international market;
-- There was no programme providing for the transfer to Brazil of aluminium industry technologies and domestic exploitation of them.

The BNDES therefore insisted in participating in the negotiations, notably in order to introduce into the project the creation of an aluminium research institute to enable Brazilian technicians to learn the technologies of this industry. However, government pressure made BNDES give its agreement for the financing plan so as to accelerate the implementation of the project.

vi) The number and diversity of the partners in the Japanese consortium complicated the co-ordination of the group. The Japanese government's involvement in the project seems to have resulted from the need to reconcile the different interests within the consortium, in order to facilitate negotiations as much with CVRD as with the Brazilian government.

vii) CVRD's lack of determination in the conduct of this project, as compared with its attitude at Carajas, also slowed the realisation of the project. The fact is that:

-- CVRD's inexperience in the aluminium industry was a handicap in the conduct of operations, despite the purchase of technology and technical assistance;
-- The insertion of the project in the Brazil-Japan co-operation agreements of 1976 and the Federal Government's involvement

in the construction of Tucurui tended to make CVRD a second-rank partner;

-- The delays in the development of Albras/Alunorte made the construction of the project coincide with the period of heaviest investment in Carajas. The limitations imposed by the Carajas financing agreement on any increase in CVRD's indebtedness made CVRD revise downwards its investments in other projects, including Albras/Alunorte;

-- The indecision within CVRD itself on the diversification strategy of the enterprise and the place to be given to development in the aluminium industry favoured CVRD's involvement in Carajas, a continuation of the company's traditional activities. Investment priority was thus given to iron ore, even though at the beginning of the 1980s the aluminium industry looked more profitable.

Difficulties during the construction phase

The changing trends of the alumina and aluminium markets during the construction phase caused tensions between the promotors of the project.

It was the construction of Alunorte that caused most of the problems. The saturation of the alumina market, caused essentially by a considerable overinvestment in the late 1970s, seemed to be a lasting phenomenon. In 1985 and 1986, as a result of the fierce competition between producers, alumina prices did not even cover the costs of the most competitive producers.

The supply of alumina (and in particular Alcoa's offer) at prices below the forecast costs of Alunorte caused the withdrawal of the Japanese shareholders at the beginning of 1987, as was provided for in the establishment agreement.

In 1985, the Japanese partners requested the revision of the way in which the price of their quota of output was fixed. The initial contract provided for a price indexed on the Alcan List Price (about $1 750 a tonne in 1979), less a 6 per cent discount. With the disappearance of the producer price, the Japanese obtained indexation of their purchase price on the LME (London Metal Exchange), this time with a discount of 1 per cent.

The Japanese partners could oppose any revision of the electricity tariff by invoking their contractual right to withdraw from Albras. The initial contract, still in force in 1989, set a tariff of 1.05 cents/kWh so long as the aluminium price does not exceed $1 400 a tonne. Above this price, the electricity tariff increases according to a formula indexed on the LME price. This arrangement was favourable to Albras during the period of depressed aluminium prices and heavily penalised Eletrobras. In fact:

a) The very substantial overshoot of the construction costs of the Tucurui hydroelectric power station as compared with the estimates made in 1976, and the resulting additional financial costs, has made this installation a very expensive energy source. The fact that the aluminium price remained below the $1 400 threshold obliged Eletrobras to sell the kWh at one-third of its average price in Brazil and one-quarter of its actual cost at Tucurui.

b) The reorganization of the finances of public enterprises demanded in particular by Brazil's creditors (IMF, World Bank) is forcing Eletrobras, now very much in deficit, to raise its tariffs. In this context, it may be envisaged in the medium term, in particular in the case of a substantial fall in the price of aluminium, that the initial conditions for Albras' electricity supply will be revised.

CONCLUSION

Albras/Alunorte is without doubt one of the major metallurgical projects of the recent past. Its history lies at the turning point between the period of oligopolistic growth in the aluminium industry and the present search for a new mode of growth in which supply and demand are better linked.

Through bringing guaranteed outlets for aluminium metal, the Japanese metallurgists were in fact the driving actors in this project. Because of their energy handicap, they were anxious to promote the production of aluminium outside Japan after the first oil shock. This international strategy was reinforced when, after the second oil shock, the Japanese aluminium producers were forced to shut down all their smelters. The Japanese metallurgists oriented their strategy in the first place to supporting operations developed outside the control of the "six sisters"[14] but without trying to establish a multinational Japanese primary aluminium industry. This strategy of support for independent producers contributed greatly to the disorganisation of the oligopoly. Furthermore, they realised that in order to buy the metal it was rarely necessary to intervene in stages further upstream. In Albras/Alunorte, with a market situation clearly in favour of metal producers who were not integrated upstream, the Japanese partners were clever enough to take advantage of their Brazilian partners' desire to develop an aluminium industry in Amazonia while limiting their own industrial and financial risk in this operation. The association of producers, processors and traders in NAAC, the interventions of financial institutions and the Japanese government, constituted a new form of investment revealing a national supply strategy. This industrial strategy may be summed up by the formula: Support the appearance of new entrants through lowering the barriers to entry, but without systematically being integrated upstream. This is what emerges from the comings and goings of the consortium in the realisation of Alunorte. It is likely that the intervention of the traders and financiers in the operation was a factor lending flexibility to the upstream and downstream relations of the NFI: up to now, the Japanese consortium has been in a position where it can adjust the degree and mode of its involvement in the project in line with evolutions in market equilibria.

For its part, CVRD, seeking to diversify its activities, thought it could take advantage of the lowering of barriers to entry to the aluminium industry after the first oil crisis to become one of the biggest integrated producers in the world. There is no doubt that the oligopolistic structure of the industry before the second oil crisis inspired CVRD to enter the market in force to establish itself as the "seventh sister". However, this strategy was possible only if the company found a large and stable outlet for its product. In this respect the alliance with the Japanese manufacturers might appear necessary. *The irony in all this is that the Japanese allied themselves with the Brazilians in order to weaken the oligopoly, while the latter associated themselves with the Japanese in order to establish a position in the oligopoly and profit from it.* But whatever CVRD's original intentions may have been, and even though the aluminium market has escaped, permanently in our opinion, from the oligopolistic control of the producers, the alliance with the Japanese consortium did enable it to develop a big smelting operation while being given some protection from the hazards of the market. The realization of Albras, in which the financial risks were equally shared with NAAC, now provides an outlet for the Alunorte alumina plant that CVRD can develop, if necessary, on its own. From the standpoint of an operator wishing to remain specialised in the exploitation of natural resources, this strategy, whose financial rationale has to be evaluated over the very long term, has in overall terms permitted the stabilization of outlets for the project despite rapidly evolving markets and made it possible to obtain part of the financing from outside actors.

Inset 1: Description of the primary aluminium production chain

The main ore used is Bauxite (Al2O3,H2O), which contains 40 to 60 per cent of aluminium oxide (alumina). The transformation of bauxite into aluminium takes place in two stages described in the following flow chart:

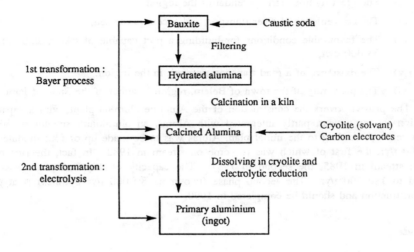

It requires on average 4 to 5 tonnes of bauxite to produce 1 tonne of aluminium.
The electrolysis of 1 tonne of aluminium consumes about 15 000 kWh.

Inset 2: Technical and economic description of the project

Albras/Alunorte is an integrated alumina and aluminium plant located in the Amazonian region of Brazil and developed jointly by CVRD (Cie Vale Rio Doce) and NAAC (Nippon Aluminium Amazon Co. Ltd.), a consortium of Japanese firms. Albras/Alunorte is located at Vila do Conde in the State of Para, about 50 kilometres from Belem. Its location was chose because of:

   i)   The abundant bauxite reserves in Amazonia;

   ii) The great hydroelectric potential of the region;

   iii) The convenience of river transport and access to the sea;

   iv) The favourable conditions for building a port capable of taking ships of up to 35 000 dwt;

   v)   The existence of a road transport network in the region;

   vi) The proximity of the town of Belem, regional capital of the State of Para.

The project covers the construction of the Alunorte alumina plant, with a capacity of 1.1 million tonnes a year, partly integrated with Albras, an aluminium smelter of 340 000 tonnes a year. According to the initial plan, Albras was to be made up of four modules, each of 80 000 t/yr, the first of which was to come on stream in 1982. In fact, the first module came on stream in 1985, the second in 1987. The capacity of this first phase was to be increased to 180 000 t/yr. The second phase (two more 80 000 t/yr potlines) is at present under construction and should be completed in 1990.

The inputs

The original plan was for Alunorte to come on stream one year after Albras, the smelter being supplied in the meantime with imported alumina. The delays that occurred in the realisation of the project modified the schedule, but the supply pattern remains the same: it is likely that the Alunorte alumina plant will come on stream with the second phase of Albras towards 1992.

Alunorte is to be supplied with bauxite from the Trombetas mine, 2 500 kilometres from Belem and operated by MRN (Mineraçao Rio do Norte). At the time of the first feasibility studies, it was envisaged to supply the plant with bauxite from the Paragominas deposit, controlled by CVRD and only 300 kilometres from Belem. This deposit, penalised by very high transport costs has never been developed.

194

The electricity is supplied by Eletronorte from its Tucurui hydroelectric power station built 300 kilometres from the complex. The Tucurui power station is dimensioned to supply 8 000 MW. It came on stream in March 1985 with an initial capacity of 4 000 MW.

The technology for Albras is that of the Mitsui Aluminium Co Ltd. It was recommended by the Japanese partners and accepted by CVRD. It was supplied in the form of a licence valid only for the basic engineering design of Albras. The total cost of the technology and the technical assistance laid down in the contract signed in January 1979 was $24.5 million. The process still used open electrolysis pots with no fume emission control[15]. In 1982, CVRD concluded a complementary contract with Mitsui to improve the technology of the process. Modules II, III and IV have less polluting hooded pots.

The alumina plant technology was supplied by Nippon Light Metals and cannot be reused in other alumina plants in the country. The process had been developed by Alcan and bought by Nippon in 1953. It cost Alunorte $15.5 million.

The overall cost of Albras is estimated in 1989 at $1.3 billion and that of Alunorte at $740 million. The State of Para and the Federal Government participated in the construction of the infrastructures. The feasibility study carried out in 1976 envisaged only $22.6 million of infrastructure investment for Albras, essentially the township and the communications system. In fact, the government took responsibility for the construction of the Tucurui hydroelectric power station, the port (with Portobras), the road network and the provision of various urban services. The construction of the Tucurui power station was certainly the biggest investment in the project. Its cost was estimated at $3.3 billion in 1981, but it was necessary to spend almost twice that sum before its inauguration in 1985.

NOTES AND REFERENCES

1. The main reason for CVRD's participation in Trombetas was the possibility of extending the production capacity initially set at 1 million tonnes a year and a feasibility study for an alumina plant with a capacity of 600 000 tonnes a year. This latter project was delayed however, because of the relative lack of interest on the part of the other partners in Trombetas. The idea was abandoned in 1973, when negotiations were started with the Japanese for the construction of an alumina plant of 1.3 million tonnes a year.

2. The other shareholders in Trombetas were: Alcan (24 per cent), Shell/Billiton (10 per cent), Norsk Hydro (5 per cent) and Reynolds Aluminium (5 per cent).

3. To make it easier to obtain Japanese financing and to tighten the links with these partners during the feasibility study and construction stages, Electronorte signed a technical co-operation agreement with the Japanese public consultant Electric Power Development Co (EPDC).

4. LMSA is a consortium of Japanese aluminium manufacturers comprising Mitsui Aluminium Co, Nippon Light Metal Co, Sumitomo Aluminium Smelting Co, Mitsubishi Light Metal Industries and Showa Aluminium Industrial.

5. The Japanese had also taken a purchase option for the whole of the CVRD quota.

6. The Brazilian government proposed this tariff because it was hoping to obtain in return low-interest credits from Japanese credit institutions for the construction of Tucurui. The feasibility studies carried out estimated the cost at O.8 cents/kWh in the case where 60 per cent of the Tucurui investment -- the consumption quota of Albras I -- was financed with interest rates of 4 per cent per annum. With interest rates of 6 per cent per annum, the cost increased to 1.0 cents/kWh.

7. The Japanese shareholders in the Asahan project were, apart from LMSA headed by Sumitomo, seven trading firms and the Overseas Economic Co-operation Fund (OECF), which was also to participate in Albras.

8. In addition to the possibility of being able to sell its services, Alcan was rather interested in Alunorte because of the project to extend its Brasilian smelter at Bahia to 150 000 tonnes a year, which would mean importing 300 000 tonnes a year of alumina.

9. The speed with which this study was completed is explained by the approaching date for the signature of economic co-operation agreements between Japan and Brazil in August 1976, for which the Brazilian government, through having the study, wanted to put pressure on the Japanese to make them get involved in Alunorte.

10. The final report of this study was presented in July 1976. Its findings have been used for certain of the descriptions in this chapter.

11. These were the five primary aluminium smelters in the LMSA, plus 10 traders, 16 aluminium consumers and processors and the Industrial Bank of Japan.

12. Breaking down NAAC's 49 per cent of the capital of Albras, the Japanese government holds 17.8 per cent, the primary metal producers 13.8 per cent, the traders 9 per cent and the metal processors 8.2 per cent.

13. The equity share of 30 per cent is less than the 40 per cent generally adopted in Brazilian projects. On the other hand, it is higher that the equity share in the direct foreign investments of Japanese firms, which rarely exceeds (except in the case of Asahan) 20 per cent.

14. Until the end of the 1970s, the aluminium market was under the control of the six major producers: Alcan, Alcoa, Reynolds, Kaiser, Péchiney and Alusuisse.

15. This technology was bought from Péchiney by Mitsui during the 1950s, and was adapted to improve the process and reduce energy consumption. This process, without the modifications introduced by Mitsui, was already used in Brazil by CBA (Cia Brasileira d'Aluminio).

Chapter X

VALESUL*

INTRODUCTION

Unlike the other projects studied in this book, Valesul is above all an import substitution project oriented towards the Brazilian domestic market for aluminium. The interest in analysing this operation is the way it highlights the difficulties encountered in trying to match the coming on stream of a relatively simple and small-scale metallurgical operation with a domestic processing industry subject to wide variations in activity. In the period of the demise of the oligopolies, marked by the destabilization of international markets, the question of the adjustment of basic industries to fluctuations in demand became a central issue. Although posed in different terms than in the case of the big export projects, at the core of the Valesul experience was the problem of finding stable outlets for an operation oriented towards the domestic market, which implied establishing new links with the consumers.

HISTORY OF THE PROJECT

-- The history of the Valesul project began in 1974 with a proposal by Reynolds to build an aluminium smelter with a production capacity of 200 000 tonnes a year at Rio de Janeiro. The Brazilian government refused the construction of a smelter entirely controlled by foreign capital and imposed a majority holding for CVRD.

-- Reynolds then refused to put up capital for the operation, but remained interested in its possible development.

---

*Chapter prepared by Isabel Marquès.

199

-- In 1975, CVRD ordered a pre-feasibility study from its consultancy subsidiary RDEP[1] for the construction of a 80 000 tonne a year aluminium smelter. The results confirmed CVRD's interest in the project, and the company issued an international call for tenders to twelve aluminium producers -- including the six sisters -- for the supply of the technology. Nine firms replied, including Péchiney and Mitsui, with whom CVRD began unsuccessful preliminary talks.

-- In March 1976, CVRD began negotiations with Reynolds for the acquisition of smelting technology. The agreement reached specified that Reynolds would take a 30 per cent share in the capital of the smelter if it should be built. This share would be financed in part through the supply of Reynolds' technology.

-- In June 1976 the President of the Republic of Brazil decided on the creation of a new public enterprise, Valesul. This was to evolve towards the "triped" model -- capital in three equal shares: public, private domestic and private international -- even though its initial composition did not follow this pattern.

-- In October 1976 the Brazilian government granted tax advantages to Valesul, in particular exemption from the import tax on capital goods. The Brazilian government, concerned about the big increase in primary aluminium imports, wanted to encourage the implantation of a smelter that would be ready for start-up before the end of the 1970s and close to the aluminium consuming centres, all the more so because the Albras/Alunorte alumina and aluminium complex in Amazonia, associated with the construction of the Tucurui hydroelectric power station, appeared unlikely to be realised before the 1980s. CVRD thus considered Valesul to be a trial aluminium smelter before the realisation of the big Amazonian projects.

-- In April 1977, CVRD and Reynolds concluded a complementary agreement specifying the conditions for Reynolds' technical assistance in Valesul. Reynolds maintained its participation in Valesul for a further year, pending confirmation of the feasibility of the project. The two companies then decided to go ahead, with the project being 60 per cent financed by outside loans. Reynolds had the option up to April 1978 to buy preferential and ordinary shares to raise its holding to up to 45 per cent. This share could be financed in part by reinvestment of the product of the sale of its technology.

-- In the course of 1978, after the project had been judged economically viable, assembly of the financing package began. The private aluminium industry in Brazil objected and put pressure on the BNDES[2], which refused to finance Valesul. Disagreements over the financing conditions caused Reynolds to virtually pull out of the project, its provision of capital being limited to 4 per cent, corresponding to the sale of its technology.

-- In November 1978 the World Bank granted Valesul a loan of $98 million in cofinancing with Chase Manhattan.

-- At the same time, the discussions held with the Royal Dutch Shell subsidiaries Billiton International Metals and Shell Brasil led to the latter taking a 35 per cent share in the capital of Valesul[3.]

-- The joint venture contract was signed in March 1979. This provided that decisions put to the general meeting should be approved by a favourable vote of at least 73 per cent of the ordinary capital. Thus CVRD, despite its majority holding, needed Shell's approval for important decisions concerning the life of the enterprise.

The shareholders could not sell their ordinary shares in Valesul, though a special derogation was granted to CVRD by the World Bank and its foreign partners in the project, allowing it to reduce its holding to 49 per cent: the agreement in fact provided that CVRD, who wanted to reduce its initial holding of 61 per cent to 49 per cent during the construction phase, could sell one-third of its excess holding each year to Brazilian private investors. If these sales were unsuccessful, CVRD, after consultation with the World Bank, would seek the opinion of an expert to define new ways of reducing its holding.

Shortly after this, Valesul signed the financing contract with the World Bank and a syndicate of commercial banks led by Chase Manhattan (see Inset 3). As planned, the financing of Valesul was on the basis of a debt/equity ratio of 60:40, or for a total investment of $368 million, loans of $220 million and equity capital of $148 million. The financial institutions involved are as follows:

i) The World Bank, with a loan of $98 million repayable over 15 years, of which three grace years, at an interest rate of 7 per cent. This loan was guaranteed by the Brazilian Treasury, for which Valesul pays the Brazilian government a commission of 3 per cent per annum. The World Bank loan was to pay for the purchase of equipment abroad ($90 million), consultancy services ($3 million) and about half the interim interest ($5 million).

ii) Chase Manhattan, leader of a syndicate of commercial banks (in cofinancing with the World Bank), with a loan of $90 million repayable over ten years, of which five grace years. These resources financed part of the working capital and paid part of the interim interest. The signature of this loan was a precondition for the World Bank's participation.

iii) The FINAME, a subsidiary of BNDES, with a loan of $34 million, financing the purchase of about 80 per cent of the domestically produced equipment.

Domestic bank financing amounted to 9.2 per cent of the total investment and 15.3 per cent of the loans subscribed. Valesul did not have the direct support of the BNDES for the construction and infrastructure expenditure because of the location of the smelter (already heavy demands on local engergy resources), the project's dependence on foreign alumina and the absence of a plan to disseminate its technology. Valesul was therefore financed 33 per cent by Brazilian resources and 67 per cent by foreign loans and equity participation by foreign firms. Expenditure in local currency during the construction phase having amounted to about 50 per cent of the total capital cost, this financing resulted in a net foreign exchange gain for the Brazilian economy during the development phase of the project.

At the end of 1981, CVRD, heavily involved in the construction of Carajas, had to sell part of its holding in Valesul. Despite the efforts made to have a pool of aluminium processors buy these shares, Brazilian private capital refused to invest in the project. This refusal by the domestic processors resulted in an increase in Shell Brasil's share, resulting in the capital of Valesul being split between CVRD (52 per cent), Royal Dutch Shell (44 per cent) and Reynolds International (4 per cent).

The smelter came on stream in 1982.

The marketing of the output was handled by Valesul itself, the shareholders not having the right to a share of production. Valesul is responsible for defining its commercial strategy[4]. If private Brazilian processors had participated in the project, the agreement provided that they would have had to take a tonnage *pro rata* to their holding.

In 1986 the shareholders negotiated the possibility of using Valesul as a subcontracting smelter. Each of them would supply alumina *pro rata* to its share in the capital and subsequently market the corresponding share of the aluminium metal. At the end of 1987, Reynolds withdrew, selling its share to CVRD. The remaining partners now supply the alumina and sell the aluminium on a *pro rata* basis, and marketing synergies have been found. CVRD's share is marketed with its share of the output from Albras, while Shell Brasil's is sold with its share of the output of Alumar, another aluminium complex realised in association with Alcoa in the north of the country.

DIFFICULTIES ENCOUNTERED

The reaction of private industry and obstacles raised by government institutions

The permanent shortage of aluminium on the Brazilian domestic market should have ensured a ready market for Valesul. However, CVRD's entry into the aluminium industry was greeted without much enthusiasm by the private producers

(Alcoa, Alcan and CBA[5]), who saw Valesul as a serious competitor on the domestic market. The 86 000 tonne a year project was then equivalent to the capacity of each of the private producers[6], who had recently extended their plants.

Because of the state support for the Valesul project, a public debate arose about its implementation. It was CBA, the only company of Brazilian origin in the aluminium sector, who opposed Valesul most strongly, supported in this by certain government agencies[7]. The main criticisms made of the project were levelled at its electricity supply. The basis for this criticism was the fact that power consumption in the region was already very high with respect to the potential, and it would be difficult to manage the installation of an additional capacity of 160 MW. Other criticisms were concerned with the project's dependence on imported alumina while the Amazonian production was not being developed.

Criticism of Valesul was particularly virulent in 1976, when the project was presented for the first time, and in 1979, when it was decided to go ahead with it. After the change of government in March 1979, the Minister of Mines and Energy suggested that the smelter should be relocated in the northeast of the country, but the threat of Shell's withdrawal and the existence of an approved financing contract meant that the construction of Valesul remained in Santa Cruz.

The reluctance of Brazilian investors

CVRD tried to attract private Brazilian capital to Valesul. After CBA's refusal to join CVRD in the project, several alternatives were studied to allow the participation of Brazilian banks, the issue of convertible shares, and the direct participation of local processors. Valesul proposed to these last a minimum participation of $12 million, corresponding to a quota of 24 per cent of the primary aluminium production. Some big processors showed interest, but the small and medium enterprises, those most affected by the difficulties in obtaining the metal in unfavourable economic conditions[8], kept away from the project.

In order to get round this difficulty, CVRD tried to set up a consortium of small consumer enterprises with ABRANFE (Brazilian Non-Ferrous Association) bringing together and co-ordinating their participation in Valesul. In fact, after the suspension of CVRD's primary aluminium importing and marketing activities[9] at the end of 1979, the small processors looked likely to take a share in the capital of Valesul to ensure their supplies, and in 1980 these enterprises announced their intention to buy 12 per cent of the shares, representing 21 per cent of the Valesul capital that CVRD wanted to dispose of.

In 1981, CVRD signed an agreement with a consortium of small processors, ANALC (Aluminion Nacional Participaçoes). Each member of the consortium who was either involved in an aluminium processing activity or held at least 40 per cent of the capital of a processing firm could obtain a share of the production of Valesul equivalent to its share in the capital.

However, the Brazilian aluminium processing industry, and its financial resources, was very hard hit by the economic crisis that came out in 1982. *From being a net importer of primary aluminium (about 100 000 tonnes a year), Brazil turned into a net exporter (80 000 to 100 000 tonnes a year).* This reversal suddenly removed the supply difficulties of the processing plants and the independent processors were thus no longer interested in investing in Valesul.

Marketing difficulties

Valesul came on stream at the worst point in the Brazilian economic crisis. Since the country was changing from being a net importer to a net exporter, Valesul was obliged to find outlets for about 50 per cent of its output on the international market, itself in a depressed state.

Valesul therefore slowed down the process of building up production, and full capacity was not reached until the end of the first quarter of 1983, when prices seemed to be rising. In addition, the sharp devaluation of the cruzeiro in 1983 improved the international competitiveness of the Valesul smelter. The Brazilian balance-of-payments deficit of 1982-83 and the government's policy of trying to obtain foreign exchange led to the creation of several export incentives[10] from which Valesul was able to benefit.

Because of the high level of fixed and debt-servicing costs, the forecasts made in 1979, based on the hypothesis of selling the output on the domestic market, whose prices were expected to remain above the international price, already showed that financial difficulties could be expected. The crisis could but worsen the situation, and Valesul's financial results were negative until 1987 -- when prices rose on the international market -- even though the company had been recording positive gross operating profits. To try to improve the profitability of the project, the shareholders examined without much success the possibility of doubling the production capacity and going into partnership with aluminium processors to achieve downstream integration.

The reversal of the situation on the international market in 1987 and the increasing scarcity of aluminium on the Brazilian domestic market[11] meant that since 1988 the Brazilian consumers have once more become interested in partnership with Valesul. What is more, the development of the industrial zone around the site of Valesul, encouraged by the fiscal policy of the State of Rio de Janeiro, favours the creation of new aluminium processing plants connected with Valesul. Three long product factories have already been built, and a foundry producing mouldings for the automobile industry is envisaged. It would thus appear that after a difficult beginning Valesul will be able in the next few years to obtain stable outlets for its product on the domestic market.

CONCLUSION: THE ACTORS' STRATEGIES

While all the conditions for a successful import substitution project appeared to be fulfilled (domestic market, national outlets, financial support), Valesul nevertheless encountered serious difficulties in its implementation and build up to full production. Some of these difficulties were due to unforeseeable changes in the economic environment, notably Brazilian, while others arose from the divergent strategies of the actors involved. These strategies were as follows:

CVRD

The world's biggest iron ore producer, CVRD wanted to develop the diversification of its activities. This process of diversification began in 1967 and was continued during the 1970s, with CVRD investing in pulp and paper, fertilizers, titanium and manganese production, iron ore pelletisation and, more recently, gold production. However, during this period it was aluminium that consituted the company's priority diversification activity. This was on the one hand because CVRD controlled major bauxite deposits discovered in the Amazon region, and on the other because, hoping to be able to take advantage of the country's great hydroelectric power potential, the government wanted to turn Brazil into one of the world's major aluminium producers.

During the 1970s, CVRD participated in the planning of the big Amazonian projects for mining bauxite and producing alumina and aluminium. Having no experience in the aluminium industry, CVRD wanted to associate with foreign enterprises to be able to take advantage of their knowledge of international markets and their mastery of the technology.

Valesul thus appeared to CVRD to be an opportunity to gain full-scale technological, marketing and management experience in aluminium smelting and to train professionals who would later be employed in Amazonia. In addition, the development of Valesul would allow CVRD to establish a commercial network on the domestic market through which it would be able to sell a substantial part of the output of its subsequent projects.

The Brazilian government

Until 1982, the non-integrated Brazilian aluminium processing industry had always been dependent on imported primary metal. At the time Valesul was approved in 1979, aluminium imports amounted to over 36 per cent of total domestic demand[12]. The forecasts made by Consider (Steelmaking and Non-Ferrous Council), taking into account the known expansion plans and the coming on stream of Valesul and Albras[13], expected the domestic aluminium deficit to continue during the 1980s. According to these forecasts for demand growth (an annual average rate of 15 per cent during the 1980s), Valesul would not suffice to satisfy the projected demand for aluminium. However, the realisation of the project should make it possible to reduce the dependence of the non-integrated processors vis-à-vis the Brazilian metal producers[14] and the *metal imports also controlled by them.*

Alcan and CBA were integrated downstream, and despite using their metal output in their own processing plants these companies remained the biggest importers of aluminium. These imports were for the most part used in the processing plants, but certain surpluses were sold on the domestic market. The independent Brazilian processors were thus highly dependent on Alcoa's Brazilian subsidiary, Alcominas, or on imports. The insufficient local production often led to the processing industry having to work below capacity. This situation seriously affected the competitiveness of the domestic processors who were not integrated upstream.

The Brazilian government therefore encouraged Valesul with the aim of regulating the supply of primary aluminium on the domestic market, as is shown by initiatives to try to promote the participation of non-integrated processors. *Furthermore, Valesul meant progress towards self-sufficiency in primary aluminium, judged strategic, and represented an import substitution investment.* At the end of the 1970s, improving the balance of trade which had been upset by the two oil crises, was a priority goal for Brazilian economic policy[15.]

The foreign companies

The foreign companies used new forms of investment in the Valesul project, characterised by:

    i)   Minority foreign capital participation in the equity capital of the project. This participation was in association with a Brazilian public enterprise as majority shareholder;

    ii) A relatively modest capital contribution, limiting the risks. The foreign capital share in the total financial resources required for developing the project amounted to 1.6 per cent for Reynolds and 14 per cent for Shell Brasil;

    iii) Reynolds' contribution corresponded strictly to the reinvestment of the royalties coming from the sale of its technology.

However, each of these two companies intervened according to its own strategy, some elements of which are discussed below.

With Valesul, Shell made its first investment in primary aluminium production. The firm had hitherto been involved in the aluminium production chain above all in bauxite and alumina, with shares in projects in Surinam, Guinea, Australia and Brazil (in MRN, for bauxite production).

In addition, for Shell-Billiton as for CVRD, participation in Valesul was an opportunity to gain industrial experience in this activity, alongside Reynolds. After Valesul, Shell-Billiton, in association with Alcoa, took a share in the Alumar project in Amazonia, 50 per cent export oriented. These two projects were the group's only primary aluminium production activities. It should be noted however that Shell's reasons for participating in these two projects are rather different. In Valesul, it was a case of learning a new trade in the aluminium sector and taking a position in a market with a strong growth potential and with the further advantage of being partly captive. Shell Brasil's decision also corresponded to the desire to reinvest in the country some of the profits realised in oil product distribution. In Alumar, Shell International's 40 per cent production-sharing interest was induced by the group's association with Alcoa, who would not authorise its partner to contribute solely to the production of alumina.

For Reynolds, the identifiable elements of the strategy are very different. In our opinion, the company recoiled from a direct investment in the project once it was not certain of being able to sell the product as it wanted on a market in which it was trying to get established. It can be assumed that Reynolds' initial decision to subscribe 30 per cent of the capital with the option to increase this share to 45 per cent was aimed at strengthening its negotiating power to obtain a share of the output proportional to its share of the capital.

The maintenance of a 4 per cent share in Valesul corresponding to the reinvestment of the product of the sale of its technology, hence a real engagement in the industrial risk of the project, is probably explained by Reynolds' not wanting to break off all industrial relations, including the sale of services, with Brazil.

Reynolds now seems to prefer to intervene on finished and semi-finished products markets with a strong growth potential. This approach means the industrial redeployment of Reynolds in Brazil. The company's withdrawal from Valesul was accompanied by the announcement of the construction of a drink can plant in Brazil. Discussions currently under way will decide the future supply pattern for this plant, which will probably be from Alcans' new rolling mill.

The World Bank

The World Bank played an active role in setting up the financing package for the project. It wanted to promote a project aimed at stabilizing the country's domestic market, substituting imports and enabling CVRD, its privileged contact in the Brazilian mining sector, to gain know-how in the aluminium industry. In fact, hoping to favour the development of an export sector capable of generating foreign exchange to help stabilize the country's balance of payments, the World Bank contributed actively to the financing of CVRD's expansion and diversification. In addition to its part in financing Valesul, the World Bank also participated in the financing of MRN and the Carajas project.

In conclusion, it would appear that Valesul was in the first place an import substitution project based on a strongly growing domestic market. It is certainly the existence of this protected outlet that made it possible, despite the mediocre forecast profitability of the project, for actors who were only beginners in the aluminium sector to have the opportunity to get hands on experience in this operation of limited size. But even though for CVRD as for Shell, this project was considered to be a secondary operation, it is difficult to see in this simplistic analysis all the reasons for its lack of success.

The fact is that the spectacular reversal of the world market trend as from 1982, and above all the prolonged crisis in the Brazilian economy, were certainly the major causes of Valesul's financial difficulties during the early years of its operation. In this situation, it was impossible to get the non-integrated processors to participate in the operation, as they were more worried about their outlets than their supplies. The period starting in 1988, marked by a relative scarcity of primary aluminium on the domestic market, seems to hold more promise of getting Valesul's customers to take a share of the capital. This new pattern would no doubt enable Valesul to better withstand the effects of another recession.

Inset 1: Technical and economic description

Valesul is a Brazilian aluminium smelter, in production since 1982. The Valesul company is 56 per cent controlled by CVRD, the big Brazilian iron ore producer. The smelter is located at Santa Cruz[16], about 60 kilometres southwest of Rio de Janeiro . The desire to keep infrastructure costs as low as possible, in view of the small size of the project, is no doubt the reason for the choice of location, close to big urban centres with aluminium consuming industries (the Rio de Janeiro - Minas Gerais - Sao Paulo axis).

The annual production capacity of the smelter is 86 000 tonnes of aluminium ingots, plates and billets. Initially, the entire output was intended for the domestic market, Brazil being a net importer of aluminium throughout the 1970s.

The main feedstock for the smelter is amumina, the consumption of which when working at full capacity is about 166 000 tonnes a year. Security of supply has been achieved by negotiating four-year contracts (extendable to eight years) with the Alcoa alumina plant[17] in Surinam and the BIDCO[18] plant in Guyana. However, the closure of the latter in 1982 obliged Valesul to buy alumina on the Rotterdam spot market. When the smelter was being built, it was expected that the Albras/Alunorte complex in the Amazonian region would come on stream in 1985, and its alumina plant was to supply Valesul. The delays in the development of Alunorte forced Valesul to continue to import alumina. The other inputs (soda, lime, fluorine, etc.) are for the most part produced in Brazil.

Inset 2: Forecast cost and profitability

The overall cost of the project was initially estimated at $370 million, the capital investment amounting to $239 million. The overall cost breaks down as follows:

	Million dollars	Per cent
Land	1.0	0.5
Equipment	126.1	52.8
Construction	58.4	24.4
Consultancy, technology, training	35.5	14.8
Start-up expenses	18.0	7.5
Estimated cost of construction	239.0	100.0
Contingency reserve	20.3	
Provision for inflation	37.8	
Total cost of construction	297.1	
Working capital	40.3	
Interim interest	32.7	
Overall cost	370.1	

In 1982, CVRD announced a reduction of $43 million in the total financing requirement. Besides the fact that during the 1970s investment costs in the mining and metallurgical sector were particularly affected by inflation, Valesul's high unit investment cost[19] is explained by the small size of the project and the anti-pollution installations (10 per cent of the total fixed investment). Furthermore, the Brazilian equipment used in constructing the smelter was 30 per cent more expensive than its equivalent on the international market. Although this equipment accounted for only 15 per cent of the cost of the installations, the exra cost involved amounted to about 5 per cent of the total[20].

Expenditure in local currency made up nearly 50 per cent of the total volume of investment, but the relative share of Brazilian equipment was about 35 per cent.

The acquisition of the technology cost $6 million, with the possibility of reusing it in other CVRD projects.

In 1978, the expected rate of return on Valesul was estimated at 10.8 per cent pre-tax and 8.7 per cent after tax, which is not very high, particularly in view of the great sensitivity of this calculation to price changes. This result is based on an assumed operating cost of about $940 per tonne (1978), excluding financial costs and depreciation, for a selling price of $1 500 per tonne (1978). In 1985, the price of aluminium on the world market ranged between $1 100 and $1 200 per tonne.

Inset 3: Management of the industrial and financial risk

The financing contract included a series of clauses limiting the risk for the financial backers and shareholders during the construction phase and the early years of smelter operation. Thus, during the construction phase:

-- The participation of the World Bank brought a guarantee for the whole of the debt of the project, the commercial loan having been contracted through cofinancing;

-- The financing plan included in case of a construction cost overrun provision of $20 million, or about 10 per cent of the physical investment, and an additional provision of $38 million to allow for additional costs due to inflation;

-- In case of the cost overrun being due to delays in construction or to poor cost estimation, the financing contract also provided for the additional necessary funds to be provided by the shareholders pro rata to their share of the capital up to a total sum of $403 million. In the case where the estimated cost of the project should exceed $403 million, any shareholder could request a revision of the cost estimate for the construction phase and propose a new financing plan for the additional requirements. This would then have to be accepted by the World Bank;

-- The financial commitments of CVRD were guaranteed by the Brazilian government;

-- In order to spread the repayments of the principal of the loans over time and relieve the financial charges at the moment of start-up, the loans contracted with the Chase Manhatten and the FINAME had repayment periods of five and seven years after grace periods of five and three years respectively;

-- The shareholders were partly guaranteed against exhange rate risks. In fact the payment of the guarantee commission to the Brazilian government (3 per cent per annum) on the whole of the World Bank financing, which brought the total interest rate on the loan to 10 per cent, could be suspended in the case of an appreciation of the dollar equal to or greater than 3 per cent.

The financial risks during the operational phase are limited by the following clauses:

i) Ban on exceeding a debt/equity ratio of 60:40 in the long-term, with short-term debts of over $3 million having to be taken into account in calculating the long-term ratio;

ii) Ban on contracting new debts that could make the debt servicing cover fall below 1.5;

iii) Ban on creating subsidiaries or investing in other enterprises without the approval of the World Bank.

While the involvement of the World Bank favoured the participation of the commercial banks, the financial capacity of the shareholders and the Brazilian government guarantee were equally decisive in the success of the financial arrangements. What is more, Reynolds' experience in the management of aluminium projects and its technological competence were favourable factors in obtaining World Bank approval for the project.

213

NOTES AND REFERENCES

1. RDEP -- Rio Doce Engenharia et Planejamento.

2. BNDES -- National Economic and Social Development Bank.

3. It should be noted that the two foreign shareholders in Valesul also participated in the MRN (Mineraçao Rio do Norte) project, producing bauxite in Amazonia. The deposit, discovered by Alcan in 1967, has been exploited by MRN since 1979. The present rate of production is 5.5 million tonnes a year. The Brazilian partners in the project are CVRD (46 per cent) and CBA (Cia Brasileira d'Aluminio) (10 per cent), the rest of the capital being held by Alcan (24 per cent), Royal Dutch Shell (10 per cent), Norsk Hydro (5 per cent) and Reynolds (5 per cent).

4. The agreement with the World Bank stipulated that this strategy must be very carefully planned in view of the commercial risks run by a new, non-integrated producer.

5. CBA -- Cia Brasileira d'Aluminio (in operation since 1955).

6. CBA and Alcan (operating in Brazil since 1950) had a primary aluminium production capicity of 59 000 tonnes and 49 000 tonnes a year respectively in 1978, increased to 88 000 and 80 000 tonnes in 1980. For its part, Alcoa had a capacity of 59 000 tonnes a year as from 1967, increased to 90 000 tonnes in 1980.

7. The BNDES refused to participate in the financing, the CACEX (Foreign Trade Financing Agency) objected to the orders for imported equipment and the INPI (National Industrial Property Institute) took a year to validate the technoligy transfer contract.

8. Aluminium imports were not subject to any kind of tax, but a deposit (compulsory transfer) of a sum equivalent to the fob price, required 360 days before the entry of the product, amounted to an indirect tax of 45 per cent, for there was no interest paid on the deposit and no adjustment for inflation.

9. In 1976, CVRD created a subsidiary, COMEC, to import and market primary aluminium, enjoying exemption from the compulsory deposit. The Brazilian government's aim was to stabilize prices on the domestic market (the shortage of primary metal had led to the appearance of a black market) and to satisfy the metal requirements of small and medium enterprises. For CVRD, the aluminium trading was to be an introduction to this market before the realisation of Valesul.

10. The incentives to export aluminium consisted in particular of a special electricity tariff and short-term soft loans equivalent to 20 per cent of the value of annual exports.

11. In 1988, the maintenance of the Brazilian domestic price below the LME price favoured aluminium exports to the extent that the government had to step in with export quotas.

12. In 1977, despite an annual average growth in production of 6 per cent between 1970 and 1977 and the development of recycling, Brazil still had to import 112 000 tonnes of aluminium.

13. According to these forecasts, with the coming on stream of Albras, 49 per cent of the production of which would be taken by the Japanese shareholders, Brazil would become both exporter and importer, but would have remained a net importer.

14. In 1979, the Brazilian primary aluminium industry was made up of three enterprises integrated upstream: Alcan Aluminium of Brazil (a subsidiary of the Alcan group); Alcominas -- became Alcoa do Brasil -- (50 per cent Alcoa, 42.5 per cent Hanna Mining and 7.5 per cent small Brazilian shareholders); and CBA (Cia Brasileira d'Aluminio), a subsidiary of the Brazilian group Votorantim.

15. The net foreign currency gain resulting from the realisation of Valesul was estimated in 1979 at $97 million a year, allowing for loan repayments and interest payments.

16. The Santa Cruz region is a priority industrialisation zone for the State of Rio de Janeiro. It now has two steelworks, a nuclear power station and two big ports. The abundance of skilled labour, the existence of port and transport infrastructures, together with the energy resources of the region were factors favouring the location of Valesul near Rio.

17. Shell acquired 40 per cent of the capital of this smelter in 1984.

18. BIDCO -- Bauxite Industry Development Company Ltd.

19. The unit investment cost per tonne of annual capacity at Valesul ($4 300) was higher than that of other projects constructed a few years earlier in Latin America, such as Venalum and Alcasa in Venezuela.

20. It is estimated that the average unit investment cost per tonne of annual capacity for aluminium in the United States at the end of the 1970s was about $2 000.

BIBLIOGRAPHY

AGLIETTA M., *Régulation et crises du capitalisme ; l'expérience des Etats-Unis*, Calmann-Lévy, 1976.

ANGELIER, J.P., *La rente pétrolière*, CNRS, Paris, 1976.

BAIN, *Barriers to New Competition*, Harvard University Press, Cambridge, 1956.

BALLMER, R.W., "The Bougainville Copper Project", *Mining Congress Journal*, April 1973.

BENZONI, Laurent, "Réflexion sur la Théorie de la rente", Université de Paris XIII, 1982.

BOMSEL, Olivier, *Dynamiques économiques des pays miniers et instabilité des marchés de matières premières minérales*. Economics of Natural Resources doctoral thesis, CERNA, Ecole des Mines, Paris, 1986.

BOMSEL, GIRAUD, de SA, "La crise de l'industrie minière" Séminaire d'Economie et de Stratégie Minières, CERNA, Ecole des Mines, Paris, 1985.

BOSSON, R. and VARON, B., *"L'industrie minière dans le Tiers-Monde"*, World Bank, Washington D.C., 1977.

CAVES and PORTER, "Market Structure, Oligopoly, and Stability of Market Shares", *Journal of Industrial Economics*, Vol. 27, pp. 289-313, 1978.

CHEVALIER, J.M., *Le nouvel enjeu pétrolier*, Calman-Lévy, Paris, 1973.

CORDON and NEARY, "Booming Sector and De-industrialisation in a Small Open Economy", *The Economic Journal 92*, pp. 825-848, December 1982.

CROWSON, P.C.F., "Investment and Future Mineral Production", *Resources Policy*, Butterworths, March 1982.

CROWSON, P.C.F., "Are Production Costs of Copper Determined by Prices of Copper?" Paper presented at the CRU/CDA Conference on the Marketing and Trading of Copper, October 1984.

CROWSON P.C.F., "What Criteria for Investing in New Capacity", *Annales des Mines*, June 1989.

DETRIE, J.P. and RAMANANTSOA, B., *Stratégie de l'entreprise et diversification*, Fernand Nathan, Paris, 1983.

DUMEL, Philippe, *Structure des marchés de matières premières et rentes minières: Application au cas du minerai de fer*. Engineering doctoral thesis, CERNA, Ecole des Mines, Paris, 1984.

GIRAUD, Pierre-Noël, *Géopolitique des ressources minières*, Economica, Paris, 1983.

GIRAUD, Pierre-Noël, *et al.*, "Evolution de la consommation de huit matières premières minérales", Séminaire d'Economie et de Stratégie Minières, CERNA, Ecole des Mines, Paris, 1985.

GRAVE, Robert T., "Inco's Soroako Nickel Project: A Case Study in Financing Large Overseas Mining Ventures", *Mining Engineers*, March 1979.

HOPPE, Richard, "Selebi-Phikwe: Concentrating and Smelting the Nickel-copper Ore", *Engineering and Mining Journal*, May 1980.

HUMPHREYS, David, "Metal Prices in the 1980s: A View from the Supply Side", *Resources Policy*, Vol. 14, No. 4, Butterworth, December 1988.

LEBEN, Charles, "Les investissements miniers internationaux dans les pays en développppement: Réflexions sur la décénnie écoulée (1976-1986)", CREDIMI, Dijon, *Journal du Droit International*, 113ème année, No. 4 - 1986.

LÜDKE, Helmut, "Ok Tedi, a New Copper Giant on the Market", *Metal Bulletin Monthly*, January 1987.

MACHADO, Raimundo, *Apontamentos para a Industria de Aluminio no Brasil*, Ed. Gorceix, Ouro Preto, 1985.

MARQUES, Isabel and de SA, Paulo, *Os maiores mineradores do Brasil* - Sous la direction de Fernandes FRC, Ed. CNPq Revista Minerios, Sao Paulo, 1981.

MARQUES, Isabel and de SA, Paulo, "The Carajas Iron Ore Project: The Strategy of a Third World State-owned Enterprise in a Depressed Market", *Resources Policy*, Butterworth, December 1985.

MANSEAU, Gilles, *Structures de financement des développements miners*, Engineering doctoral thesis, CERNA, Ecole des Mines, Paris, 1979.

MIKESELL, Raymond F., *Foreign Investment in Mining projects: Case Studies of Recent Experiences*, Oelgeschlager, Gunn & Hain, Publishers, Inc., Cambridge, Mass., 1982.

MIKESELL, Raymond F., *Foreign Investment in Copper Mining*, Resources for the Future Inc., 1985 (?).

NANKANI, G., *Developing Problems of Mineral Exporting Countries*, Staff working paper No. 354, Washington D.C., 1979.

NAPPI, C., "Pricing Behaviour and Market Power in North American Non-ferrous Metal Industries", *Resources Policy*, Butterworth, September 1985.

NEARY and VAN WIBERGEN, *Natural Resources and the Macroeconomy*, Blackwell, 1986.

O'FAIRCHEALLAIGH, Cirian, "The Marketing of Copper Concentrates: The Case of BCL", *Mining Magazine*, June 1984.

OMAN, Charles, *New Forms of International Investment in Developing Countries*, OECD Development Centre, Paris, 1984.

OMAN, Charles *et al.*, *New Forms of Investment in Developing Country Industries: Mining, Petrochemicals, Automobiles, Textiles, Food*, OECD Development Centre, Paris, 1989.

PINTZ, William S., *OK Tedi: Evolution of a Third World Mining Project*, Mining Journal Books Ltd, 1984.

PORTER, Michael, *Choix stratégiques et concurrence*, Economica, Paris, 1980.

RADETZKI, Marian, "Changing Structures in the Financing of the Mineral Industries in the LDCs", *Development and Change*, Sage, London and Beverley Hills, Vol. 11, 1980.

RADETZKI, Marian and VAN DUYNE, Carl, "The Response of Mining Investment to a Decline in Economic Growth", *Journal of Development Economics 15*, North Holland, 1984.

RICARDO, David, *The Principles of Political Economy and Taxation*.

ROBERTS, "Assessing the Impact of the Slack Demand for Metals", *Resources Policy*, Vol. 14, No. 2, Butterworth, June 1988.

ROBERTSON, Roland R., "Colombia's Cerro Matoso", *Engineering and Mining Journal*, May 1985.

de SA, Paulo, *Stratégie des opérateurs miniers internationaux*, CERNA, Study distributed by l'Observatoire des Matières Premières, Paris, 1986.

de SA, Paulo *et al.*, *Intervention des opérateurs pétroliers dans le secteur minier*, Annex to the Boisson Report on the Mining and Metallurgical Industries, Groupe de Travail "Matières Premières Minérales", Commissariat Général du Plan, Paris, 1986.

de SA, Paulo, *Evolution des programmes d'exploitation minière*, CERNA study for l'Observatoire des Matières Premières, Paris, 1987.

de SA, Paulo, *La crise de l'industrie minière*, Doctoral thesis in the economics of natural resources, CERNA, Ecole des Mines de Paris, 1988.

de SA, Paulo, "Structural Changes and Price Formation in the Minerals and Metals Industries", *Resources Policy*, Vol. 14, No. 4, Butterworth, December 1988.

TILTON, John, "Changing Trends in Metal Demand and the Decline of Mining and Mineral Processing in North America", duplicated note, Colorado School of Mines, Golden, 1986.

TILTON, John, "Atrophy in Metal Demand", Material and Society, Vol. 10, No. 3, 1986.

VALENTINE, R.J., "How Selebi-Phikwe Ni-Cu Project Overcame Early Production Problems?", *World Mining*, November 1987.

ZINSER, James E., "The Cerro Matoso Nickel Project in Colombia", in *Foreign Investment in Mining Projects*, co-ordinated by R. Mikesell, Oelgeschlager, Gunn & Hain, Publishers, Inc., Cambridge, Mass., 1982.

ZRAICK, Samir, "Financiamento Projeto Carajas", *CVRD Review*, Vol. IV, No. 12, December 1983 and February 1985.

ABBREVIATIONS

AAC	Anglo-American Corporation
ABRANFE	Brazilian Non-Ferrous Association
ADB	African Development Bank
AESDF	Arab Economic and Social Development Fund
AMZA	Amazonie Mineraçao SA
ANALC	Aluminion Nacional Participaçoes
BCL	Bamangwato Concessions Ltd (Botswana)
BCL	Bougainville Copper Proprietary Limited
BIDCO	Bauxite Industry Development Company Ltd (Guyana)
BNDES	National Economic and Social Development Bank (Brazil)
BRGM	Bureau de Recherches Géologiques et Minières
BRST	Botswana RST Ltd
CACEX	Foreign Trade Financing Agency (Brazil)
CBA	Cia Brasileira d'Aluminio
CCCE	Caisse Centrale de Coopération Economique (French Development Bank)
CIDA	Canadian International Development Agency
CMSA	Cerro Matoso SA (Colombia)
CRA	Conzinc Rio Tinto of Australia Ltd
CVRD	Cie Vale Rio Doce (Brazil)
ECSC	European Coal and Steel Community
ECGD	Export Credits Guarantee Department
EIB	European Investment Bank
FIL	Falconbridge International Ltd
IBRD	International Bank for Reconstruction and Development (World Bank)
IDC	Industrial Development Corp (of South Africa)
IFI	Instituto de Fomento Industrial (Colombia)
IMF	International Monetary Fund

INPI	National Industrial Property Institute
JICA	Japan International Cooperation Agency
KE	Kupfer Exploration Gesellschaft
KFW	Kreditanstalt für Wiederaufbau (German Development Bank)
LME	London Metal Exchange
LMSA	Light Metals Smelters Association (Japan)
MG	Metallgesellschaft
MRN	Mineraçao Rio do Norte
NA	Norddeutsche Affinerie
NAAC	Nippon Aluminium Amazon Co
NBHC	New Broken Hill Consolidated Ltd
OECF	Overseas Economic Co-operation Fund (Japan)
OPEC	Organization of Petroleum Exporting Countries
OPIC	Overseas Private Investment Corp (US)
OTDC	Ok Tedi Development Company
OTML	Ok Tedi Mining Limited
PGC	Programme Grande Carajas (Brazil)
PNG	Papua-New Guinea
RDEP	Rio Doce Engenharia et Planejamento
RST	Rhodesian Selection Trust
RTM	Rio Tinto Minera (Spain)
SAFA	Société Arabe du Fer et de l'Acier (Mauritania)
SNIM	Société Nationale Industrielle et Minière (Mauritania)
UNDP	United Nations Development Programme
USAID	US Agency for International Development
ZCCM	Zambia Consolidated Copper Mines (Chapter 1 note 9)

WHERE TO OBTAIN OECD PUBLICATIONS
OÙ OBTENIR LES PUBLICATIONS DE L'OCDE

Argentina – Argentine
Carlos Hirsch S.R.L.
Galeria Güemes, Florida 165, 4° Piso
1333 Buenos Aires
  Tel. 30.7122, 331.1787 y 331.2391
Telegram: Hirsch-Baires
Telex: 21112 UAPE-AR. Ref. s/2901
Telefax:(1)331–1787

Australia – Australie
D.A. Book (Aust.) Pty. Ltd.
648 Whitehorse Road (P.O. Box 163)
Vic. 3132 Tel. (03)873.4411
Telex: AA37911 DA BOOK
Telefax: (03)873.5679

Austria – Autriche
OECD Publications and Information Centre
4 Simrockstrasse
5300 Bonn (Germany) Tel. (0228)21.60.45
Telex: 8 86300 Bonn
Telefax: (0228)26.11.04

Gerold & Co.
Graben 31
Wien I Tel. (0222)533.50.14

Belgium – Belgique
Jean De Lannoy
Avenue du Roi 202
B-1060 Bruxelles
  Tel. (02)538.51.69/538.08.41
Telex: 63220 Telefax: (02)538.08.41

Canada
Renouf Publishing Company Ltd.
1294 Algoma Road
Ottawa, Ont. K1B 3W8 Tel. (613)741.4333
Telex: 053–4783 Telefax: (613)741.5439
Stores:
61 Sparks Street
Ottawa, Ont. K1P 5R1 Tel. (613)238.8985
211 Yonge Street
Toronto, Ont. M5B 1M4 Tel. (416)363.3171

Federal Publications
165 University Avenue
Toronto, ON M5H 3B9 Tel. (416)581.1552
Telefax: (416)581.1743
Les Publications Fédérales
1185 rue de l'Université
Montréal, PQ H3B 1R7 Tel.(514)954–1633

Les Éditions La Liberté Inc.
3020 Chemin Sainte-Foy
Sainte-Foy, P.Q. G1X 3V6
  Tel. (418)658.3763
Telefax: (418)658.3763

Denmark – Danemark
Munksgaard Export and Subscription Service
35, Norre Sogade, P.O. Box 2148
DK-1016 Kobenhavn K
  Tel. (45 33)12.85.70
Telex: 19431 MUNKS DK
  Telefax: (45 33)12.93.87

Finland – Finlande
Akateeminen Kirjakauppa
Keskuskatu 1, P.O. Box 128
00100 Helsinki Tel. (358 0)12141
Telex: 125080 Telefax: (358 0)121.4441

France
OECD/OCDE
Mail Orders/Commandes par correspon-
dance:
2 rue André-Pascal
75775 Paris Cedex 16 Tel. (1)45.24.82.00
Bookshop/Librairie:
33, rue Octave-Feuillet
75016 Paris Tel. (1)45.24.81.67
  (1)45.24.81.81
Telex: 620 160 OCDE
Telefax: (33-1)45.24.85.00

Librairie de l'Université
12a, rue Nazareth
13602 Aix-en-Provence Tel. 42.26.18.08

Germany – Allemagne
OECD Publications and Information Centre
4 Simrockstrasse
5300 Bonn Tel. (0228)21.60.45
Telex: 8 86300 Bonn
  Telefax: (0228)26.11.04

Greece – Grèce
Librairie Kauffmann
28 rue du Stade
105 64 Athens Tel. 322.21.60
Telex: 218187 LIKA Gr

Hong Kong
Swindon Book Co. Ltd
13–15 Lock Road
Kowloon, Hong Kong Tel. 366.80.31
Telex: 50.441 SWIN HX
Telefax: 739.49.75

Iceland – Islande
Mal Mog Menning
Laugavegi 18, Postholt 392
121 Reykjavik Tel. 15199/24240

India – Inde
Oxford Book and Stationery Co.
Scindia House
New Delhi 110001 Tel. 331.5896/5308
Telex: 31 61990 AM IN
Telefax: (11)332.5993
17 Park Street
Calcutta 700016 Tel. 240832

Indonesia – Indonésie
Pdii-Lipi
P.O. Box 269/JKSMG/88
Jakarta12790 Tel. 583467
Telex: 62 875

Ireland – Irlande
TDC Publishers – Library Suppliers
12 North Frederick Street
Dublin 1 Tel. 744835/749677
Telex: 33530 TDCP EI Telefax : 748416

Italy – Italie
Libreria Commissionaria Sansoni
Via Benedetto Fortini, 120/10
Casella Post. 552
50125 Firenze Tel. (055)645415
Telex: 570466 Telefax: (39.55)641257
Via Bartolini 29
20155 Milano Tel. 365083
La diffusione delle pubblicazioni OCSE viene
assicurata dalle principali librerie ed anche
da:
Editrice e Libreria Herder
Piazza Montecitorio 120
00186 Roma Tel. 679.4628
Telex: NATEL I 621427
Libreria Hoepli
Via Hoepli 5
20121 Milano Tel. 865446
Telex: 31.33.95 Telefax: (39.2)805.2886
Libreria Scientifica
Dott. Lucio de Biasio "Aeiou"
Via Meravigli 16
20123 Milano Tel. 807679
Telefax: 800175

Japan – Japon
OECD Publications and Information Centre
Landic Akasaka Building
2-3-4 Akasaka, Minato-ku
Tokyo 107 Tel. 586.2016
Telefax: (81.3)584.7929

Korea – Corée
Kyobo Book Centre Co. Ltd.
P.O. Box 1658, Kwang Hwa Moon
Seoul Tel. (REP)730.78.91
Telefax: 735.0030

**Malaysia/Singapore –
Malaisie/Singapour**
University of Malaya Co-operative Bookshop
Ltd.
P.O. Box 1127, Jalan Pantai Baru 59100
Kuala Lumpur
Malaysia Tel. 756.5000/756.5425
Telefax: 757.3661
Information Publications Pte. Ltd.
Pei-Fu Industrial Building
24 New Industrial Road No. 02–06
Singapore 1953 Tel. 283.1786/283.1798
Telefax: 284.8875

Netherlands – Pays-Bas
SDU Uitgeverij
Christoffel Plantijnstraat 2
Postbus 20014
2500 EA's-Gravenhage Tel. (070)78.99.11
Voor bestellingen: Tel. (070)78.98.80
Telex: 32486 stdru Telefax: (070)47.63.51

New Zealand –Nouvelle-Zélande
Government Printing Office
Customer Services
P.O. Box 12–411
Freepost 10–050
Thorndon, Wellington
Tel. 0800 733–406 Telefax: 04 499–1733

Norway – Norvège
Narvesen Info Center – NIC
Bertrand Narvesens vei 2
P.O. Box 6125 Etterstad
0602 Oslo 6
  Tel. (02)67.83.10/(02)68.40.20
Telex: 79668 NIC N Telefax: (02)68.19.01

Pakistan
Mirza Book Agency
65 Shahrah Quaid-E-Azam
Lahore 3 Tel. 66839
Telex: 44886 UBL PK. Attn: MIRZA BK

Portugal
Livraria Portugal
Rua do Carmo 70–74
1117 Lisboa Codex Tel. 347.49.82/3/4/5

**Singapore/Malaysia
Singapour/Malaisie**
See "Malaysia/Singapore"
Voir "Malaisie/Singapour"

Spain – Espagne
Mundi-Prensa Libros S.A.
Castello 37, Apartado 1223
Madrid 28001 Tel. (91) 431.33.99
Telex: 49370 MPLI Telefax: 575.39.98
Libreria Internacional AEDOS
Consejo de Ciento 391
08009 –Barcelona Tel. (93) 301–86–15
Telefax: 575.39.98

Sweden – Suède
Fritzes Fackboksföretaget
Box 16356, S 103 27 STH
Regeringsgatan 12
DS Stockholm Tel. (08)23.89.00
Telex: 12387 Telefax: (08)20.50.21
Subscription Agency/Abonnements:
Wennergren–Williams AB
Box 30004
104 25 Stockholm Tel. (08)54.12.00
Telex: 19937 Telefax: (08)50.82.86

Switzerland – Suisse
OECD Publications and Information Centre
4 Simrockstrasse
5300 Bonn (Germany) Tel. (0228)21.60.45
Telex: 8 86300 Bonn
Telefax: (0228)26.11.04
Librairie Payot
6 rue Grenus
1211 Genève 11 Tel. (022)731.89.50
Telex: 28356
Maditec S.A.
Ch. des Palettes 4
1020 Renens/Lausanne Tel. (021)635.08.65
Telefax: (021)635.07.80
United Nations Bookshop/Librairie des Na-
tions-Unies
Palais des Nations
1211 Genève 10
  Tel. (022)734.60.11 (ext. 48.72)
Telex: 289696 (Attn: Sales)
Telefax: (022)733.98.79

Taiwan – Formose
Good Faith Worldwide Int'l. Co. Ltd.
9th Floor, No. 118, Sec. 2
Chung Hsiao E. Road
Taipei Tel. 391.7396/391.7397
Telefax: (02) 394.9176

Thailand – Thalande
Suksit Siam Co. Ltd.
1715 Rama IV Road, Samyan
Bangkok 5 Tel. 251.1630

Turkey – Turquie
Kültur Yayinlari Is–Türk Ltd. Sti.
Atatürk Bulvari No. 191/Kat. 21
Kavaklidere/Ankara Tel. 25.07.60
Dolmabahce Cad. No. 29
Besiktas/Istanbul Tel. 160.71.88
Telex: 43482B

United Kingdom – Royaume-Uni
H.M. Stationery Office
Gen. enquiries Tel. (071) 873 0011
Postal orders only:
P.O. Box 276, London SW8 5DT
Personal Callers HMSO Bookshop
49 High Holborn, London WC1V 6HB
Telex: 297138 Telefax: 071.873.8463
Branches at: Belfast, Birmingham, Bristol,
Edinburgh, Manchester

United States – États-Unis
OECD Publications and Information Centre
2001 L Street N.W., Suite 700
Washington, D.C. 20036–4095
  Tel. (202)785.6323
Telex: 440245 WASHINGTON D.C.
Telefax: (202)785.0350

Venezuela
Libreria del Este
Avda F. Miranda 52, Aptdo. 60337
Edificio Galipan
Caracas 106
  Tel. 951.1705/951.2307/951.1297
Telegram: Libreste Caracas

Yugoslavia – Yougoslavie
Jugoslovenska Knjiga
Knez Mihajlova 2, P.O. Box 36
Beograd Tel. 621.992
Telex: 12466 jk bgd

Orders and inquiries from countries where
Distributors have not yet been appointed
should be sent to: OECD Publications
Service, 2 rue André-Pascal, 75775 Paris
Cedex 16.
Les commandes provenant de pays où
l'OCDE n'a pas encore désigné de dis-
tributeur devraient être adressées à : OCDE,
Service des Publications, 2, rue André-
Pascal, 75775 Paris Cedex 16.

OECD PUBLICATIONS, 2 rue André-Pascal, 75775 PARIS CEDEX 16
PRINTED IN FRANCE
(41 90 05 1) ISBN 92-64-13382-8 – No. 45139 1990